Remembering Lexington

W. Gay Reading

Trade Paper Press

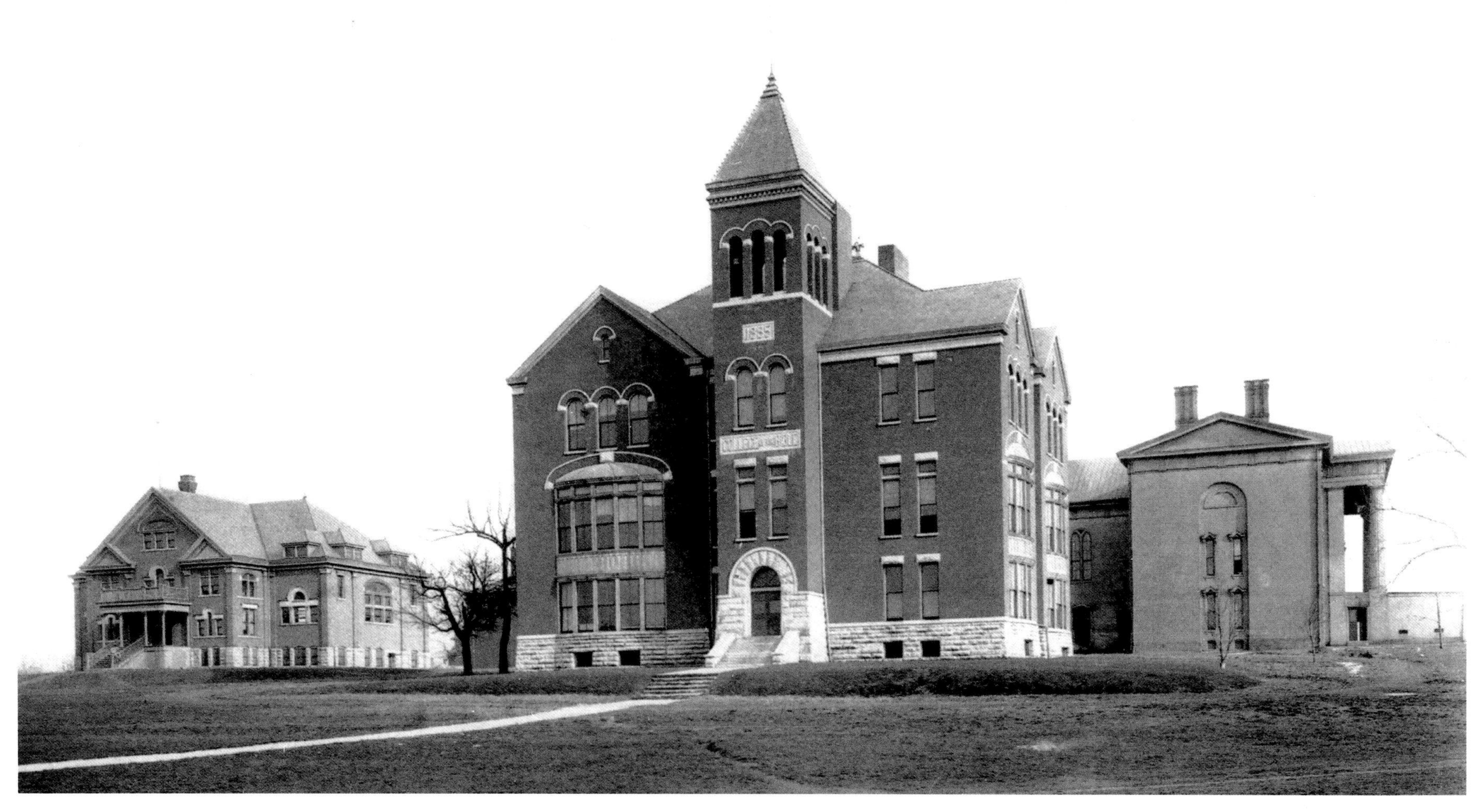

College of the Bible (built 1895) at Transylvania University (then Kentucky University), 1898.

Remembering Lexington

Turner Publishing Company
200 4th Avenue North • Suite 950
Nashville, Tennessee 37219
(615) 255-2665

Remembering Lexington

www.turnerpublishing.com

Library of Congress Control Number: 2010902278

ISBN: 978-1-59652-604-4

Printed in the United States of America

10 11 12 13 14 15 16—0 9 8 7 6 5 4 3 2 1

Contents

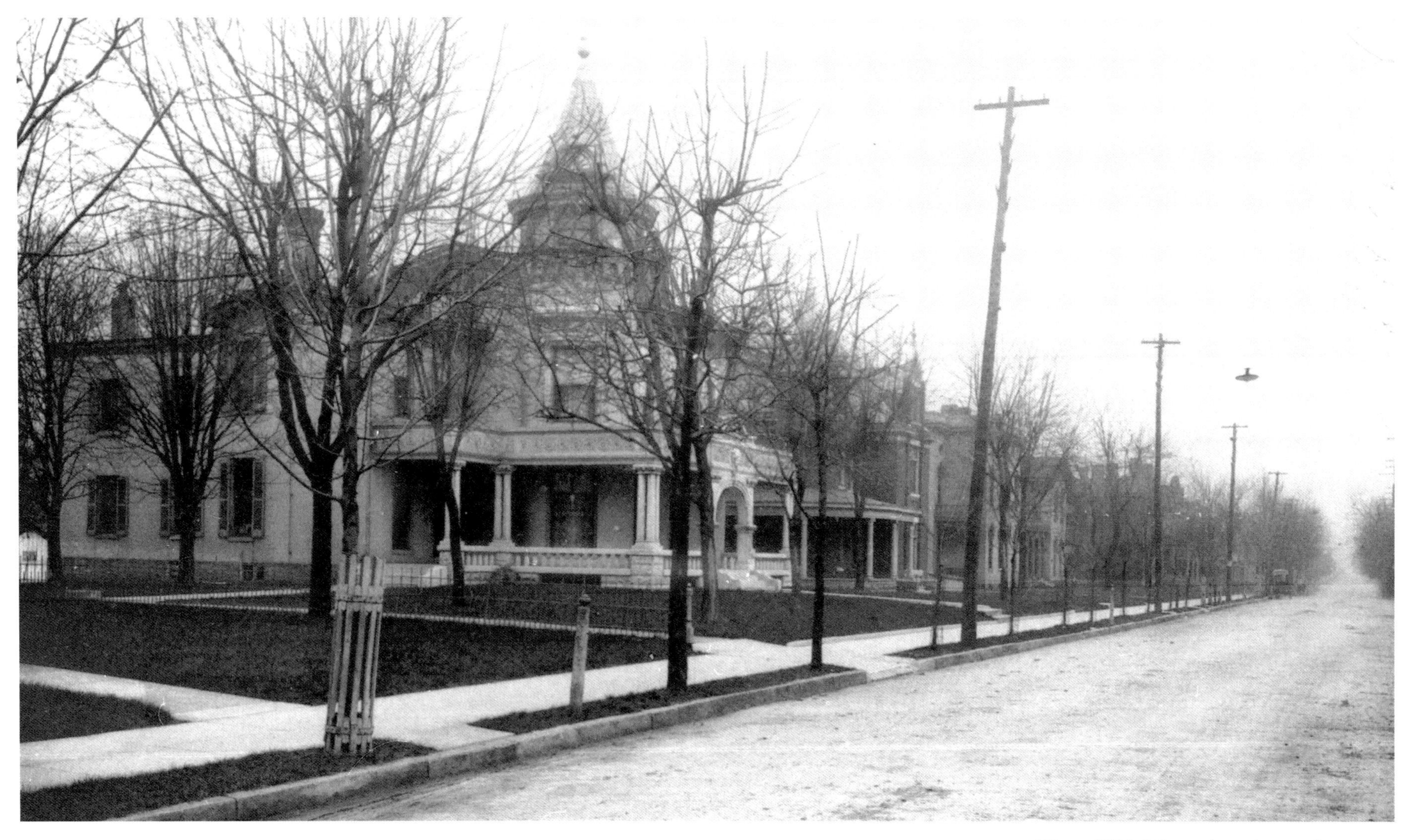

View of Third Street, late nineteenth century.

Acknowledgments

This volume, *Remembering Lexington,* is the result of the cooperation and efforts of many individuals and organizations. It is with great thanks that we acknowledge the valuable contribution of the following for their generous support.

Equus Standardbred Station
Georgetown College
University of Kentucky Libraries
Transylvania University Special Collections Library
Lexington Opera House/Lexington Center Corporation
Keeneland
Kentucky American Water Company

Our appreciation goes to Tamara Farnsworth for her professional guidance and assistance in research and verification.

We would also like to thank the following individuals for their valuable contribution and assistance in making this work possible:

Jason Flahardy, Audio Visual Archivist, University of Kentucky Libraries
Luanne Franklin, Program Director, Lexington Opera House
BJ Gooch, Special Collections Librarian and University Archivist, Transylvania University Library
Susan Lancho, Communications Manager, Kentucky American Water
Cathy Schenck, Librarian, Keeneland Library
Glen Edward Taul, Ph.D., Director, Archives, Georgetown College

Preface

Lexington has thousands of historic photographs that reside in private and public archives. These photographs give us an important link to the city's past. During a time when Lexington is looking ahead and evaluating its future course, many people are wondering how to treat the city's past. These decisions affect every aspect of the city—architecture, public spaces, commerce, and infrastructure—and these, in turn, affect the way that people live their lives. This book seeks to provide easy access to a valuable, objective look into Lexington's history.

The power of photographs is that they are less subjective than words in their treatment of history. Although the photographer can make subjective decisions regarding subject matter and how to capture and present it, photographs seldom interpret the past to the extent textual histories can. For this reason, photography is uniquely positioned to offer an original, untainted look at the past, allowing the viewer to learn for himself what the world was like a century or more ago.

The project represents countless hours of review and research. The researchers and writer have reviewed thousands of photographs in numerous archives. We greatly appreciate the generous assistance of the archivists listed in the acknowledgments of this work, without whom this project could not have been completed.

The goal in publishing this work is to provide broader access to a set of extraordinary photographs. We hope to inspire and provide insight and perspective using the past as a lesson for the future. Equally important, this book seeks to preserve the past with respect and reverence.

The photographs we have selected for this book represent the technology of that era. With the exception of touching up imperfections that have accrued with the passage of time and cropping where necessary, no changes have been made. The focus and clarity of many images are limited to the technology and the ability of the photographer at the time they were recorded.

The work is divided into eras. Beginning with some of the earliest known photographs of Lexington, the first section records events from the Civil War era through the end of the nineteenth century. The second section spans the first two decades of the twentieth century. The third section moves through the Great Depression. The final section takes a look at the World War II era up to the 1970s.

In each of these sections we have made an effort to capture various aspects of life through our selection of photographs. People, commerce, transportation, infrastructure, religious institutions, and educational institutions are included to provide a broad perspective.

We encourage readers to reflect as they walk down Main Street, through Gratz Park, or visit Transylvania. Streetcar tracks once ran down Broadway, houses and shopping centers now sit on land where horses once grazed, and the site of the city's first marketplace is once again bustling with downtown businesses. It is the publisher's hope that in utilizing this work, longtime residents will learn something new, and new residents will gain insight on where Lexington has been, so that each can contribute to its future.

—Todd Bottorff, Publisher

Streetcar center at Lexington's fourth courthouse. The courthouse was built in 1883-84 and burned in 1897.

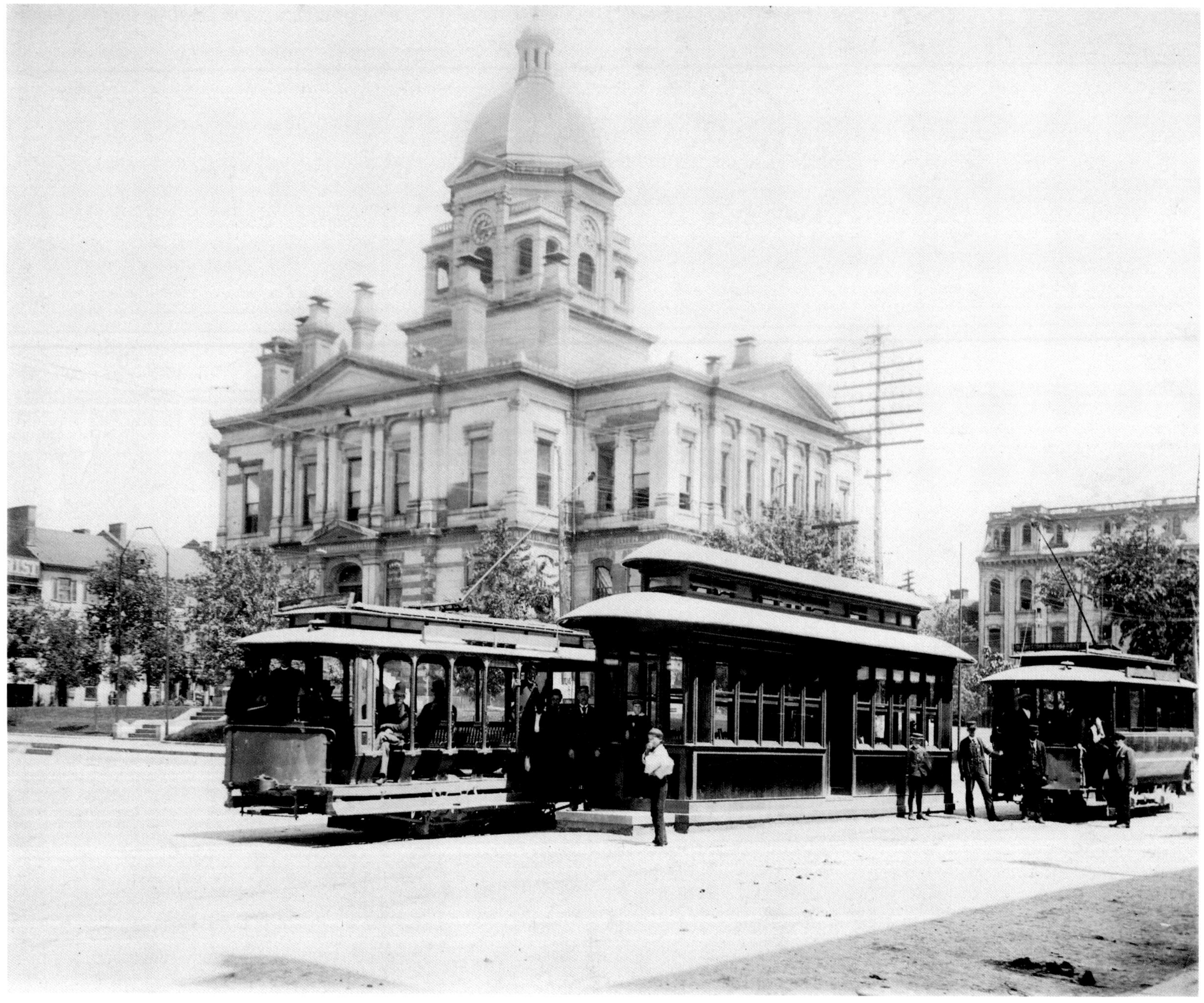

The Postwar Nineteenth Century

(1870s–1899)

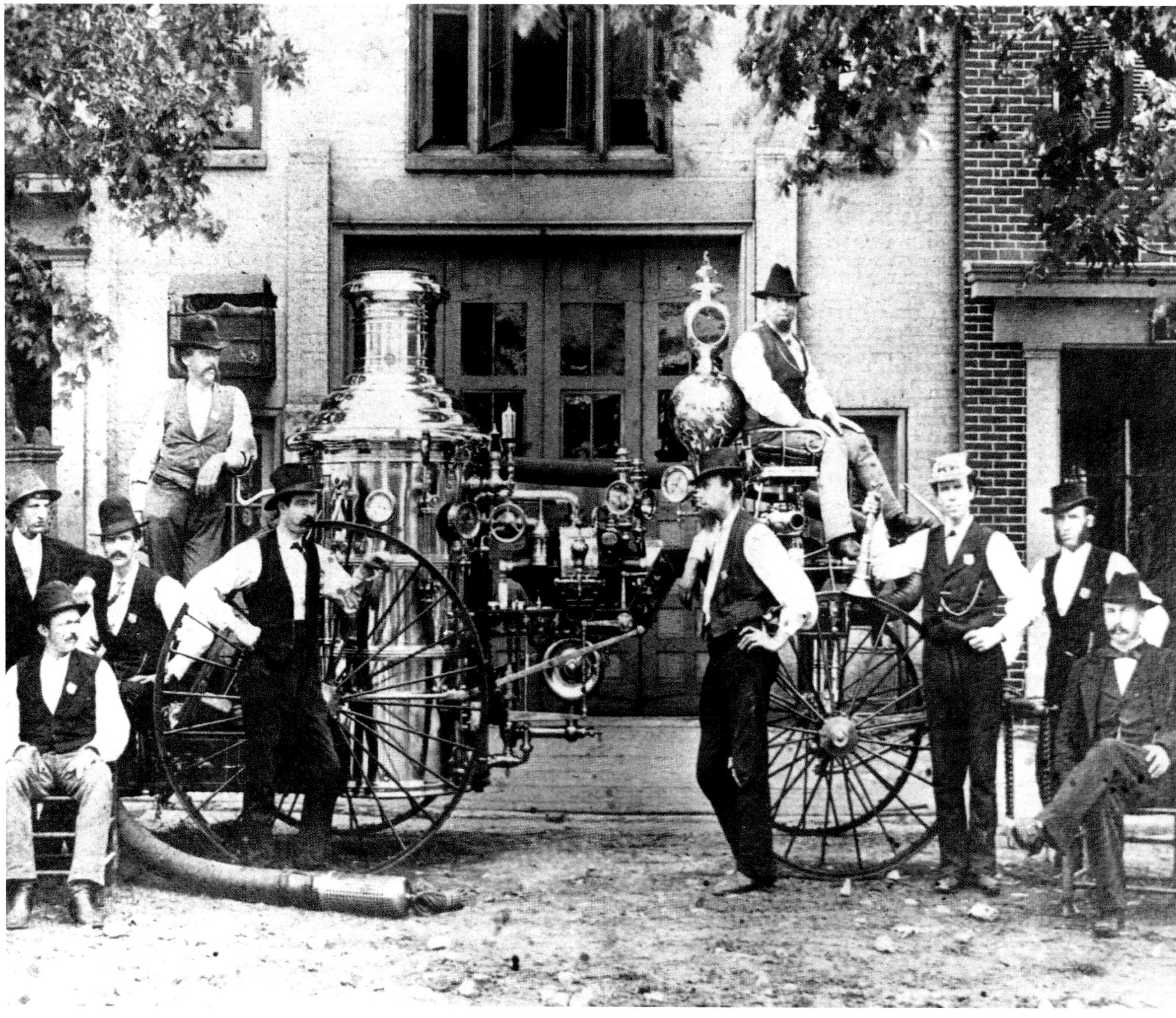

Lexington Fire Department on Short Street, ca. 1875.

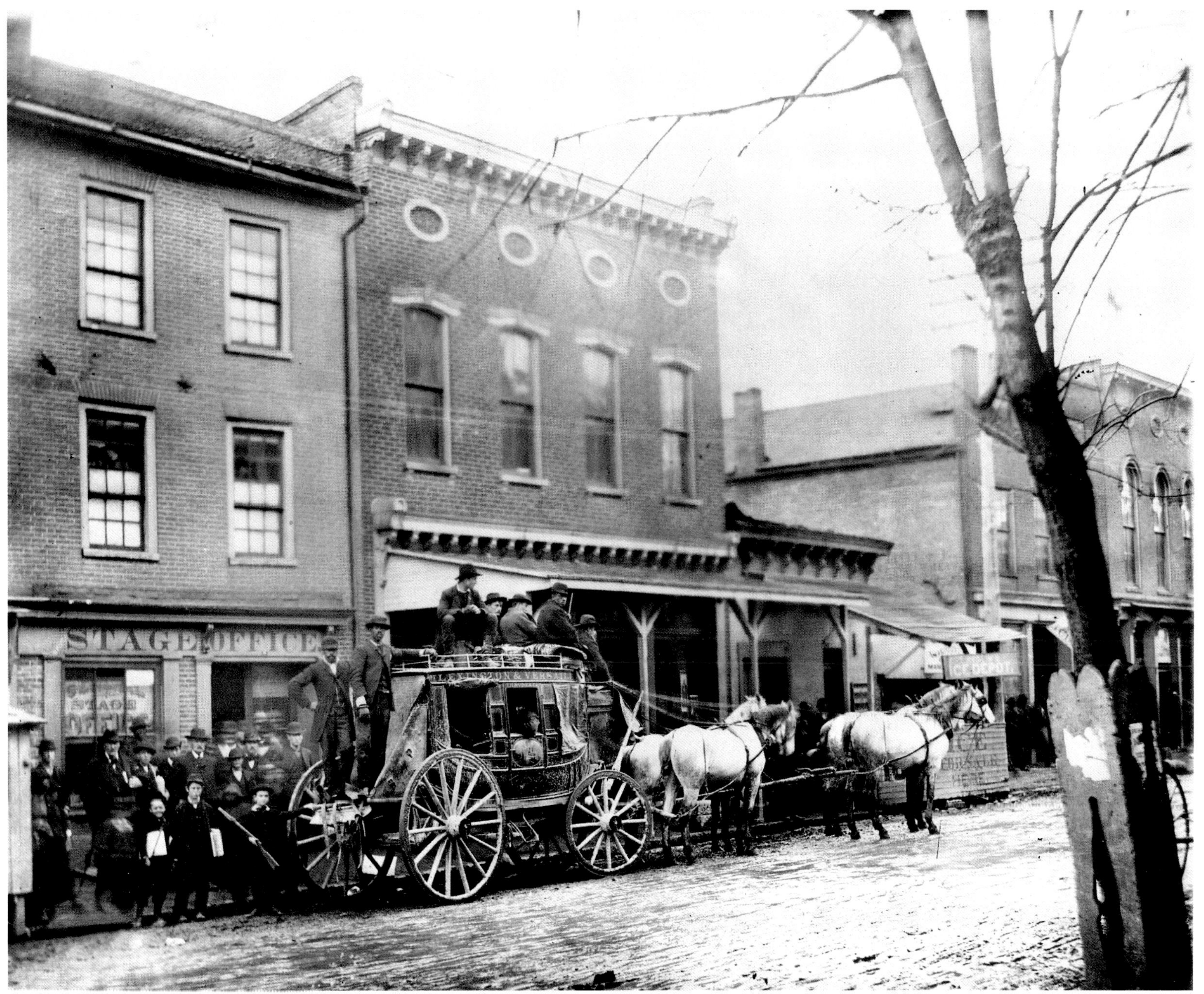

Stagecoach stop on Short Street, ca. 1885.

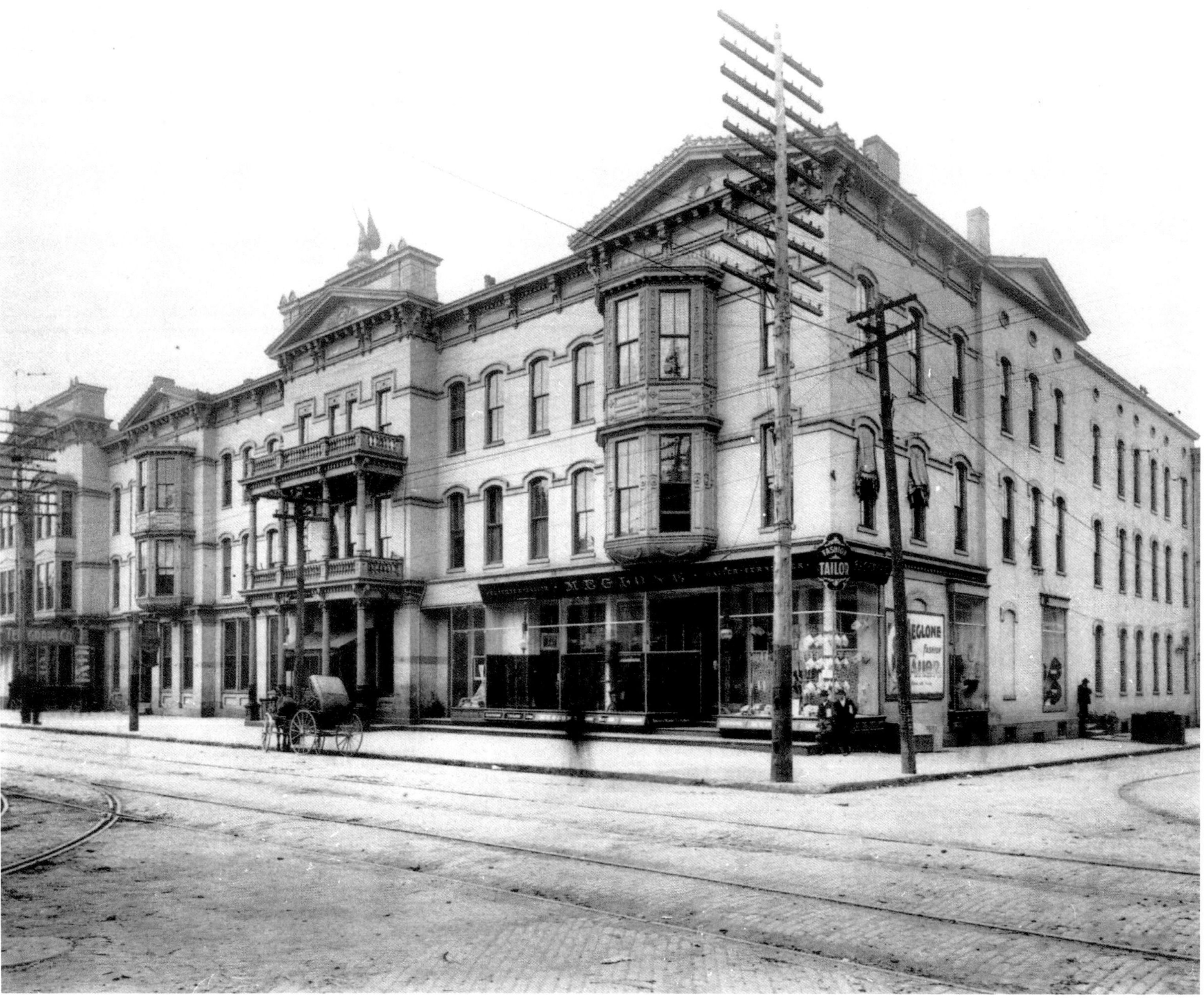

Phoenix Hotel on Main, built in the 1870s.

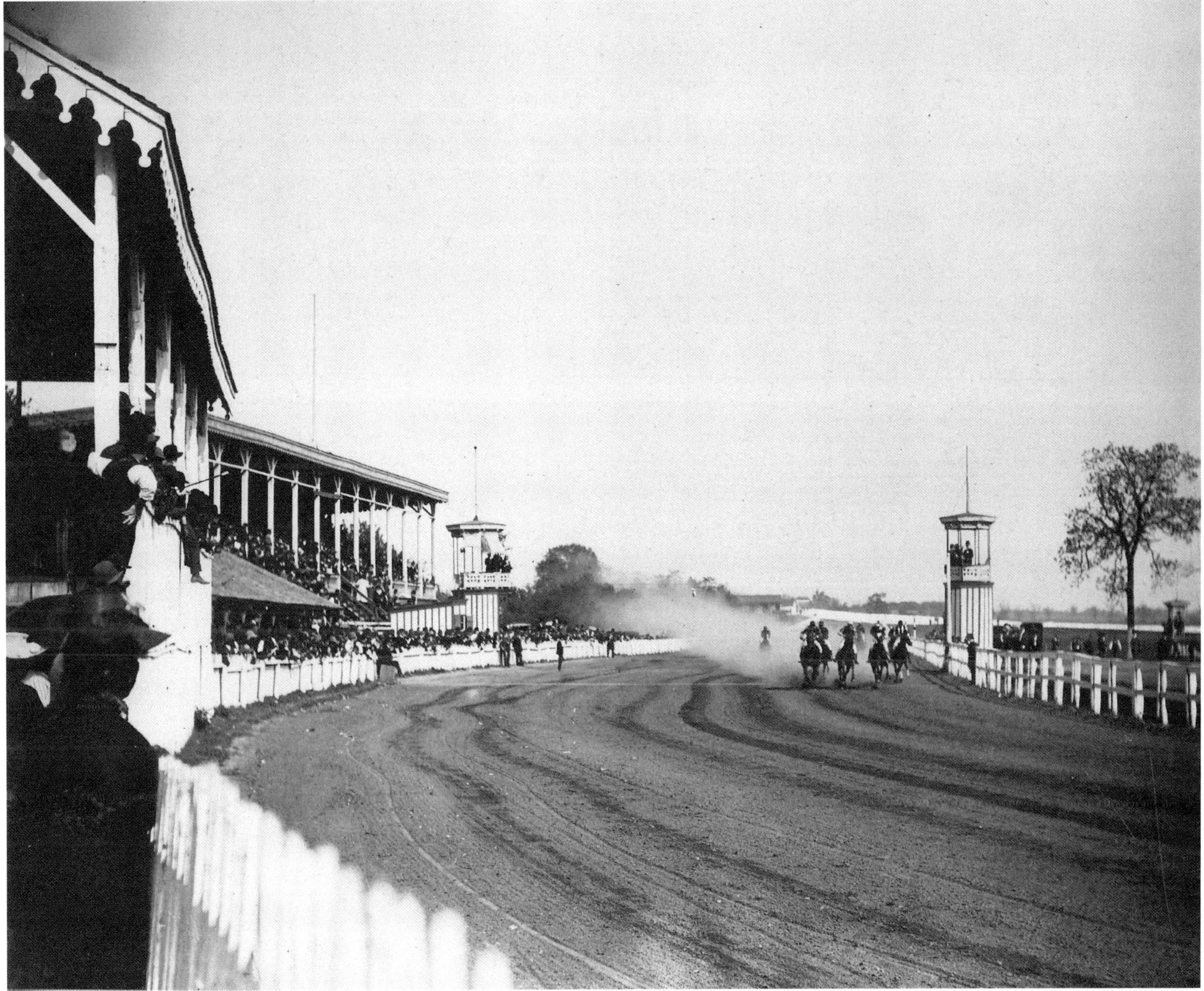

Racetrack of the Kentucky Association for the Improvement of the Breeds of Stock, 1888. This grandstand was replaced in 1889.

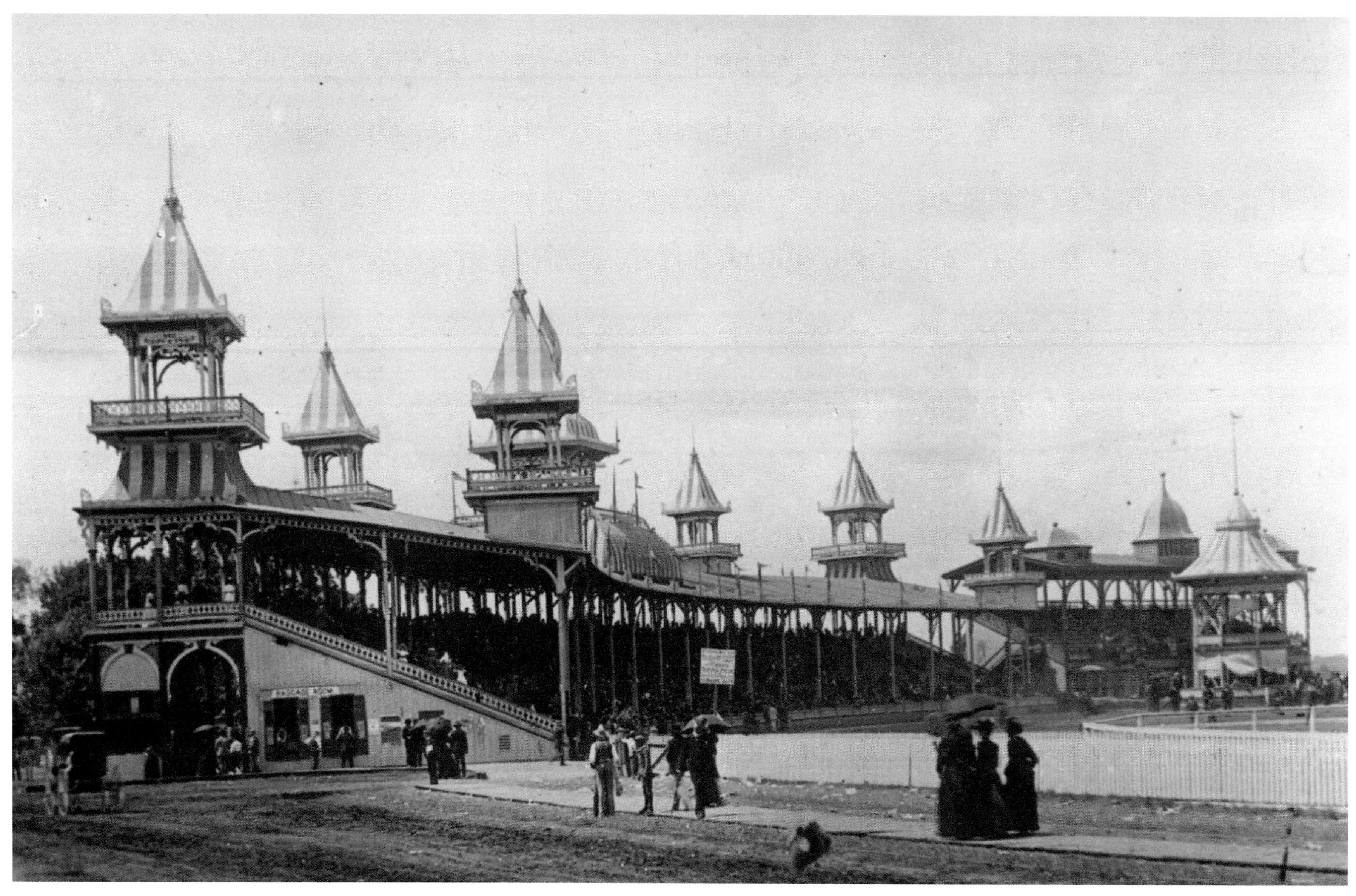

Grandstand and trotting track at the fairgrounds ("The Red Mile"), ca. 1882.

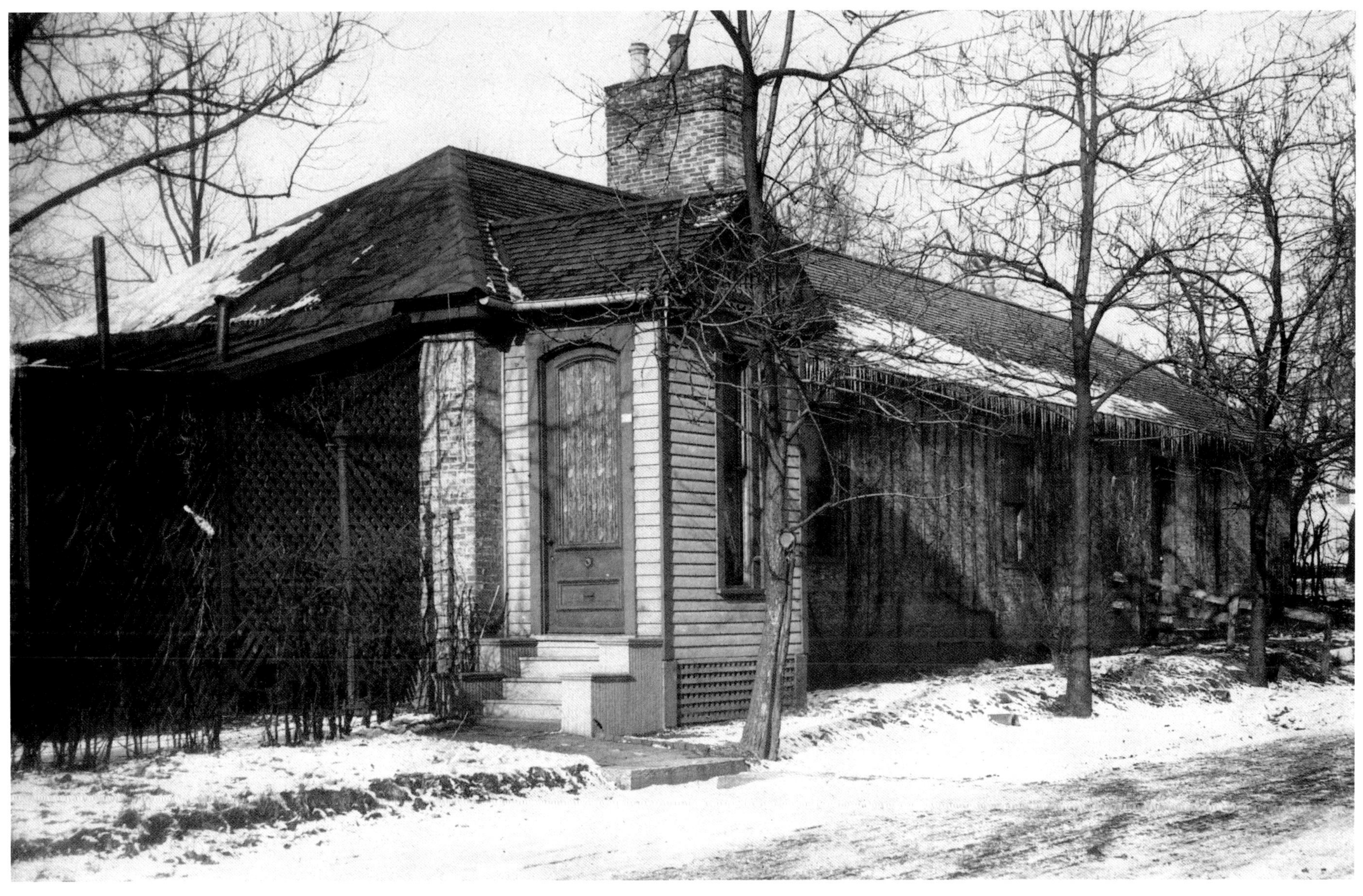

Kitchen in Graz Park (the only remaining part of the original Transylvania University campus) as it looked when occupied by Howard Graz, ca. 1880.

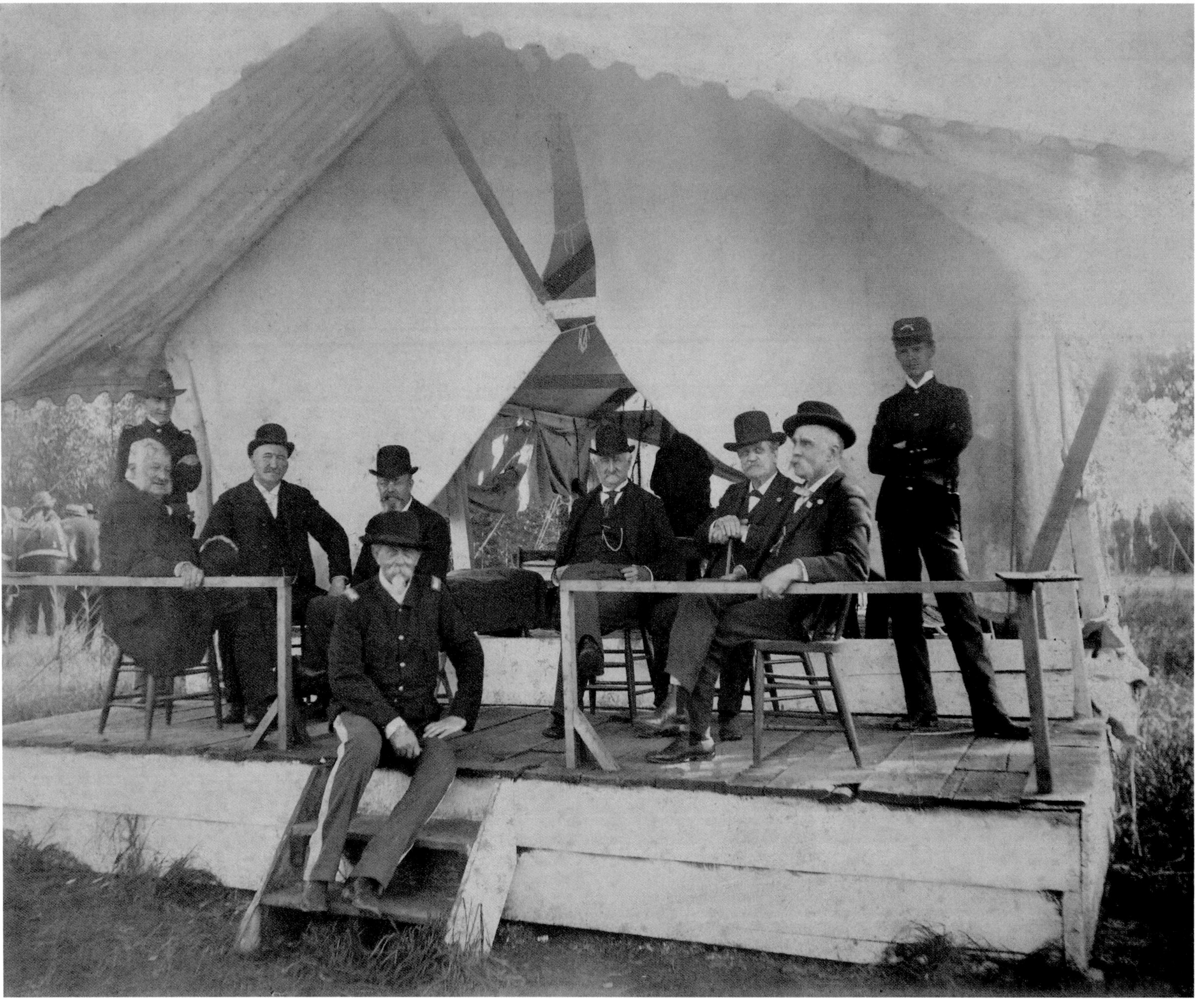

Old soldiers' reunion (some in Union uniforms), late nineteenth century.

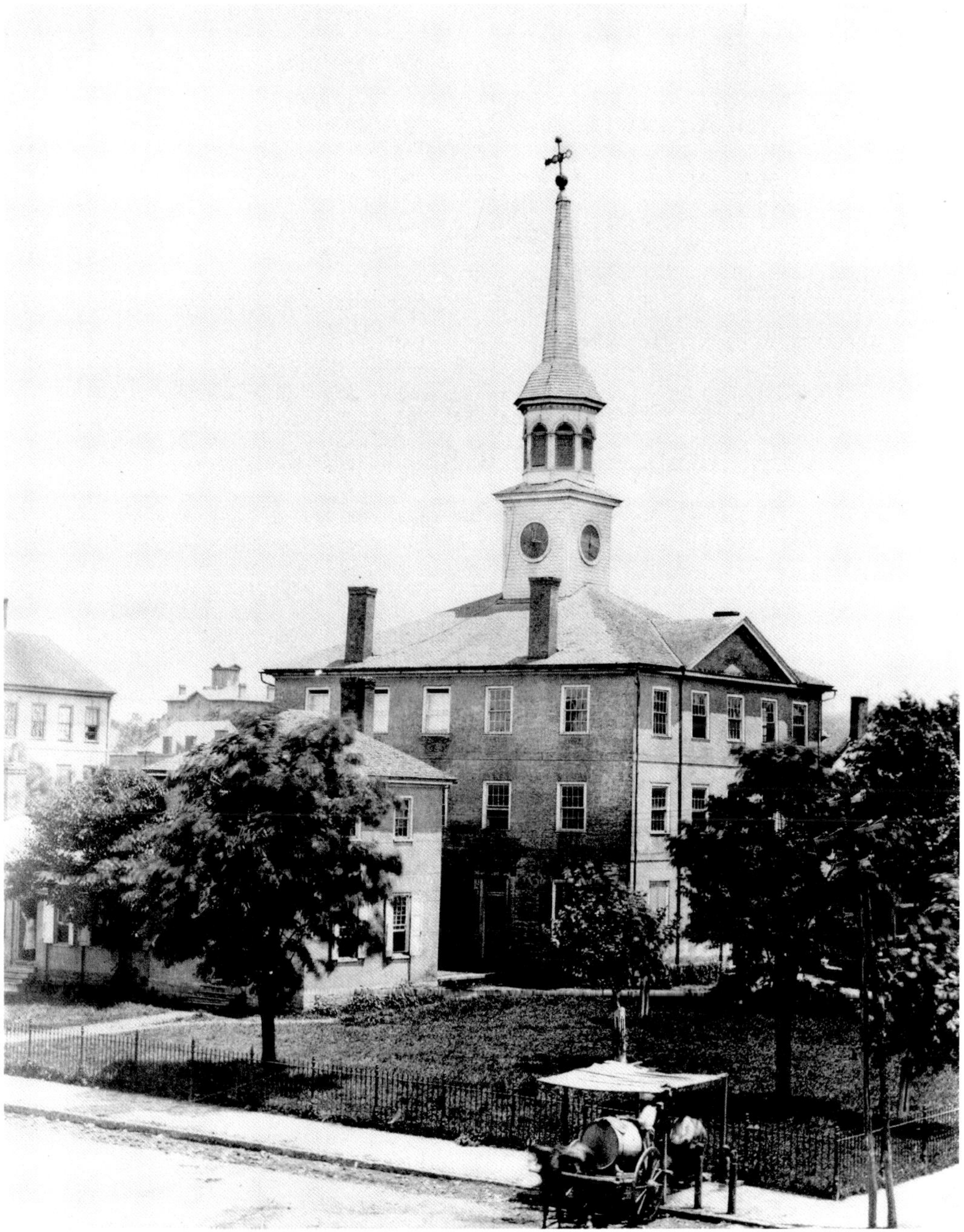

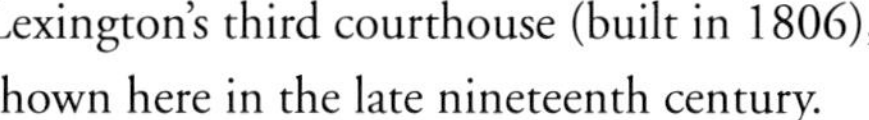

Lexington's third courthouse (built in 1806), shown here in the late nineteenth century.

Sheriff's office on Upper Street. It burned in 1897.

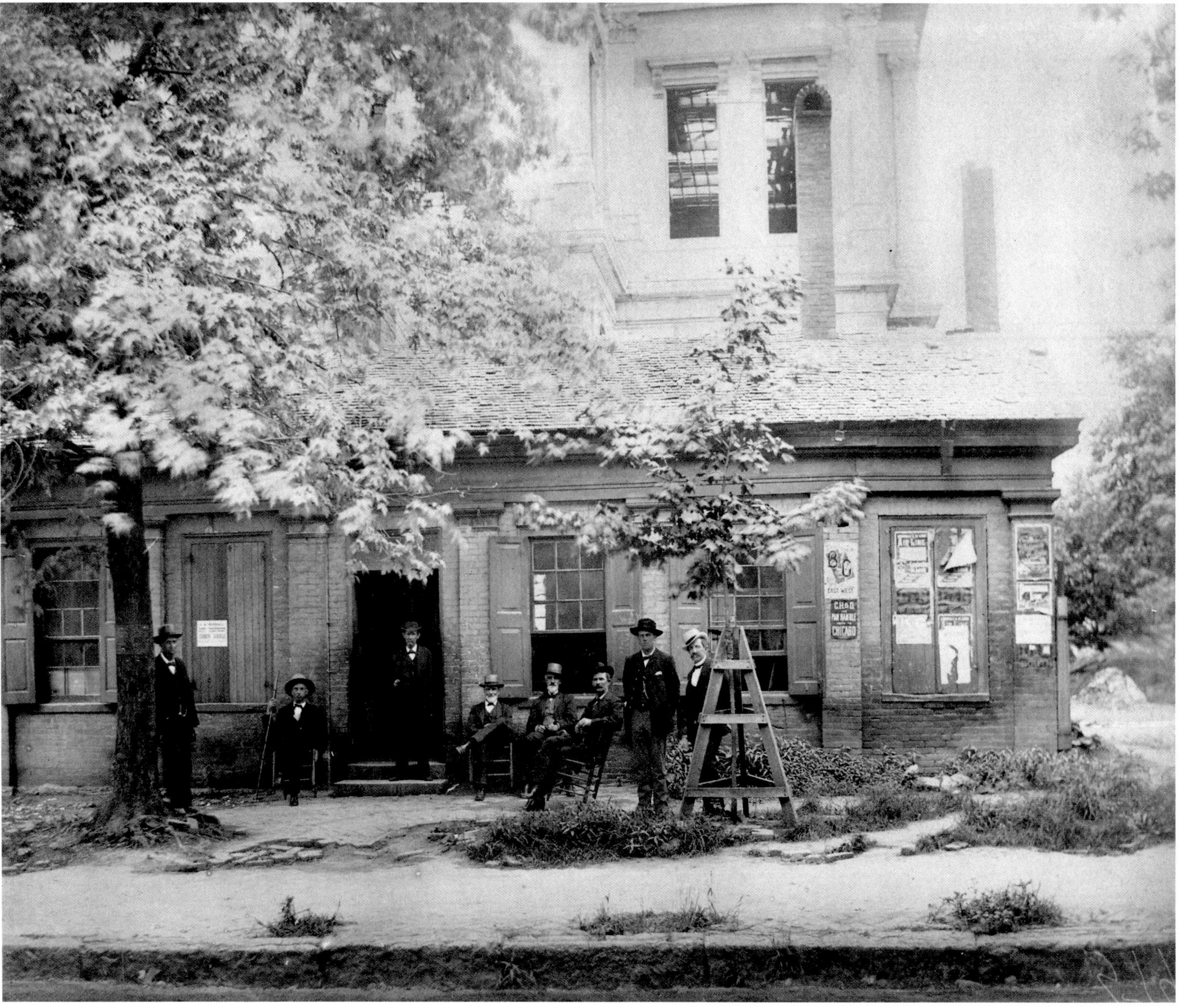

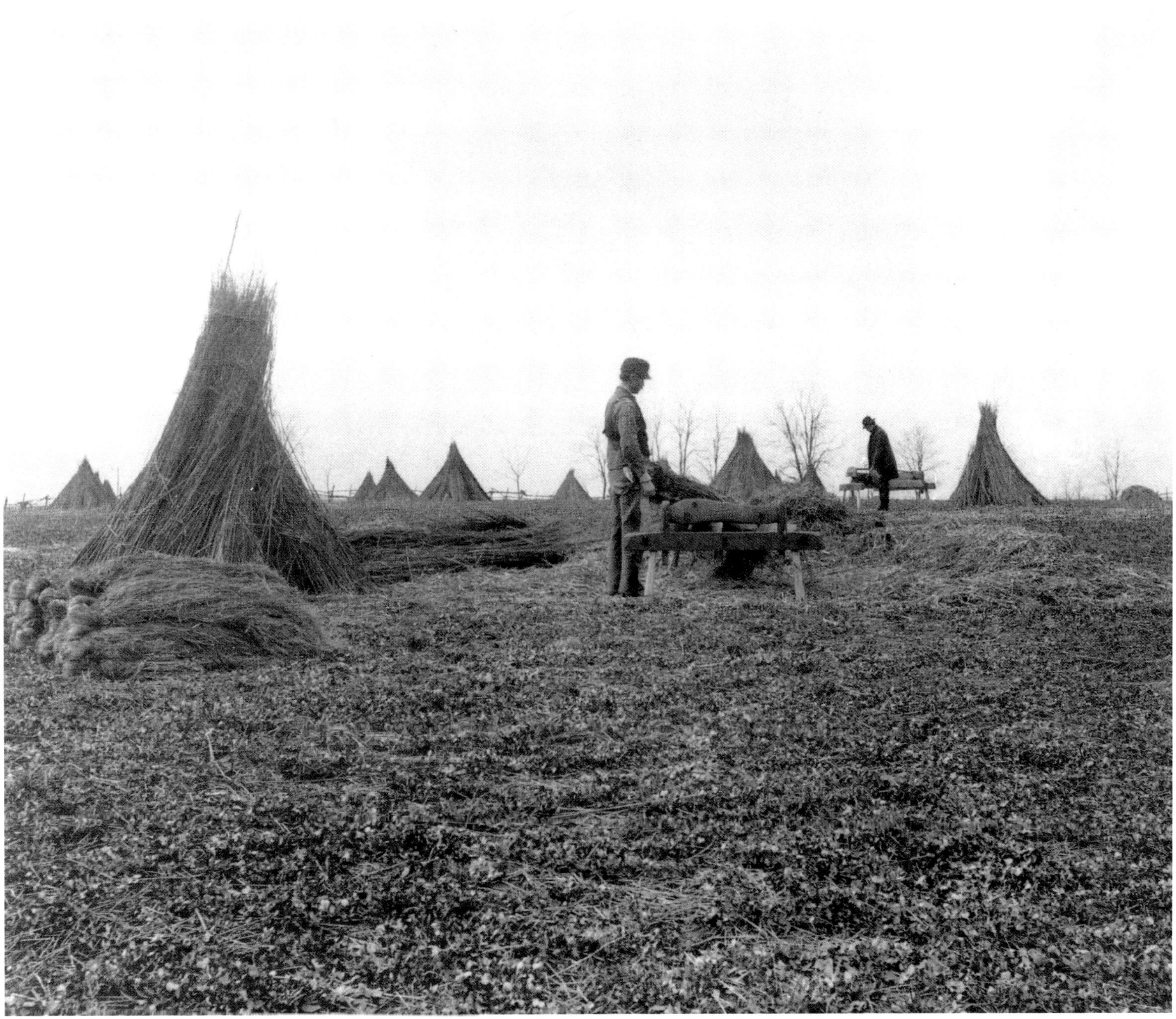

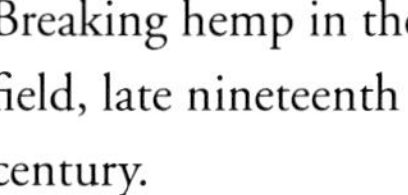

Breaking hemp in the field, late nineteenth century.

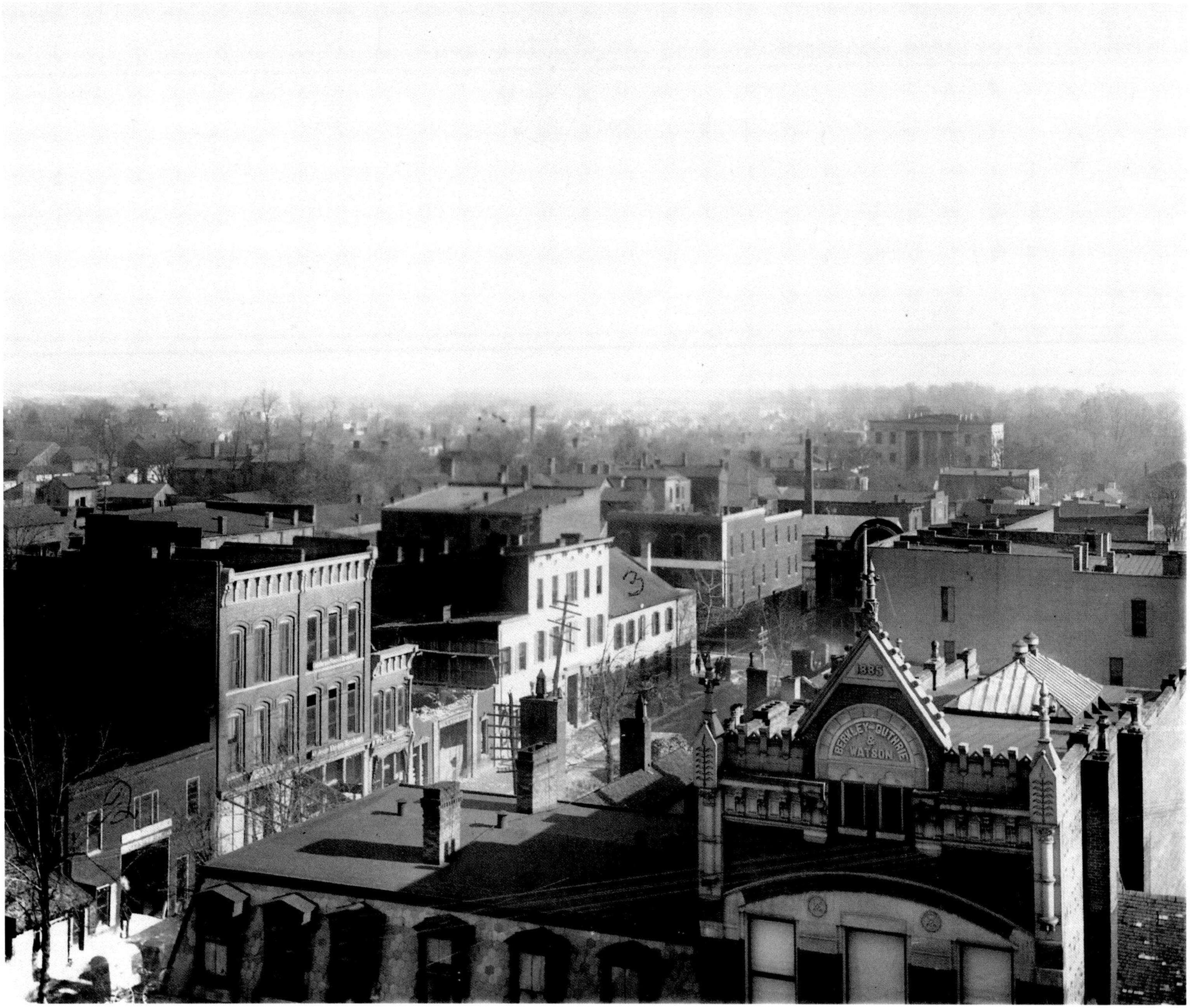

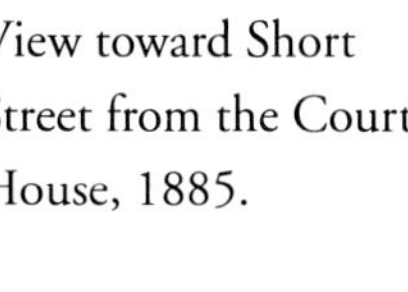

View toward Short Street from the Court House, 1885.

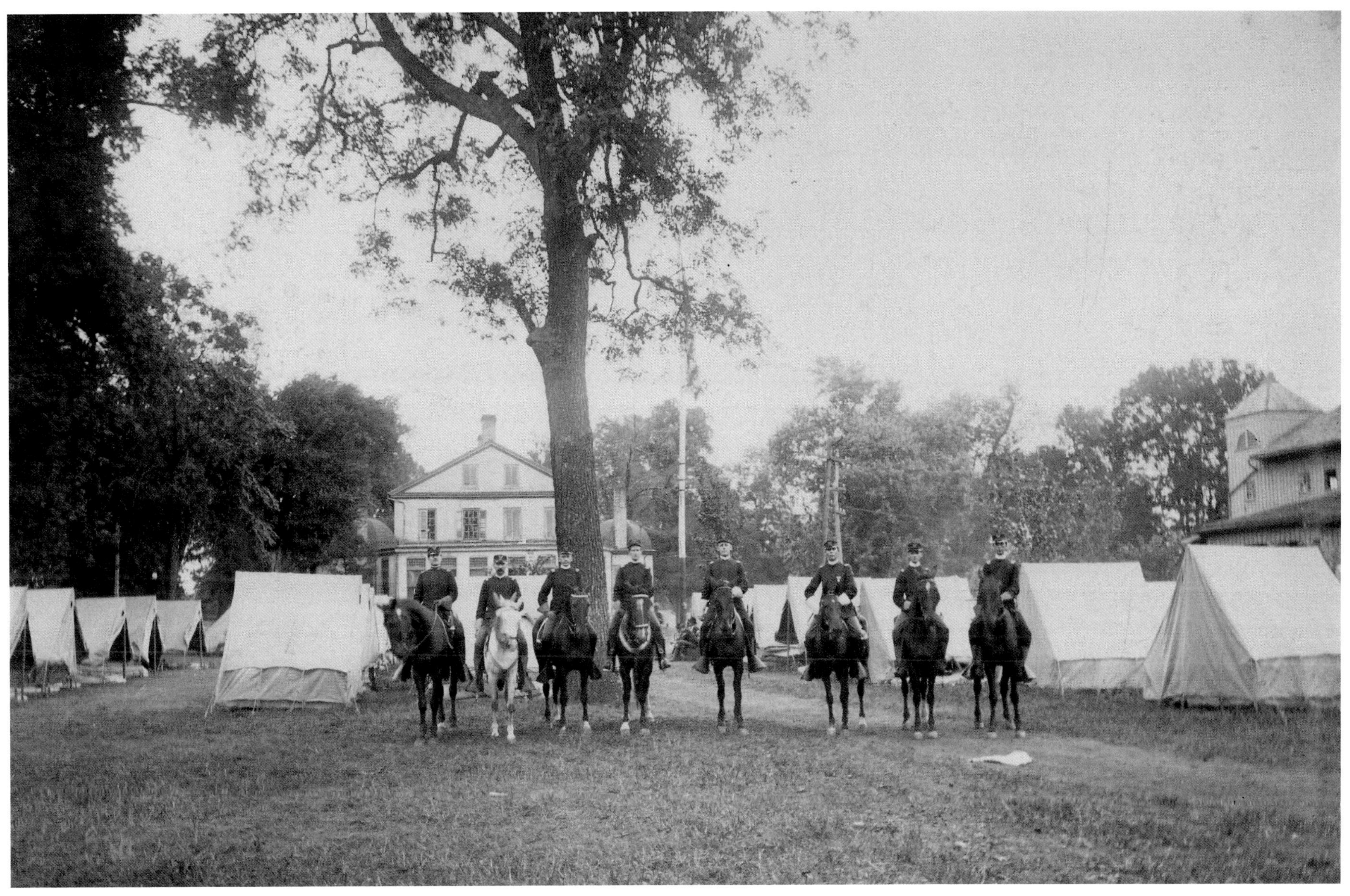

Kentucky State Guard encamped in Woodland Park, 1899.

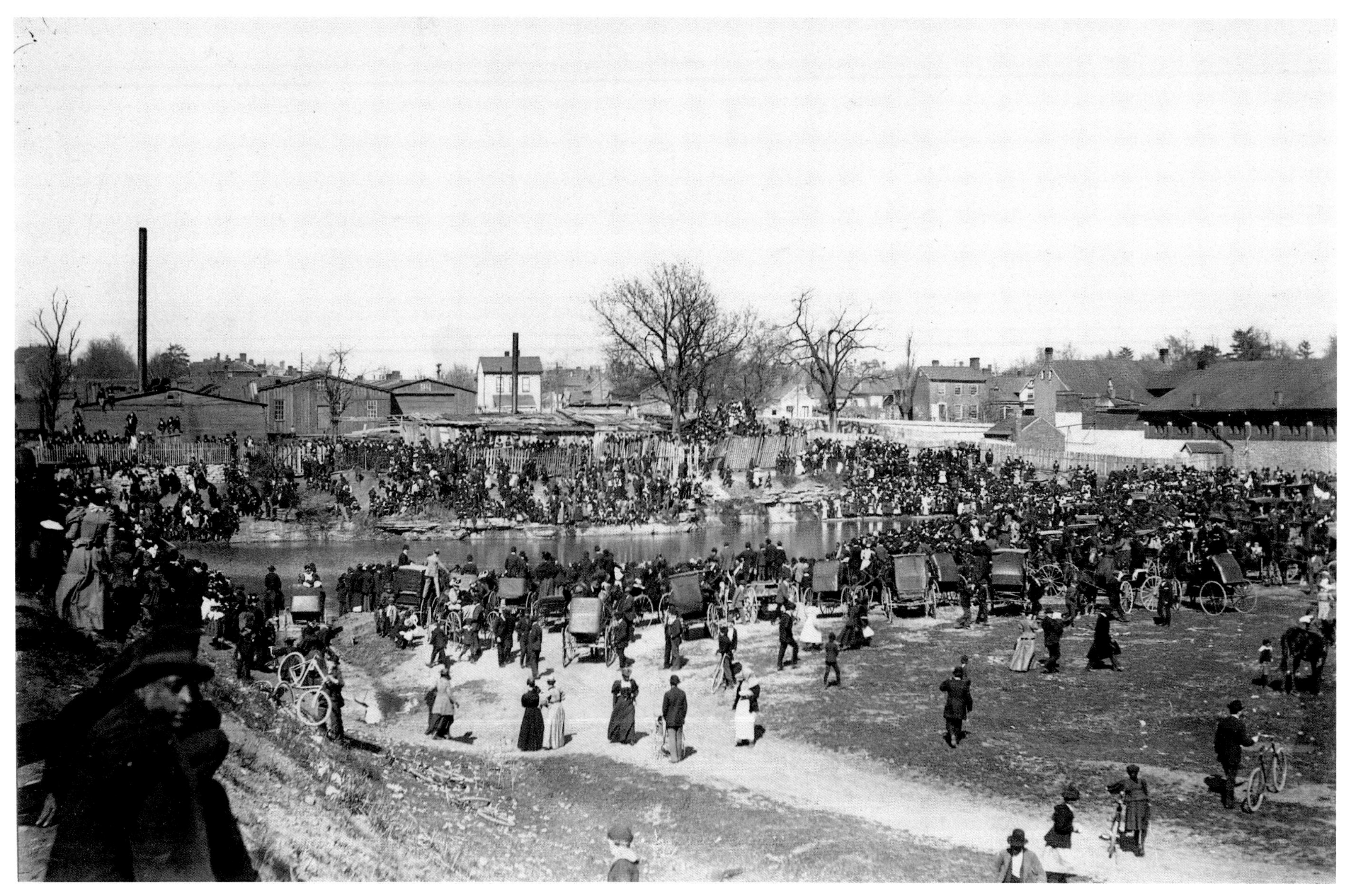

African-American Baptism at Work House pond, late nineteenth century.

Lexington Post Office, 1898.

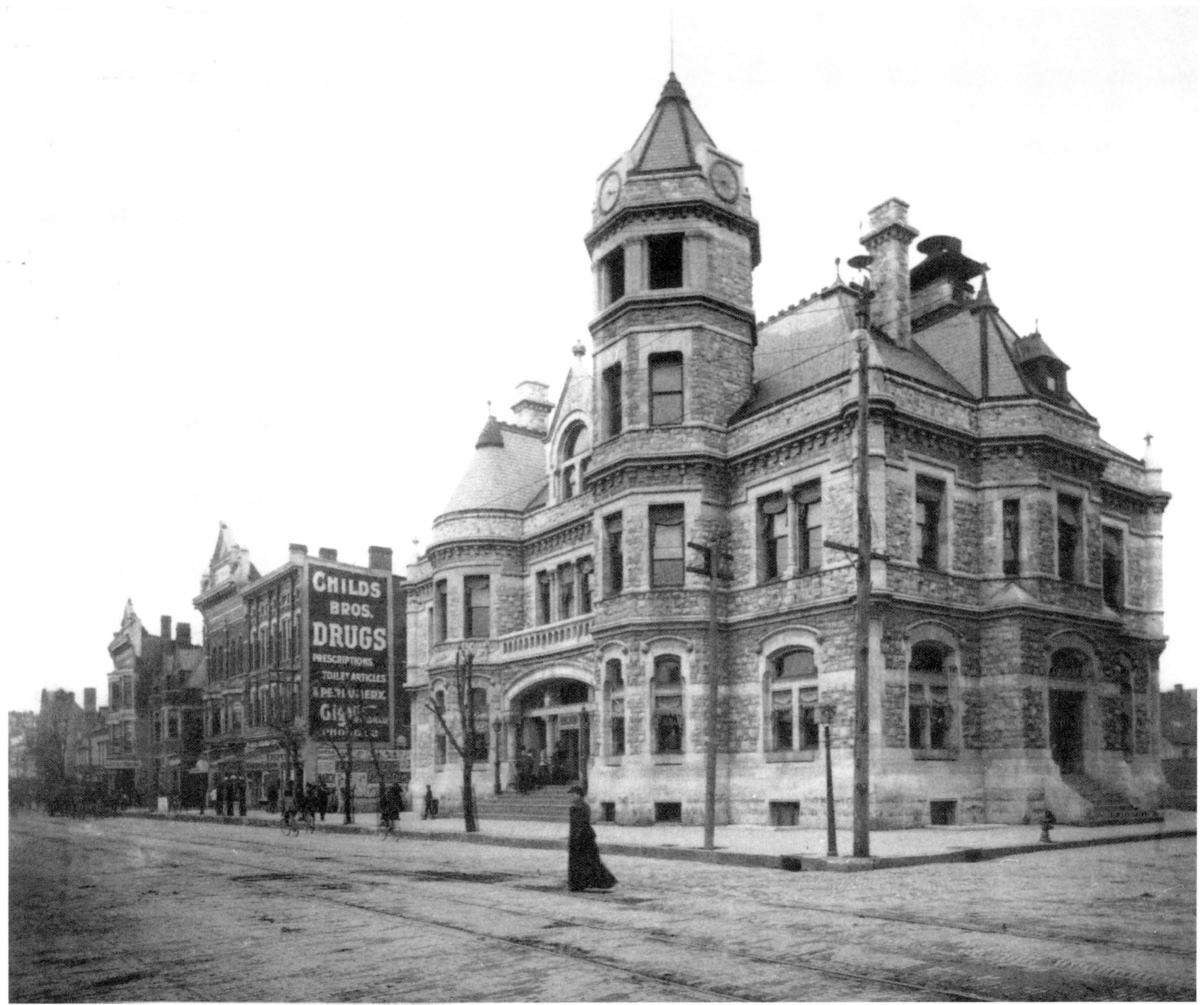

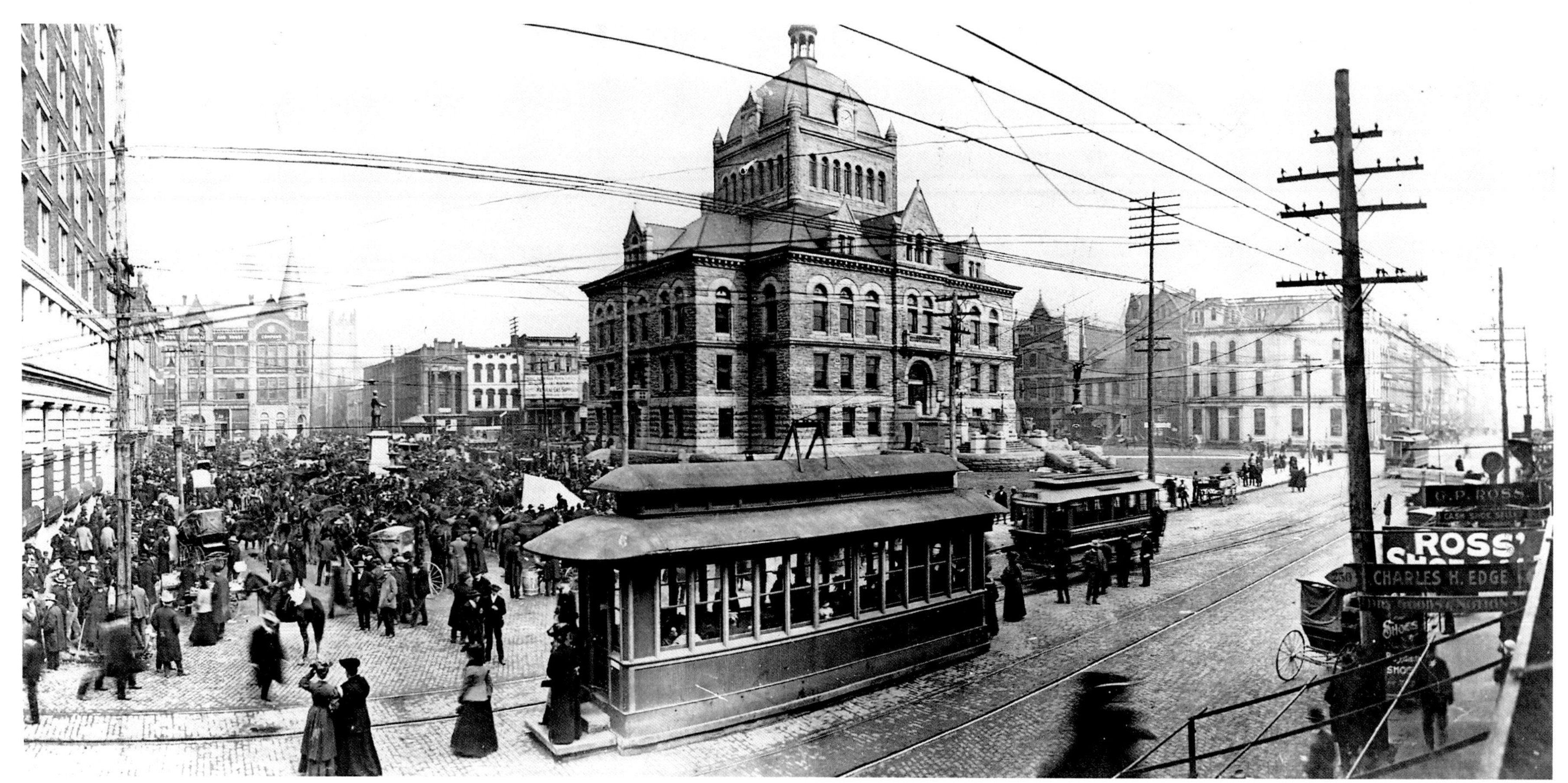

Courthouse facing north on Cheapside, 1890s.

Court day on Cheapside looking south, 1897.

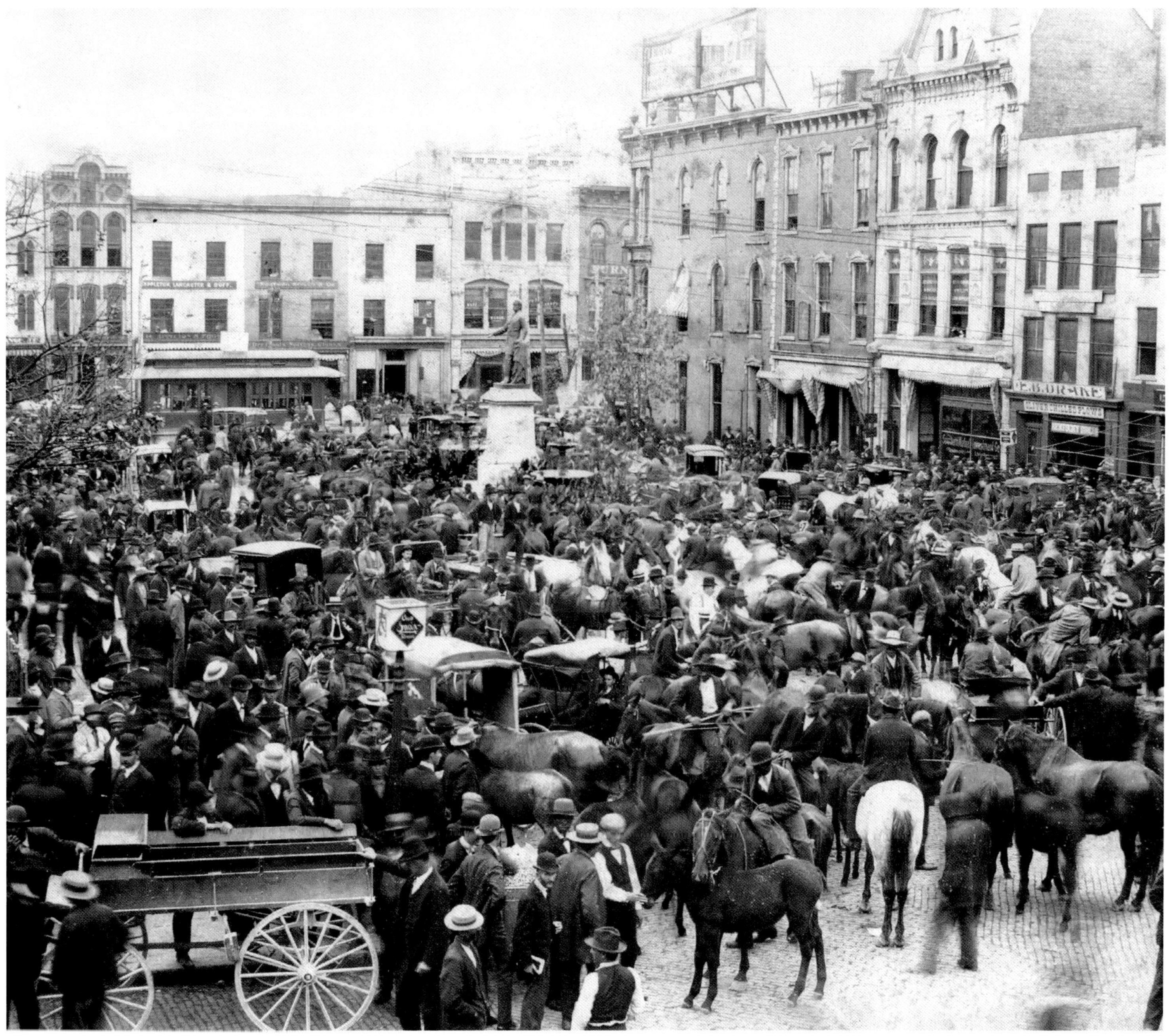

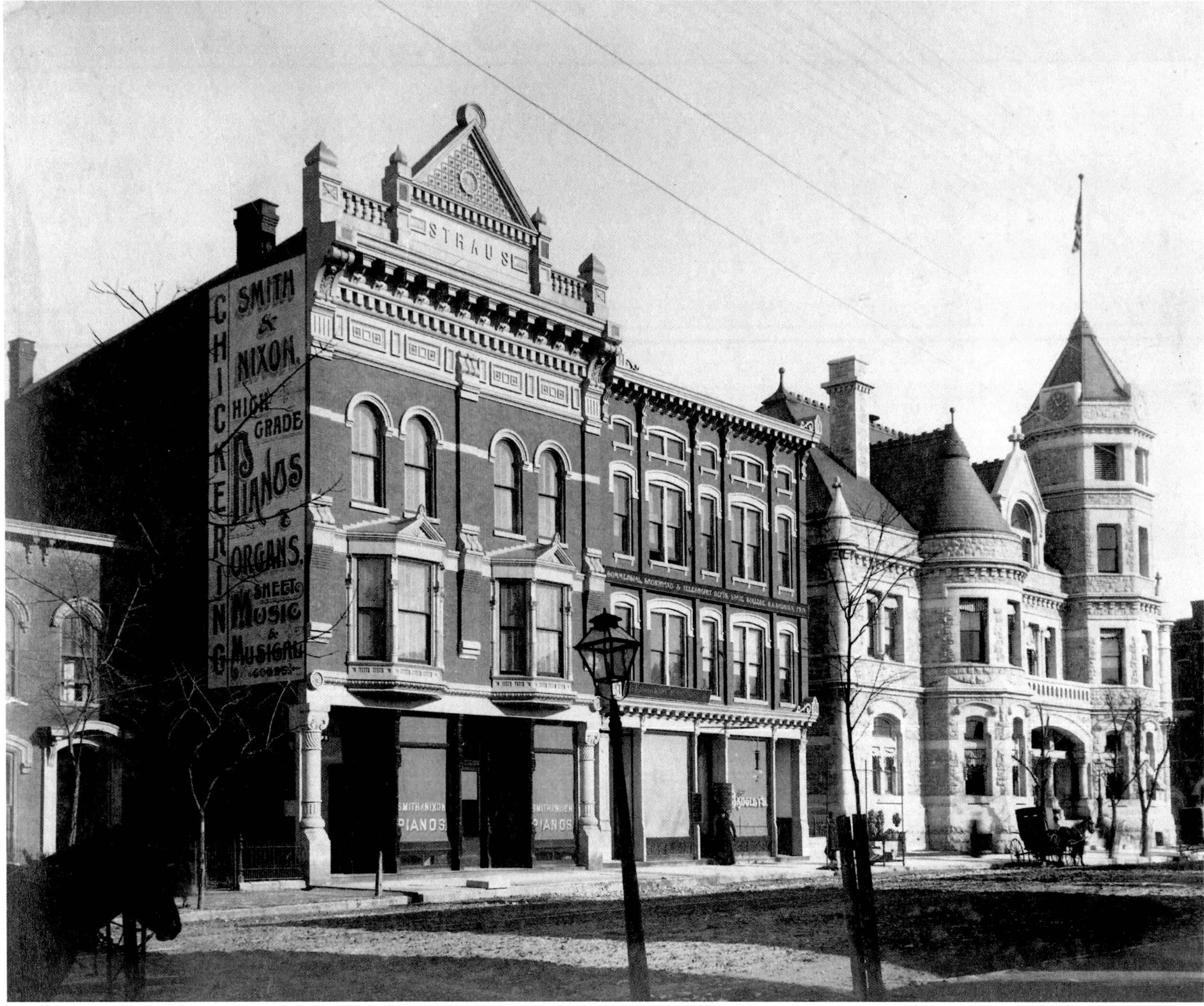

The Straus Building, located next to the post office, 1889.

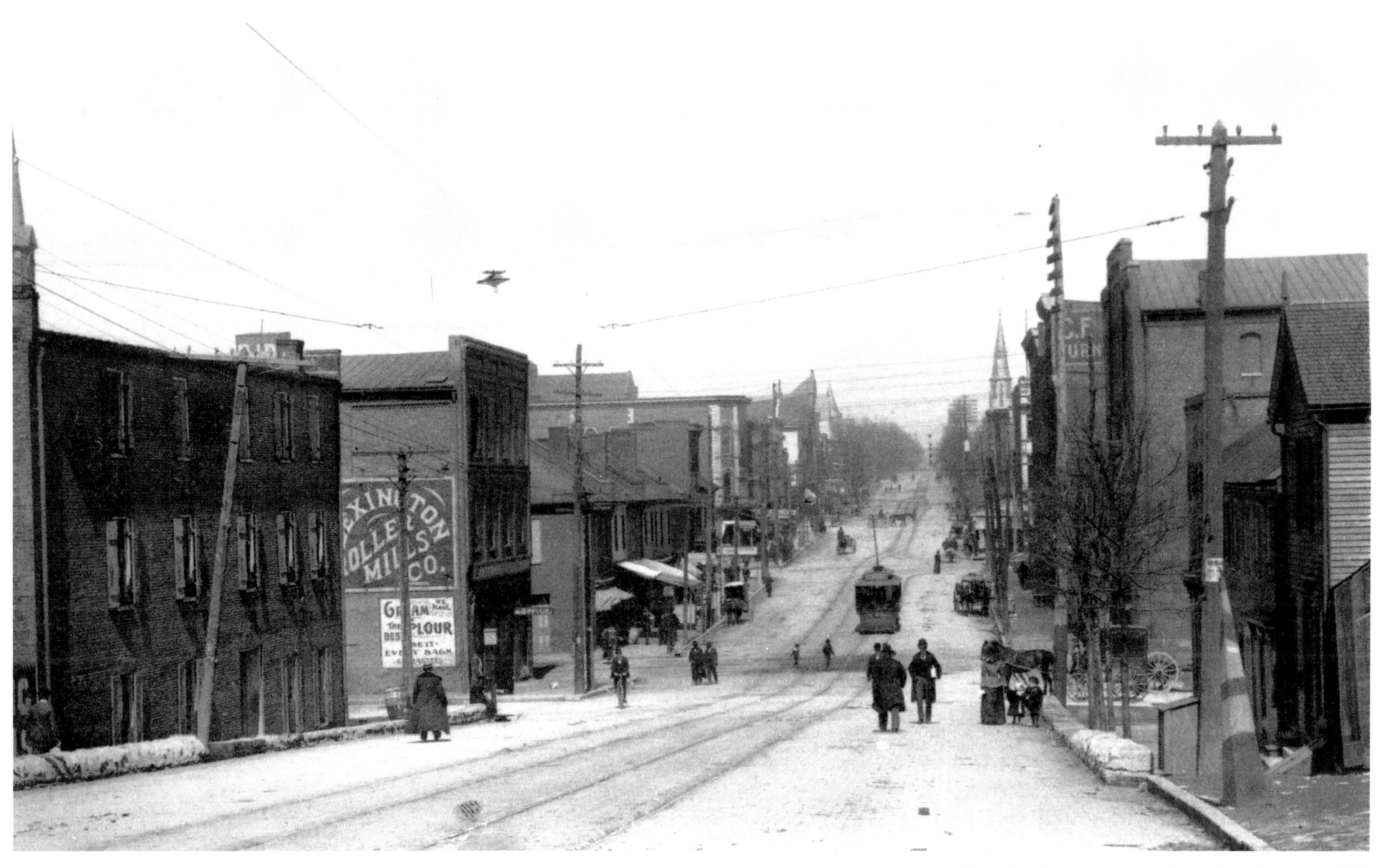

View showing streetcar tracks on Broadway, ca. 1898.

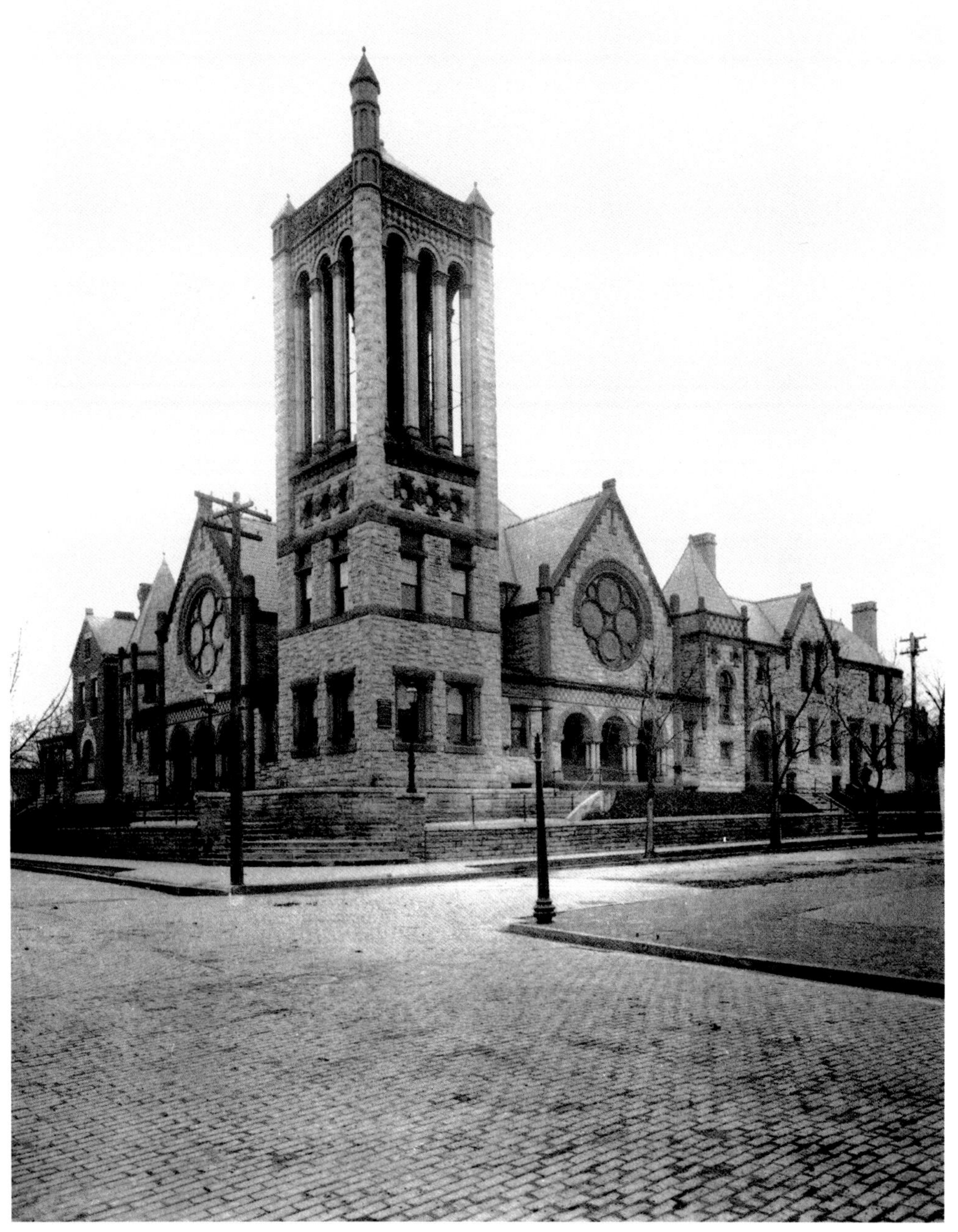

Central Christian Church (built 1893-94), late nineteenth century.

Lexington Cemetery entrance, 1898.

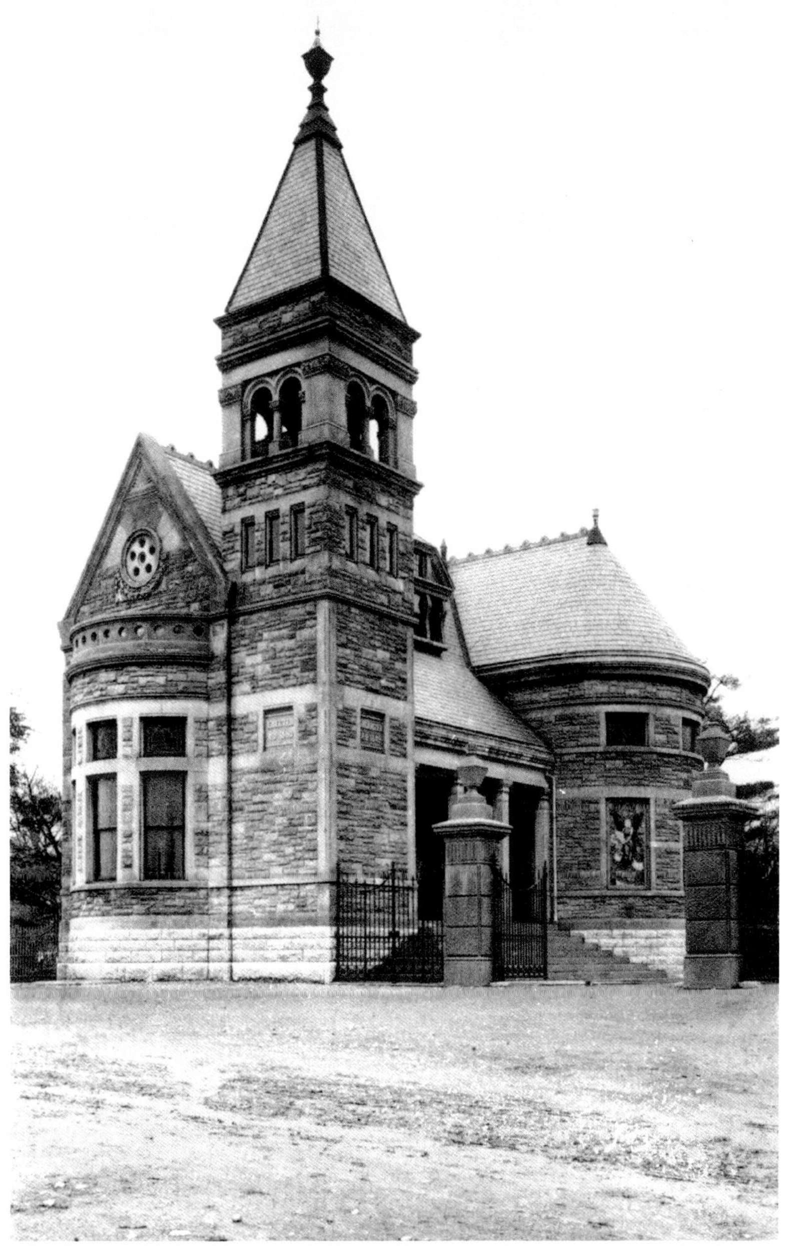

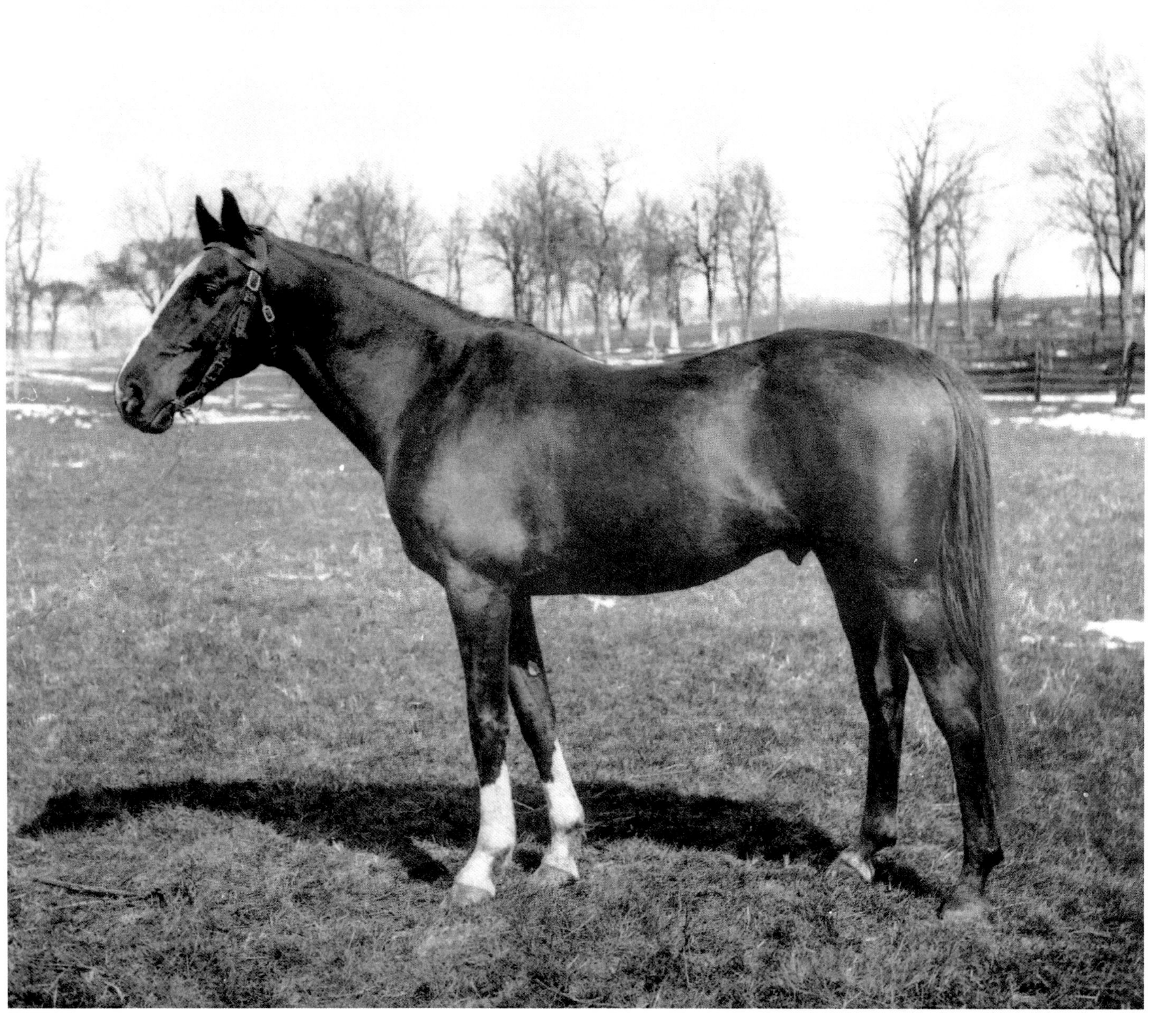

Named Hanover (1884–1899), this racehorse won 32 of his 50 starts. In 1889, he was purchased by Colonel Milton Young, who sent him to his McGrathiana Farm near Lexington. Hanover led U.S. sire lists in four successive years.

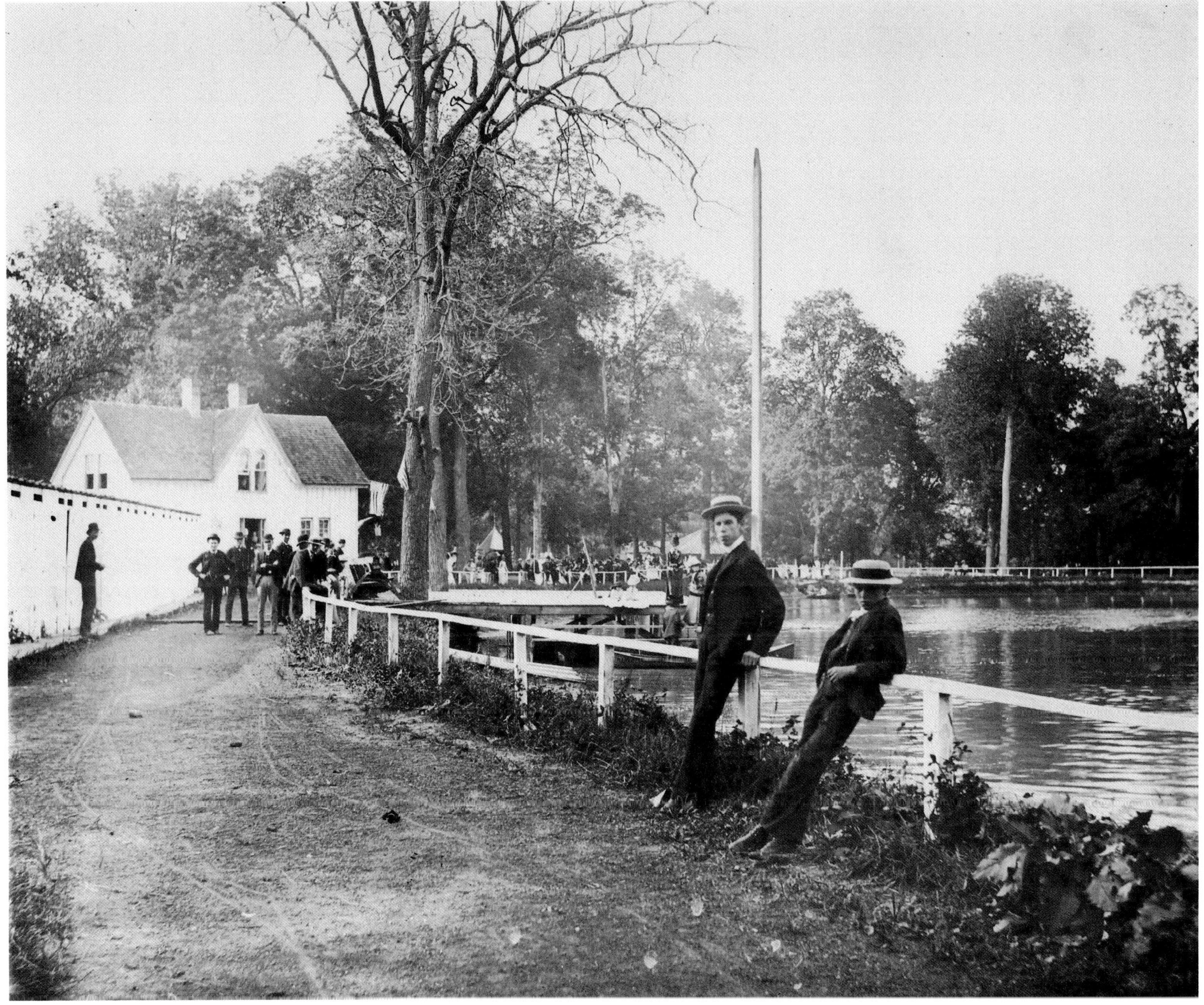

Chenosa Lake in Woodland Park, 1890. The lake was filled in around 1895.

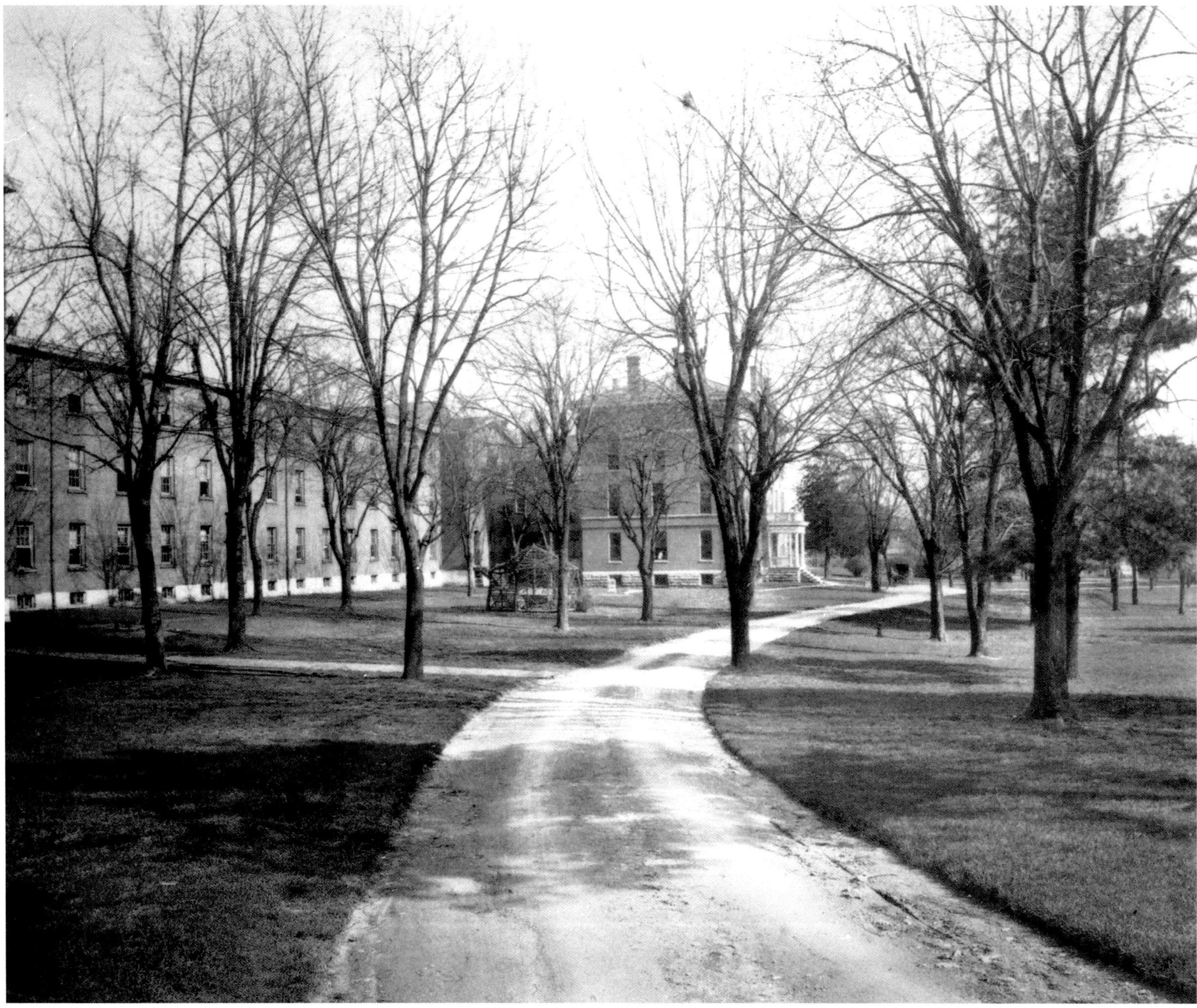

Eastern Kentucky Asylum for the Insane (established in 1816), was the second-oldest in the nation. The asylum is shown here in 1898.

Mule-drawn trolleys at Woodland Park, late 1890s.

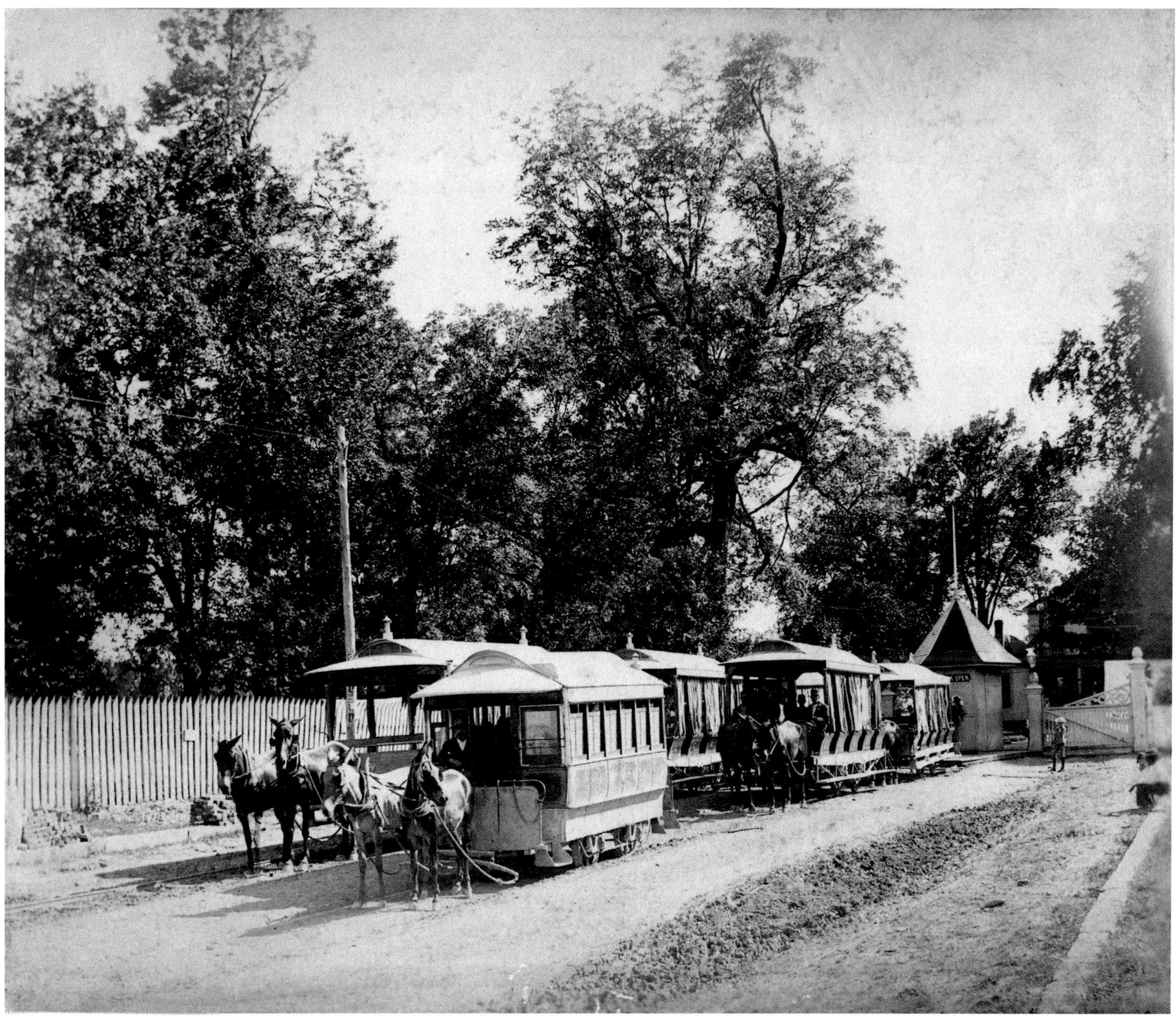

Lexington Opera House interior view, late 1890s.

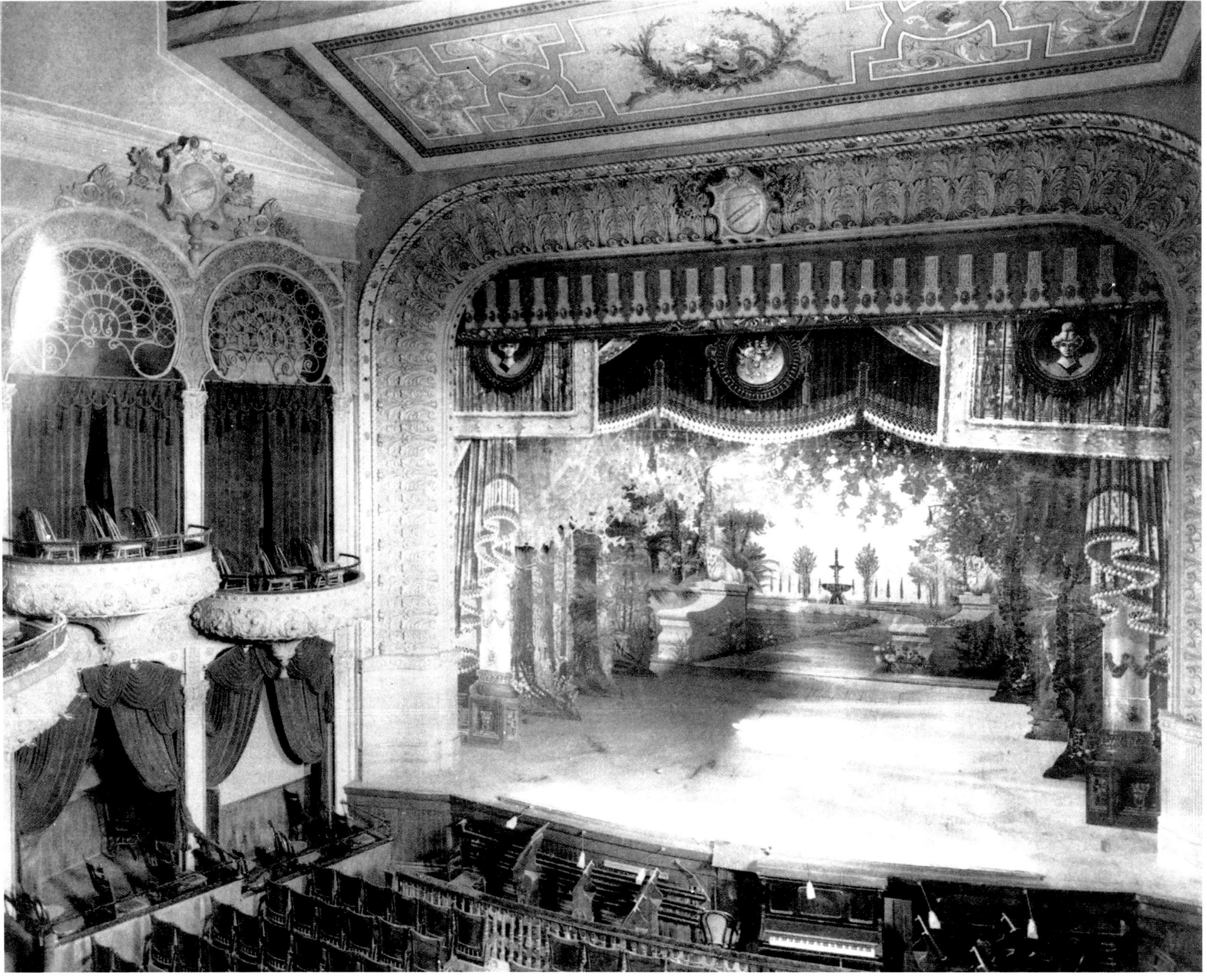

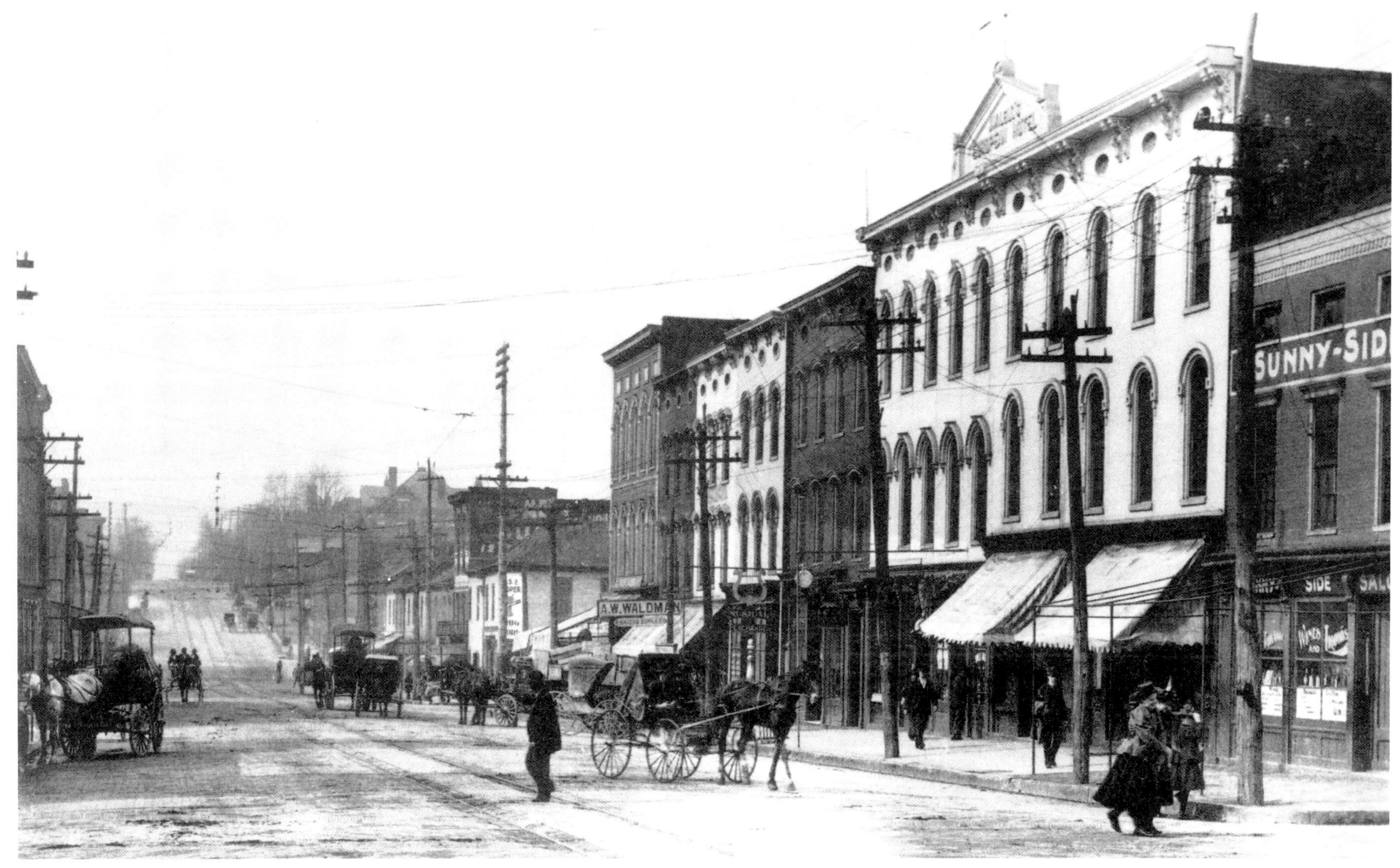

A view of Broadway, 1898.

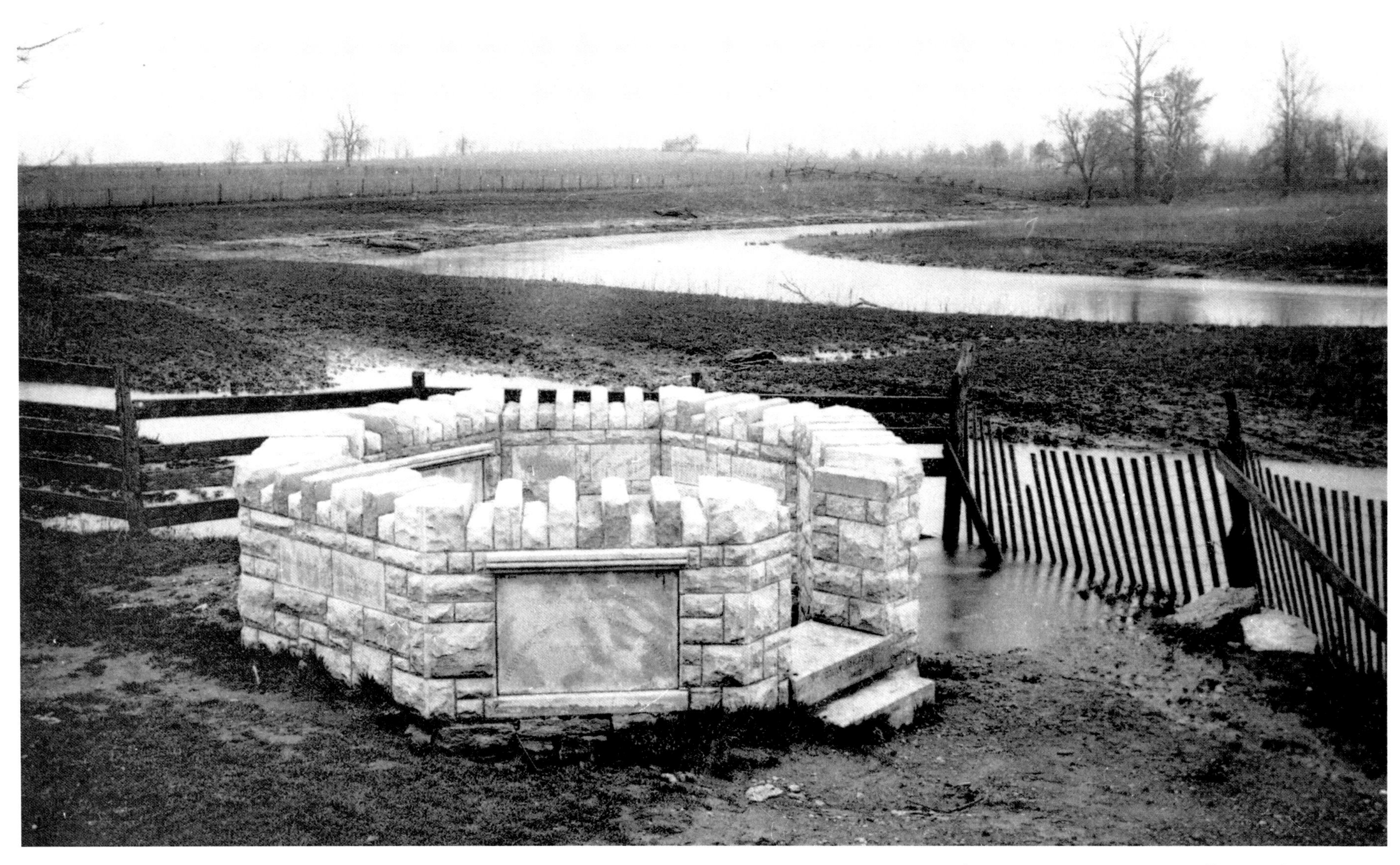

Memorial at Bryan Station spring, site of historic fort, ca. 1898.

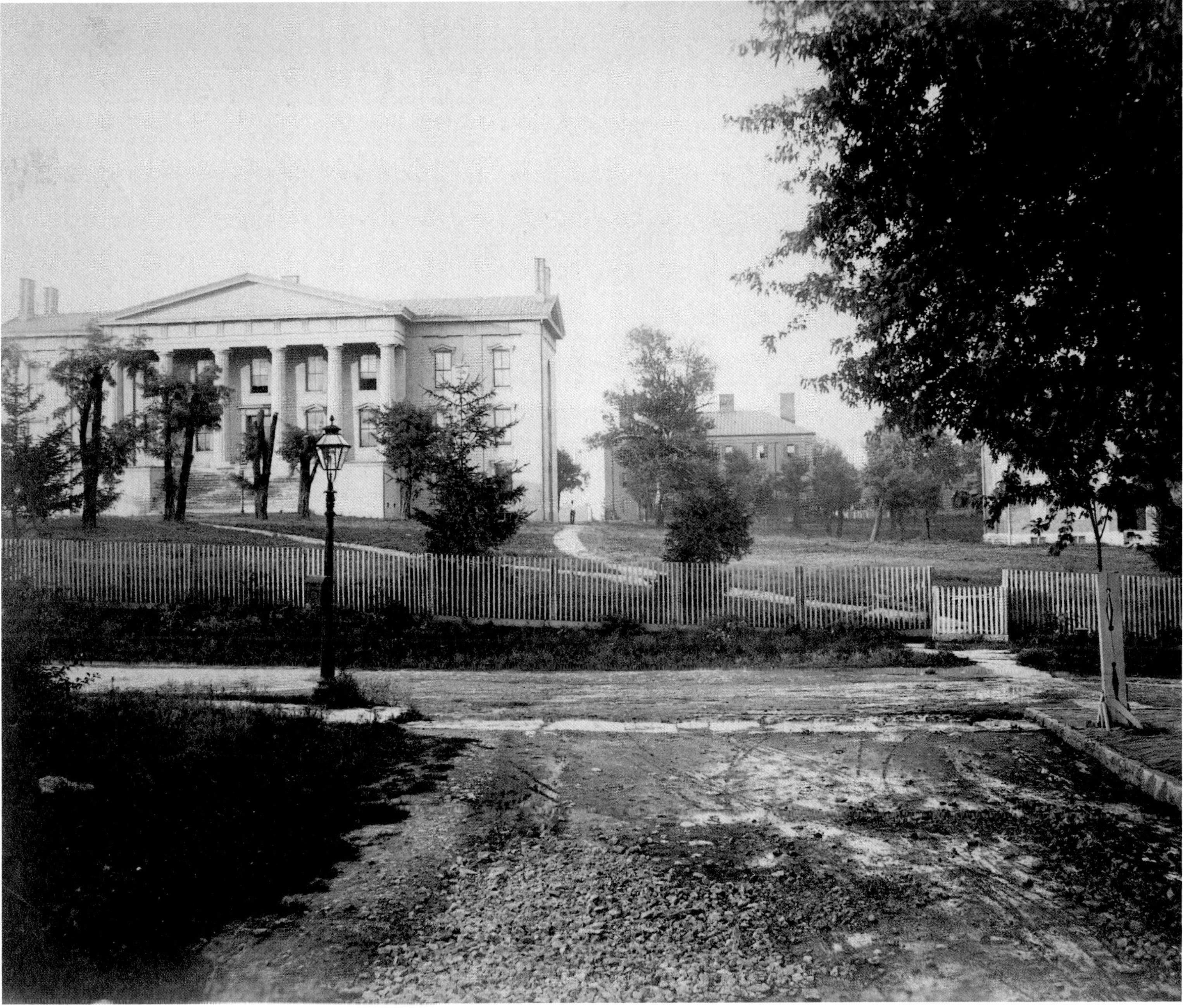

"Old Morrison" of Transylvania University seen from Graz Park, late nineteenth century.

Monument to John C. Breckinridge on Cheapside, 1898.

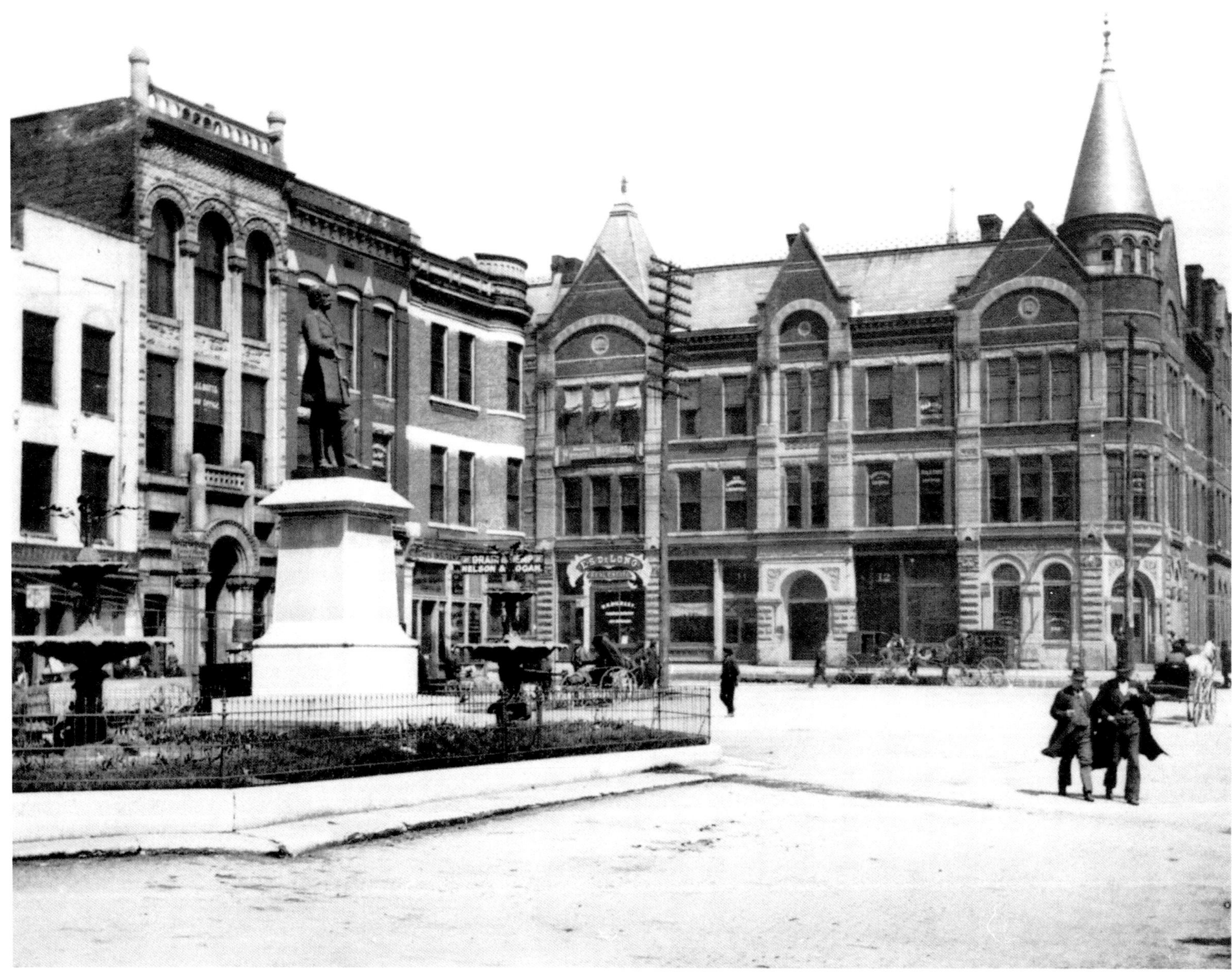

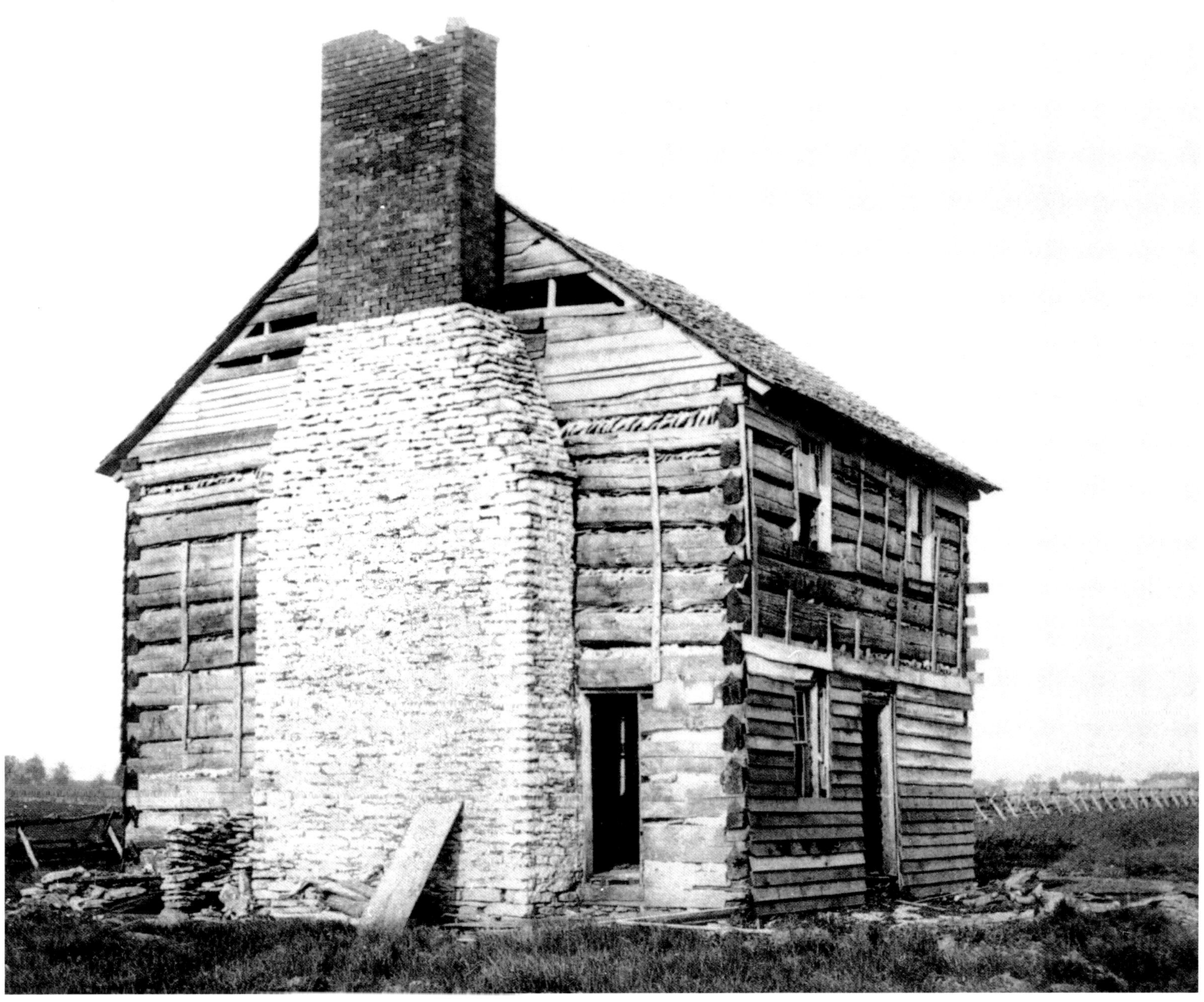

Masterson's Station (site of first Methodist Church conference in Kentucky in 1790), 1898.

Lyon Firehouse on Limestone, late nineteenth century.

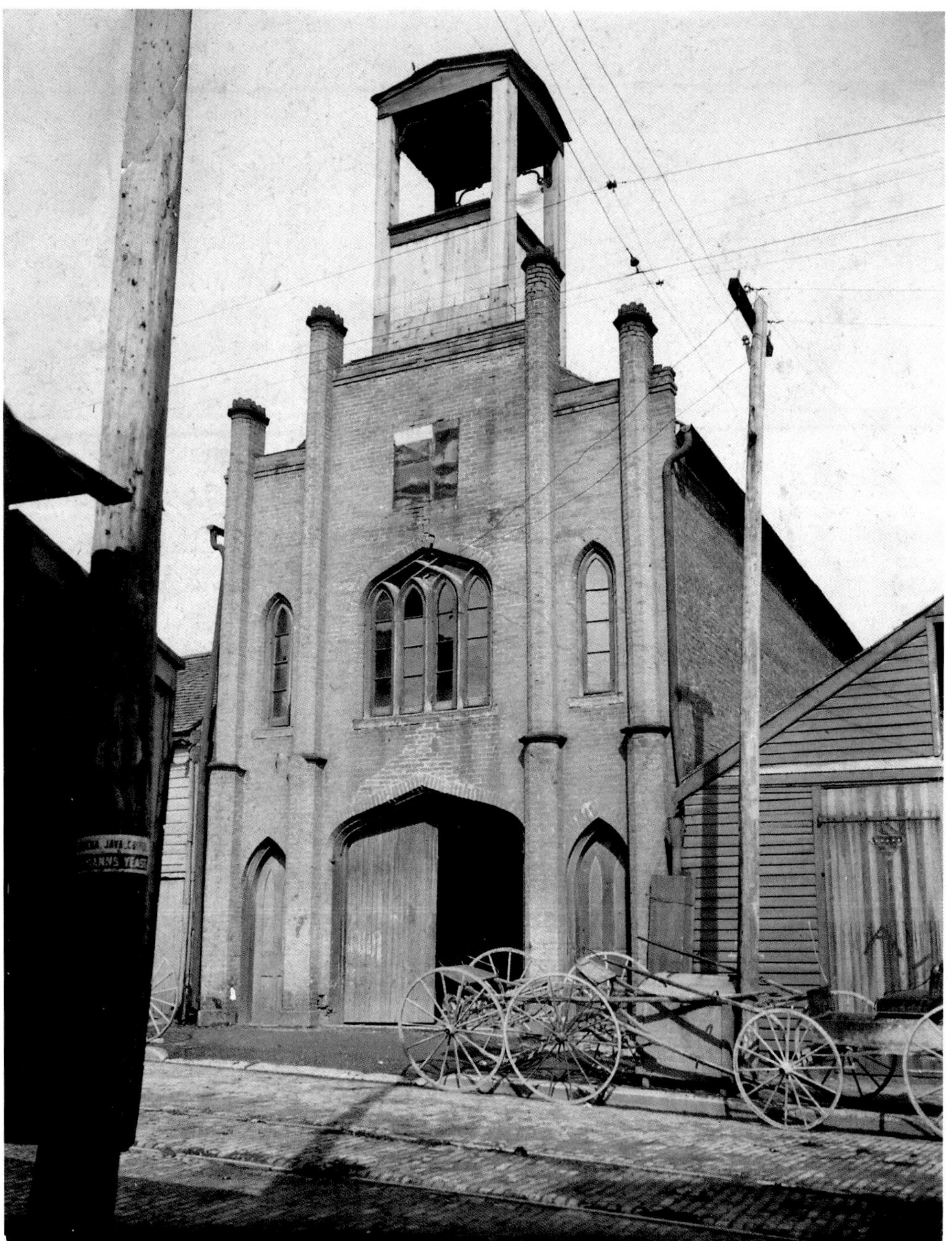

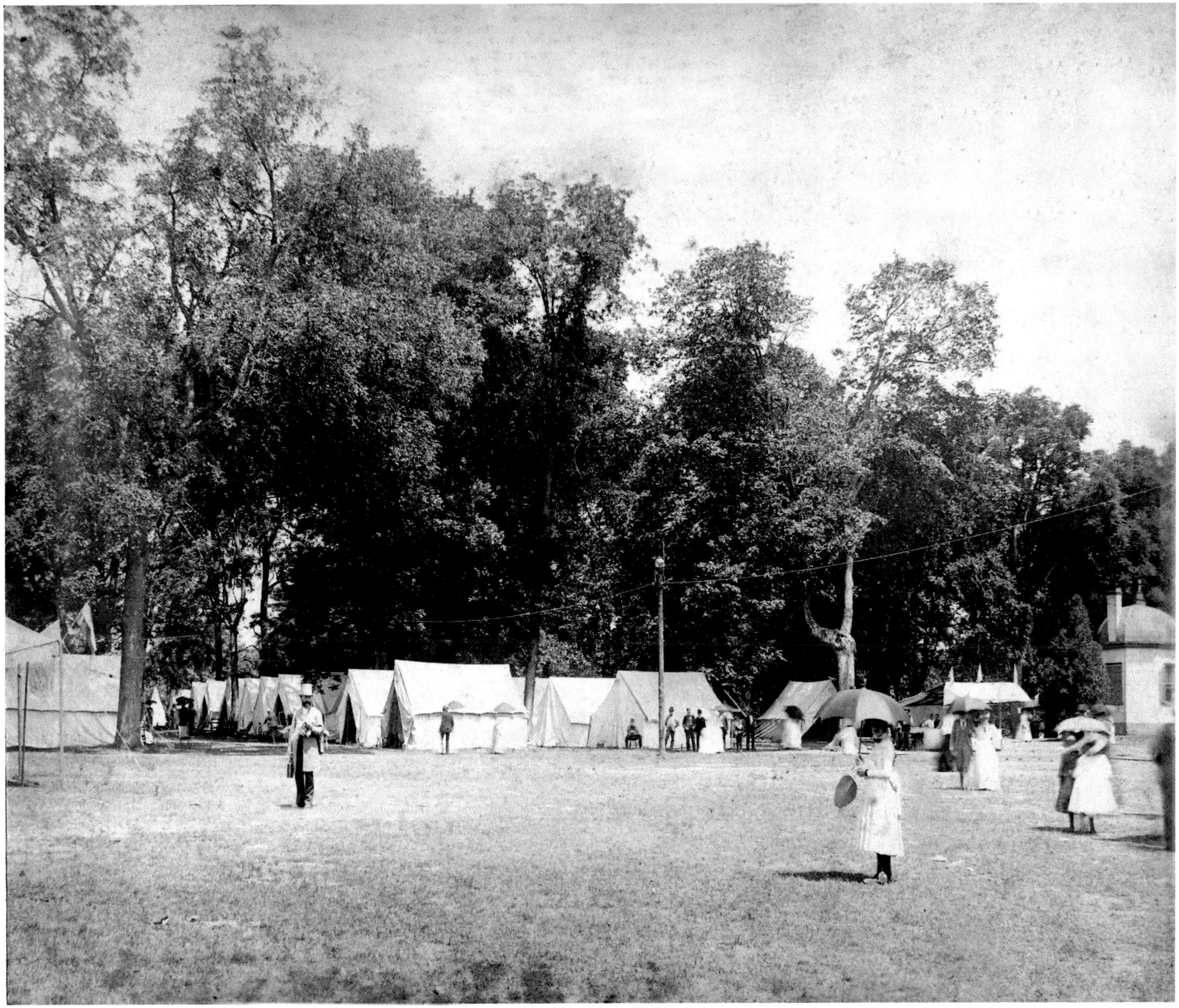

Revival in Woodland Park, late nineteenth century.

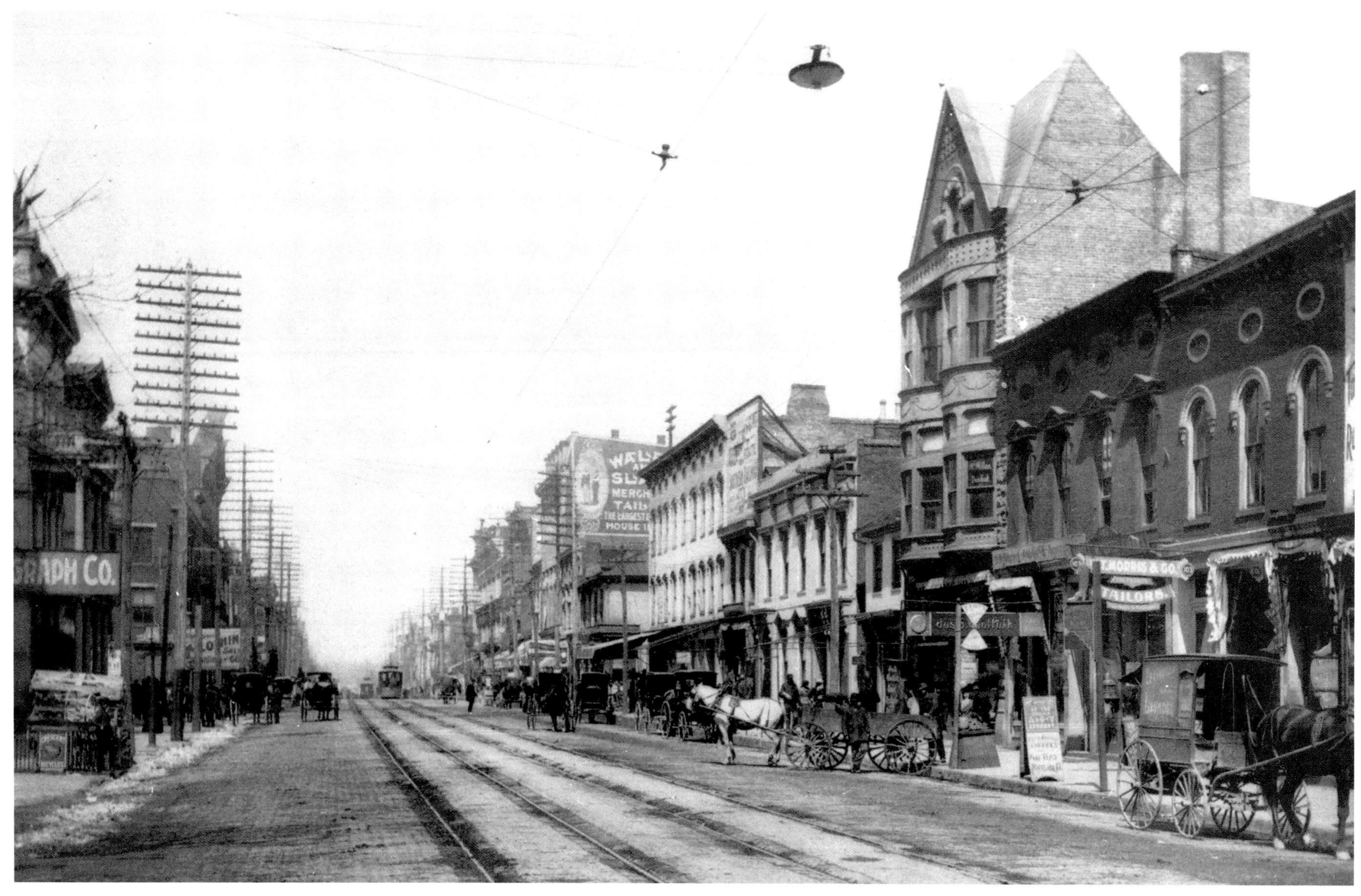

A view of Main Street, 1898.

Hamilton Female College, ca. 1898. Founded in 1869 as Hocker Female College, it became part of Transylvania University in 1903.

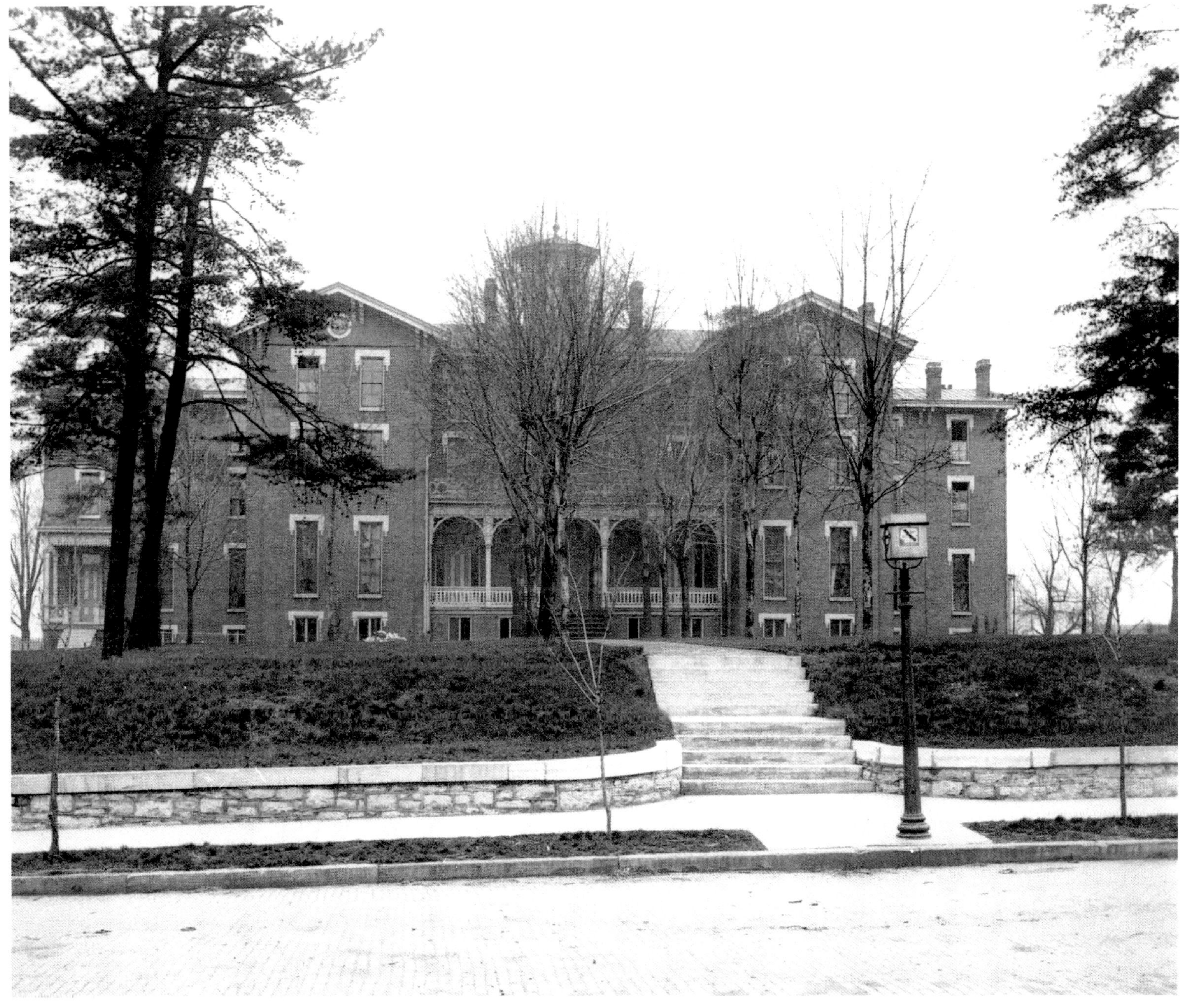

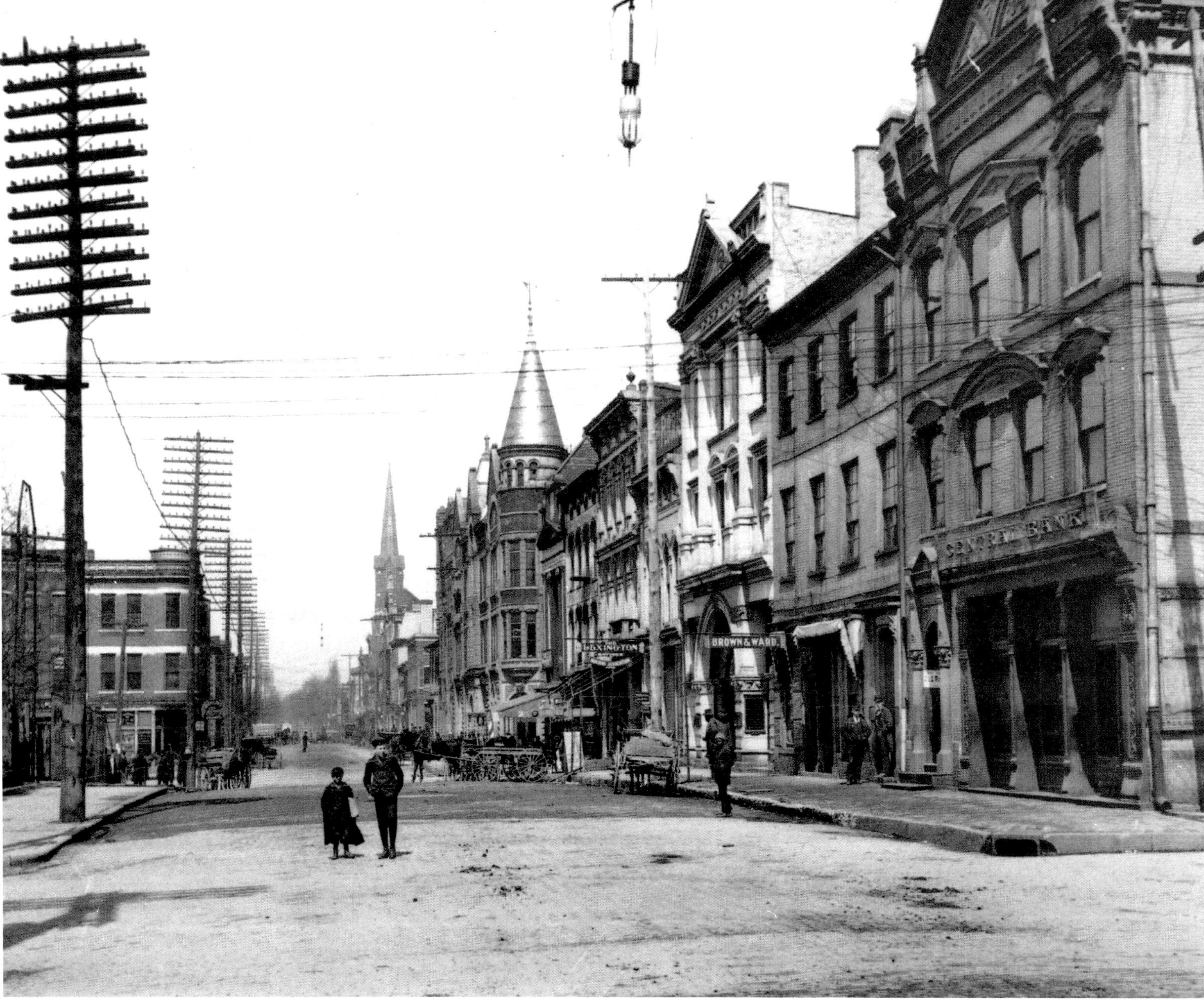

A view of Short Street, ca. 1898.

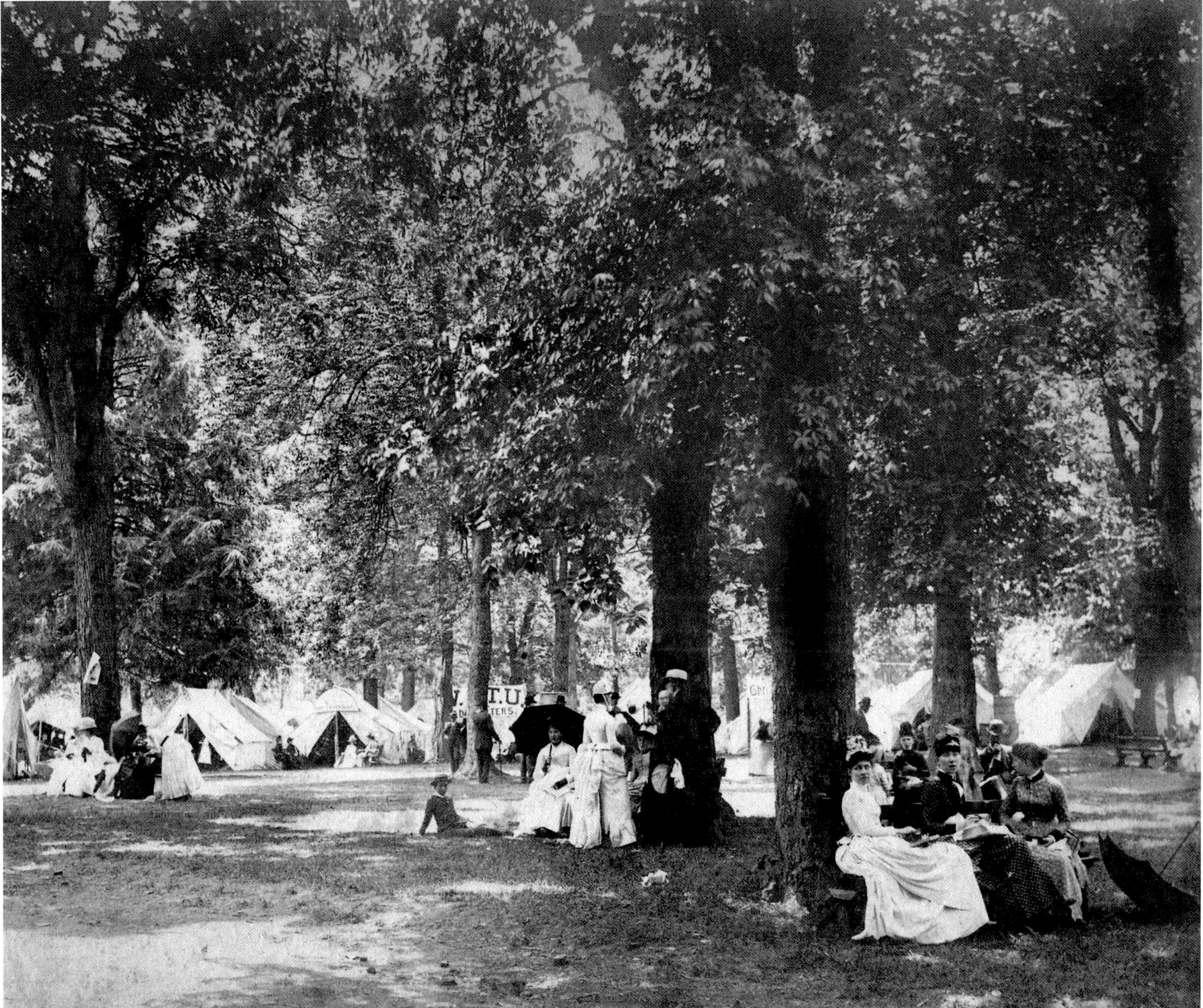

Women and Christian Temperance Union convocation in Woodland Park, late nineteenth century.

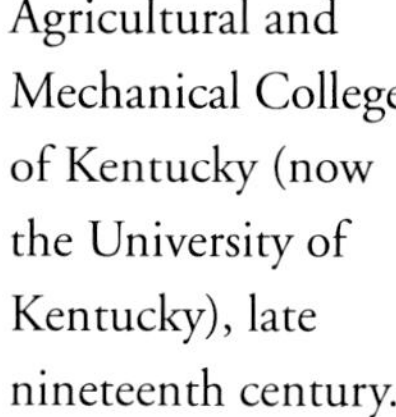

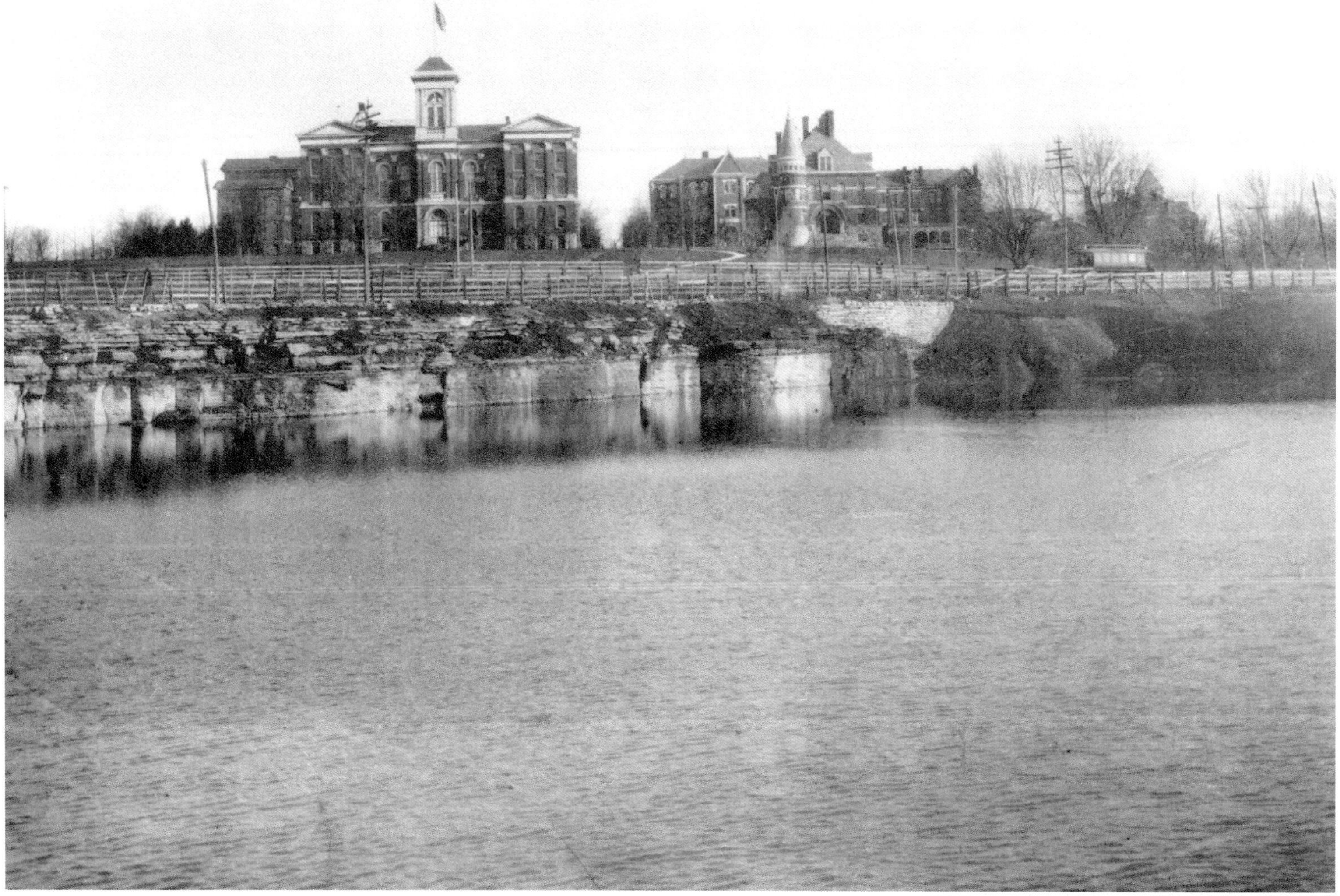

Agricultural and Mechanical College of Kentucky (now the University of Kentucky), late nineteenth century.

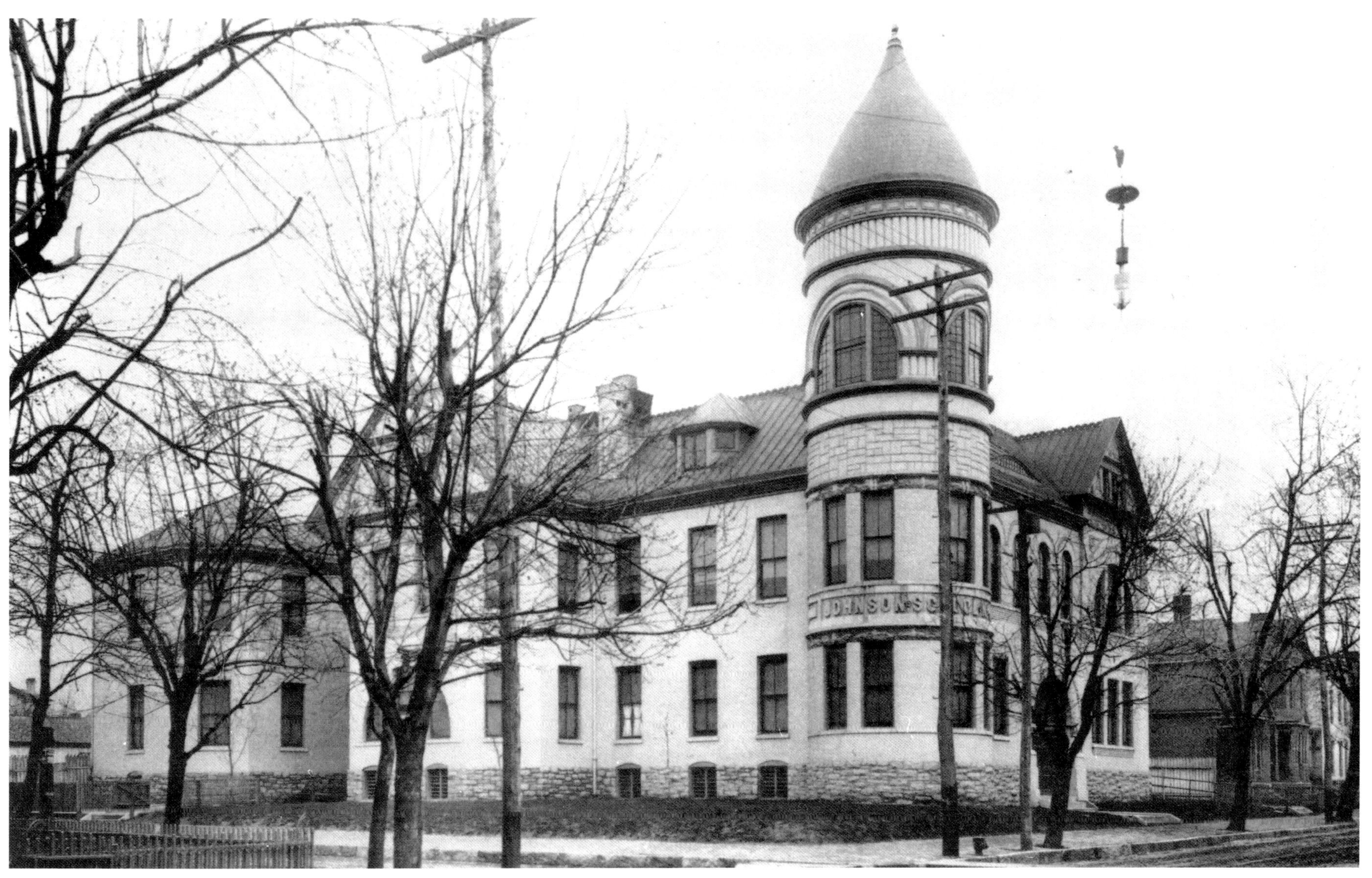

Johnson School, late nineteenth century.

Stable on South Limestone, 1898.

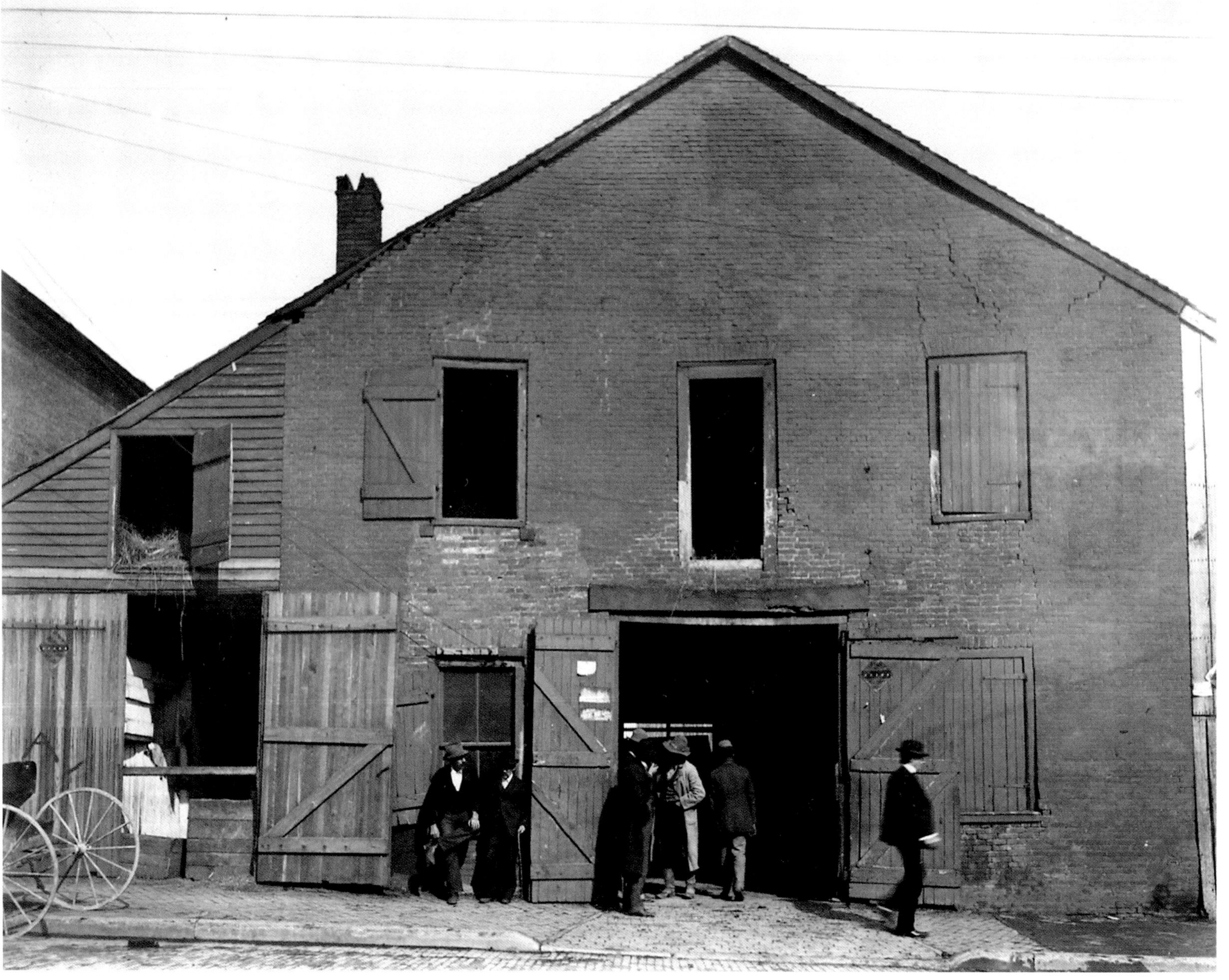

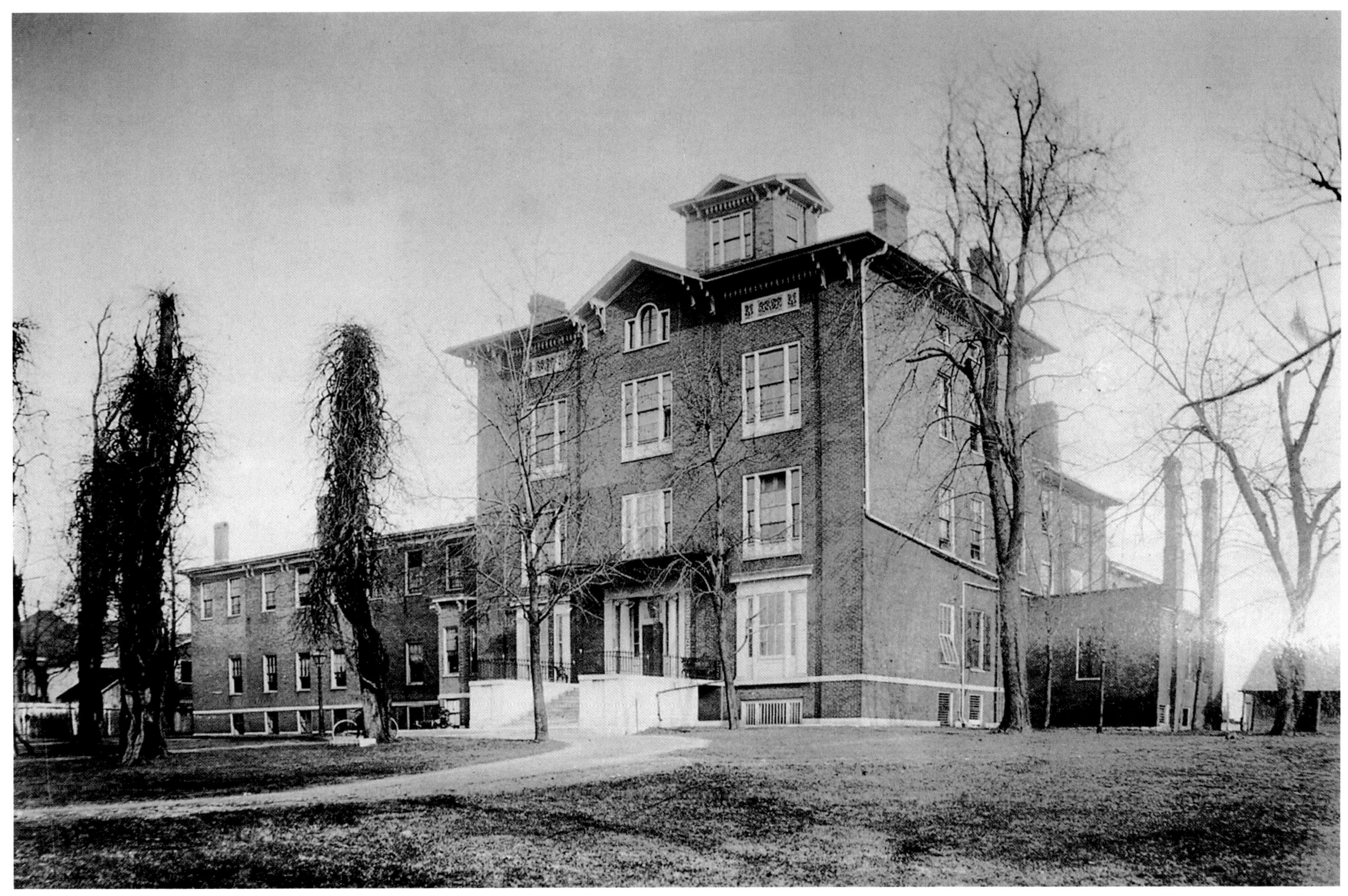

Sayre Female Institute, late nineteenth century. Founded in 1854 as the Transylvania Female Seminary, it was renamed the Sayre Female Institute in 1954 and moved to a five-acre tract that included two small houses and a brick mansion on North Limestone.

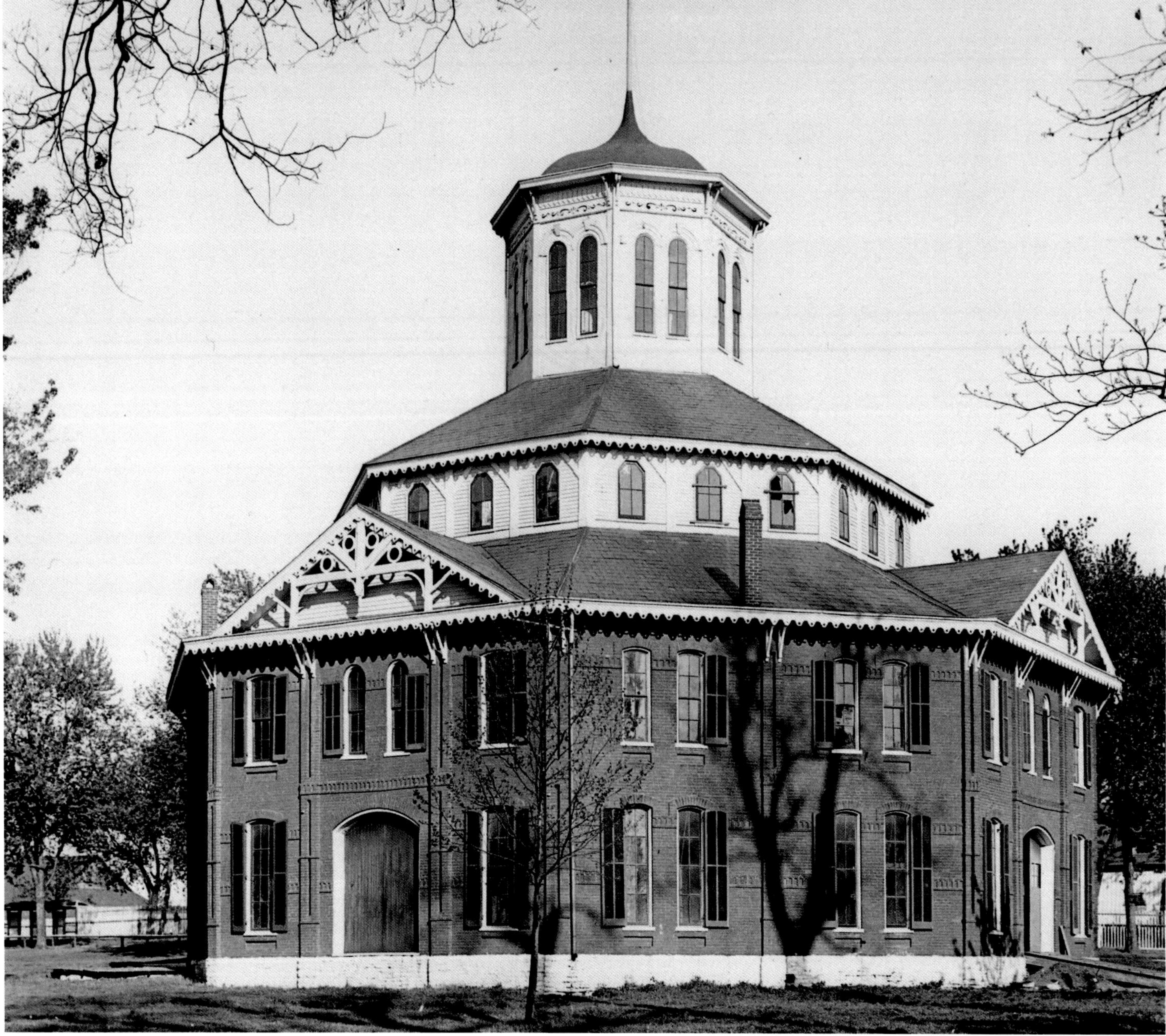

Floral Hall at the Red Mile, built 1882.

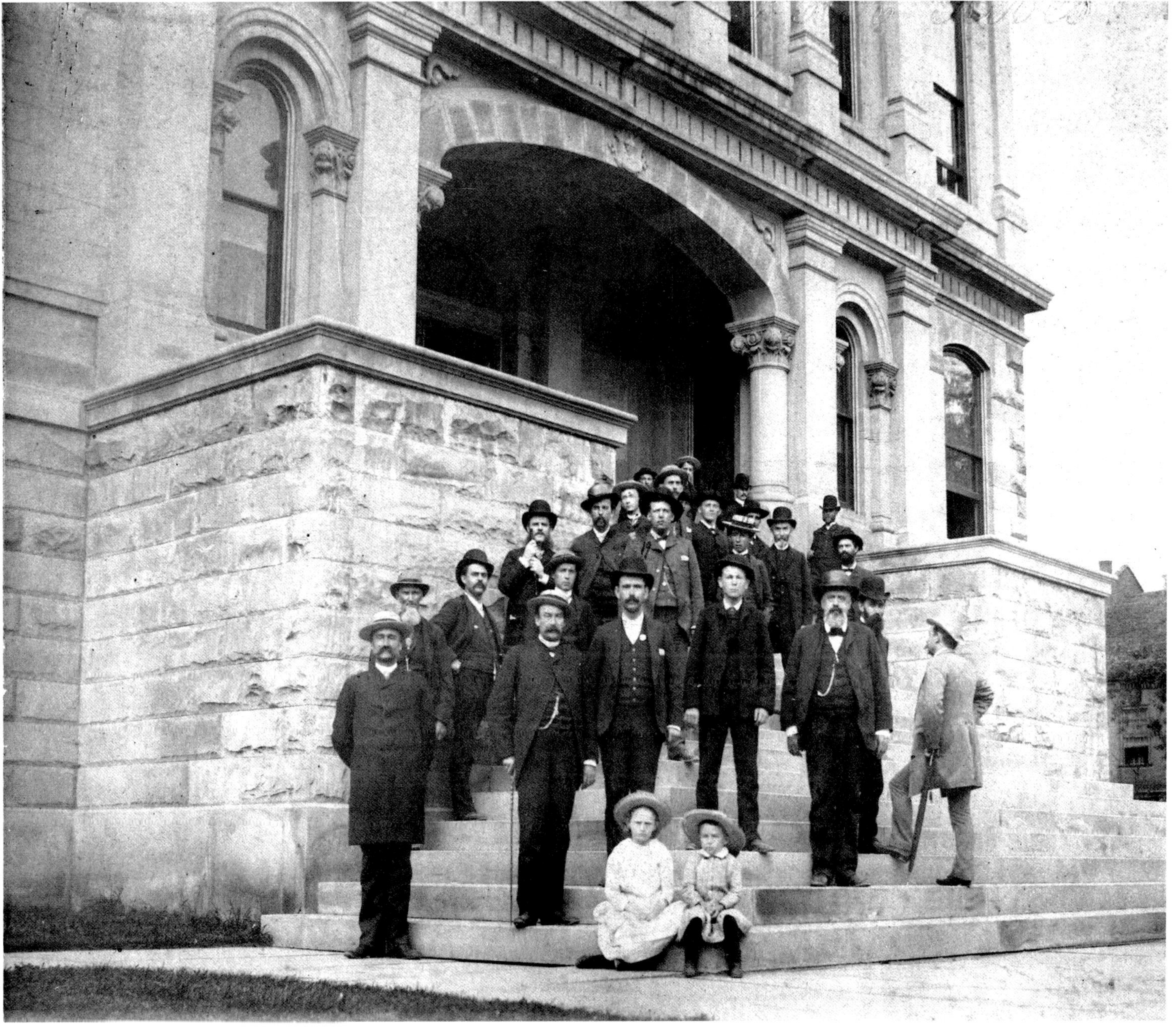

Assembly on steps of the fourth courthouse, late nineteenth century.

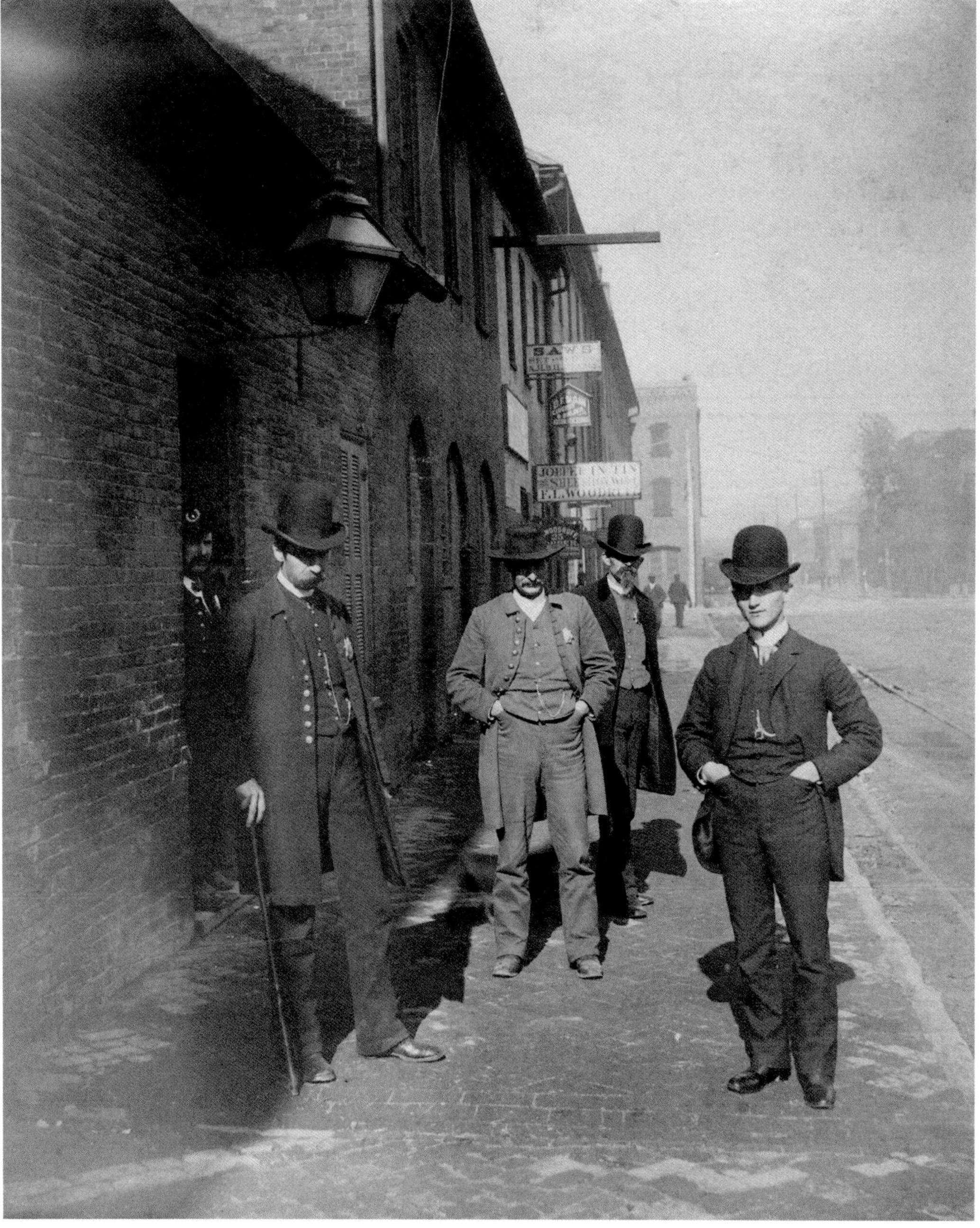

Officers and gentlemen stand beside the police station on Water Street, early 1900s.

Growth from Slumber

(1900–1919)

Mary Dodd's class at East Hickman School, 1901.

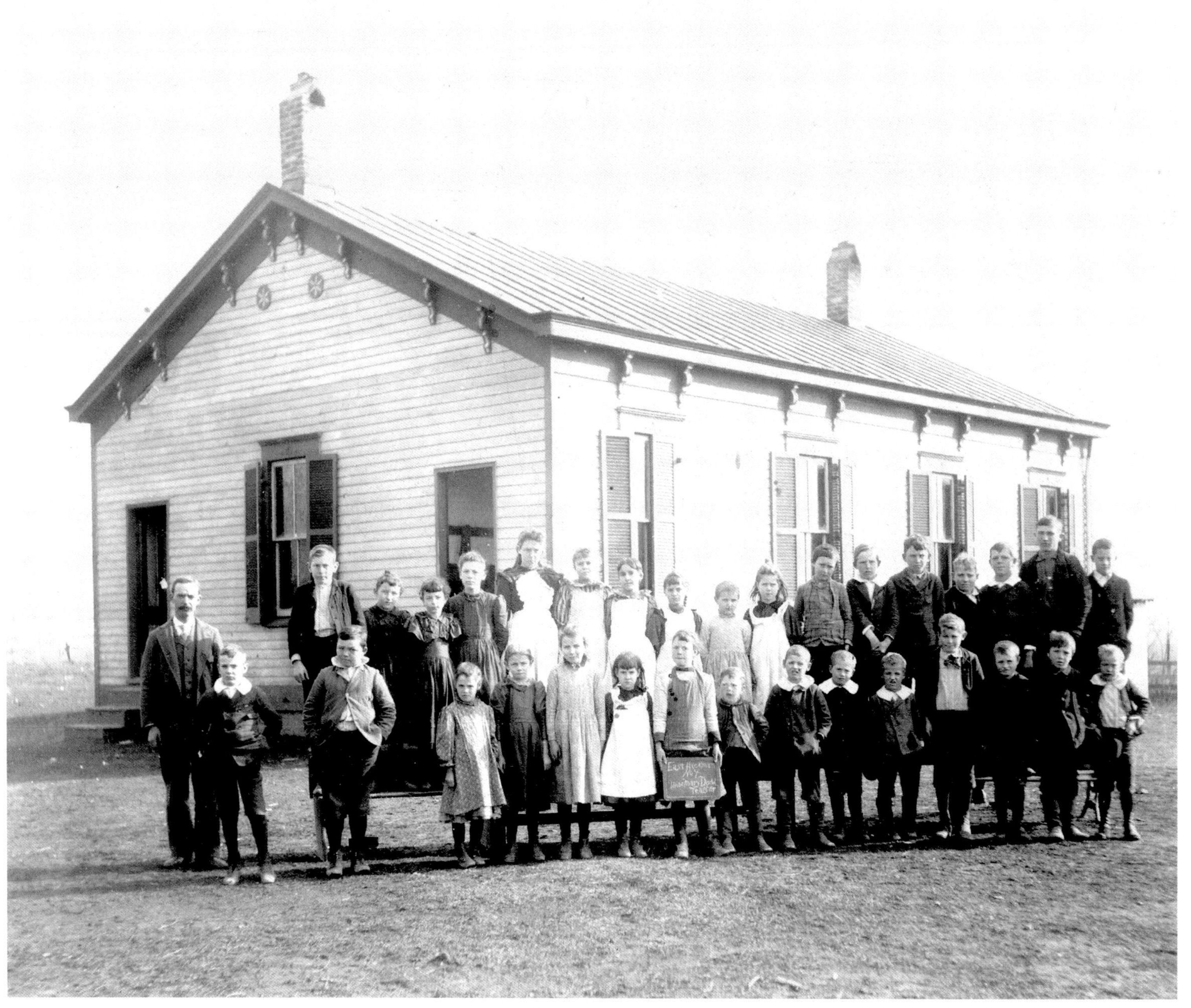

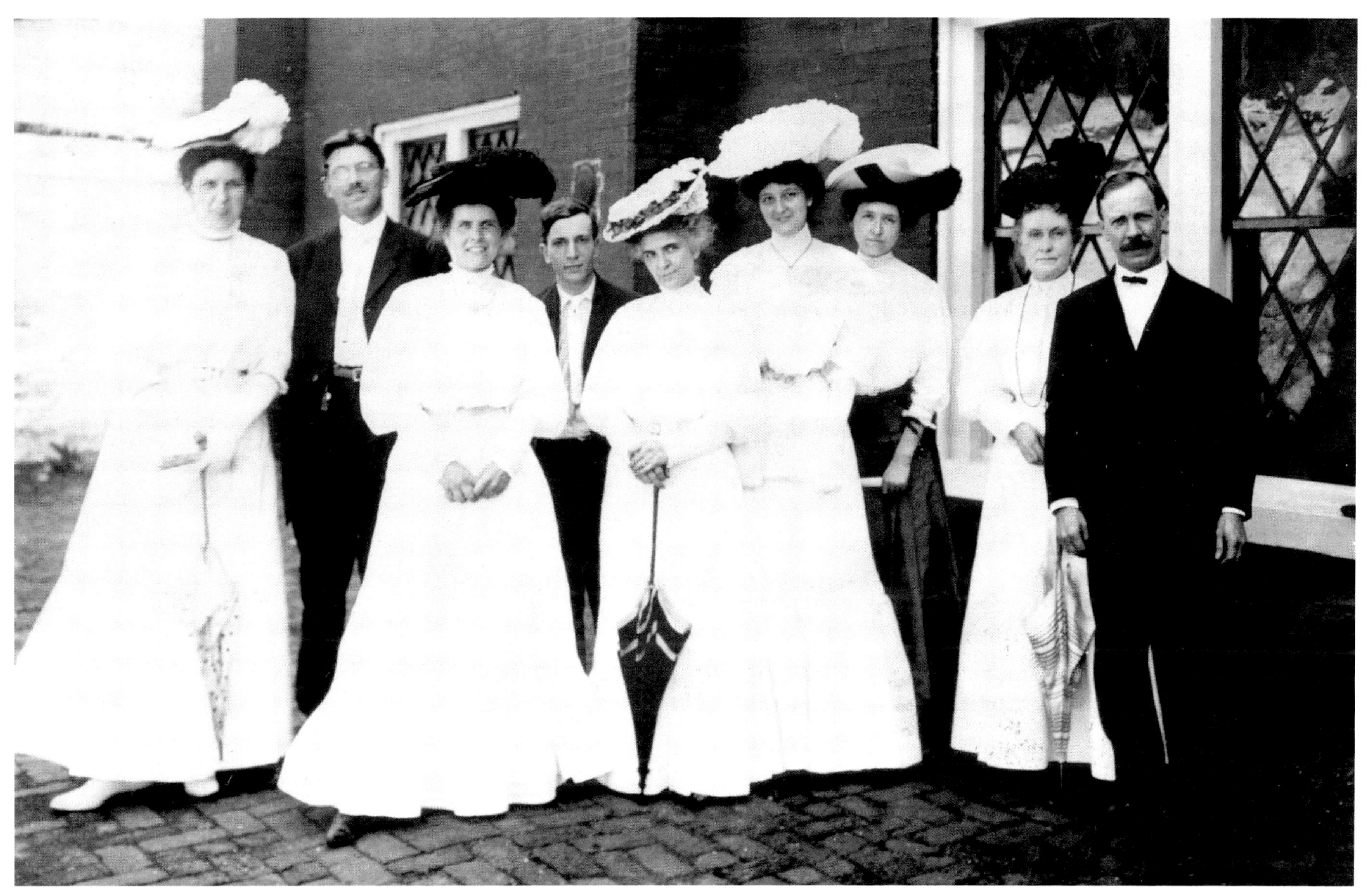

Choir of the Second Presbyterian Church, early twentieth century.

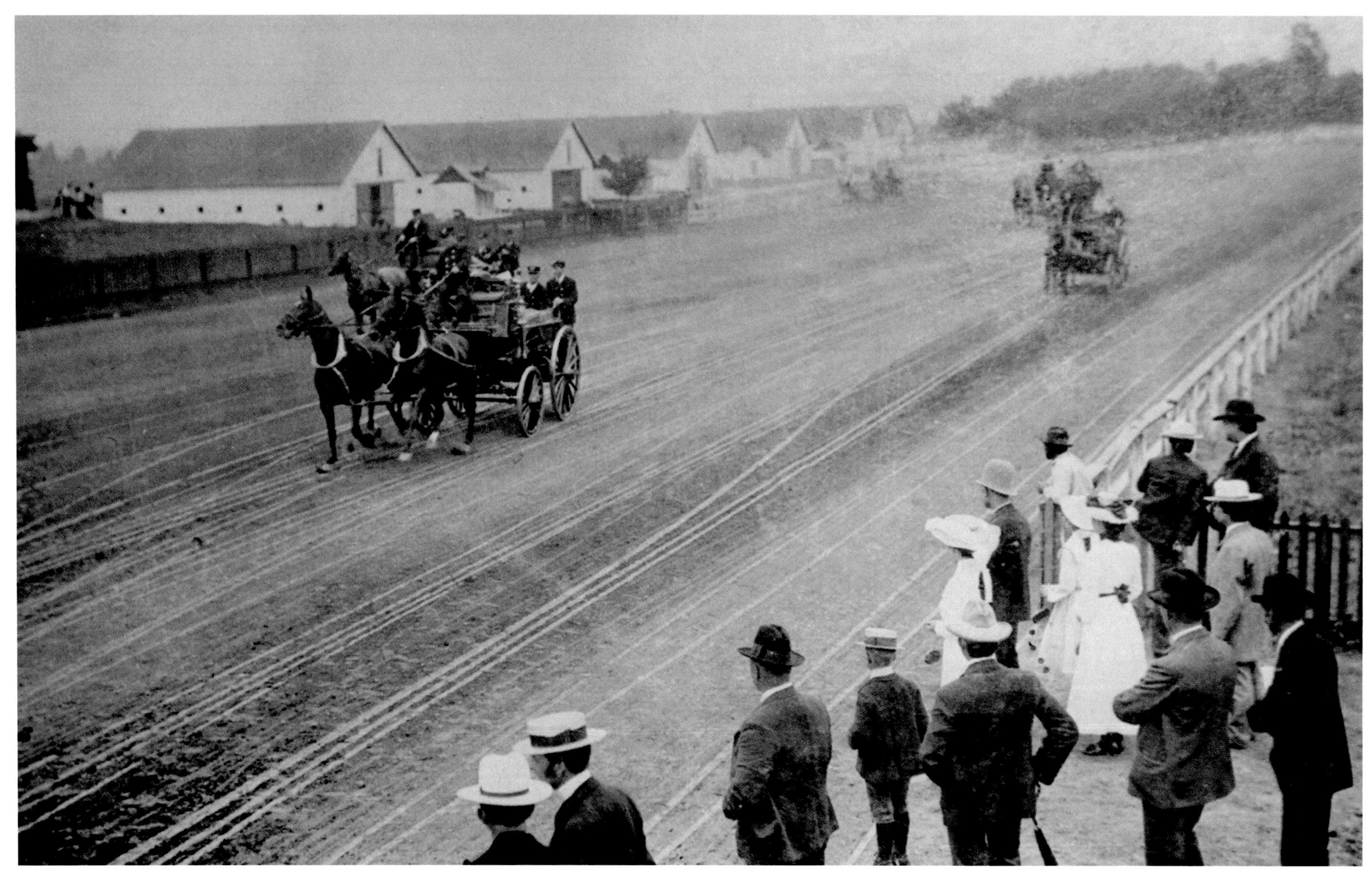

Fire companies race at the trotting track, ca. 1900.

Henry Howard Gratz in Gratz Park, 1900.

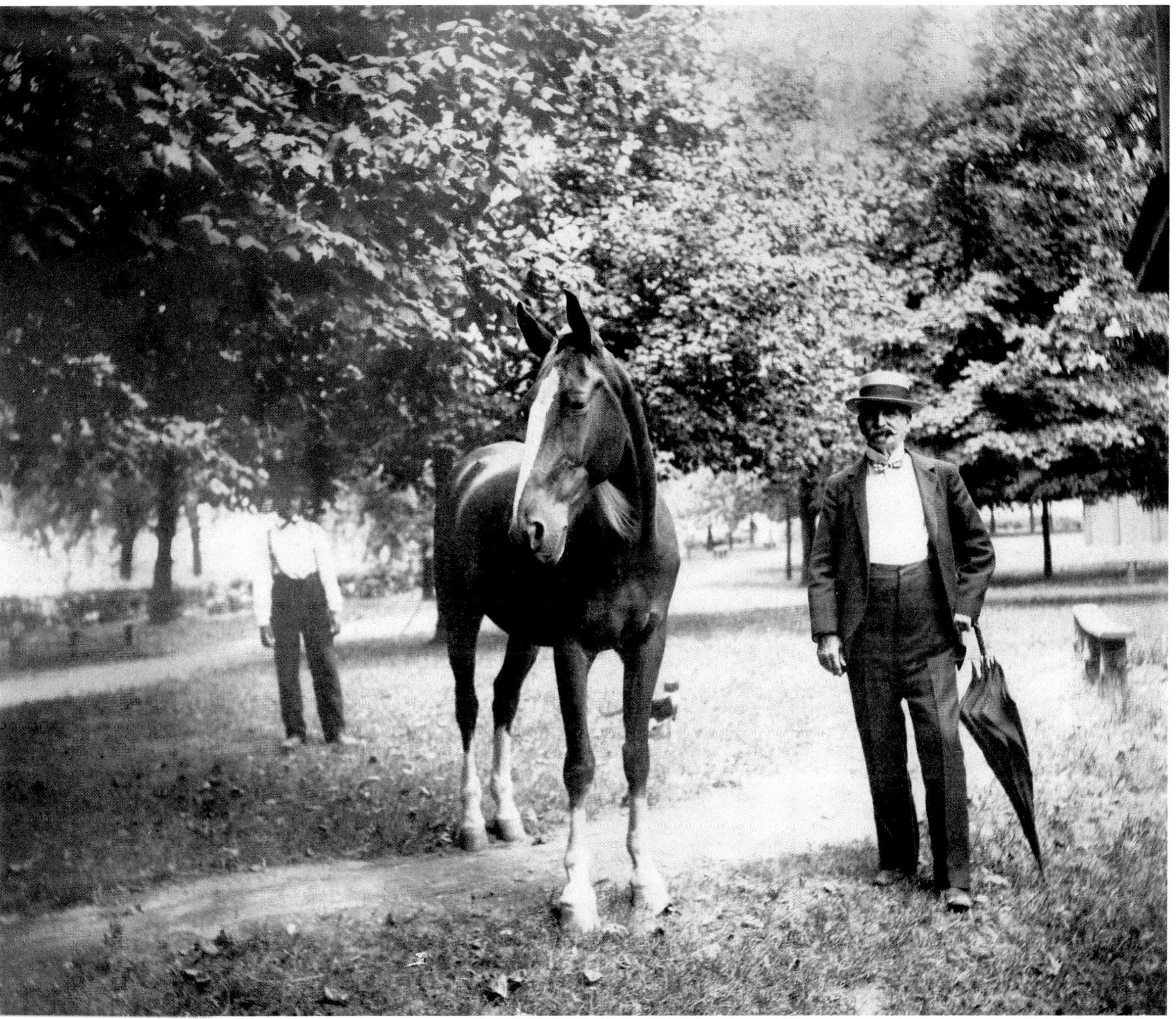

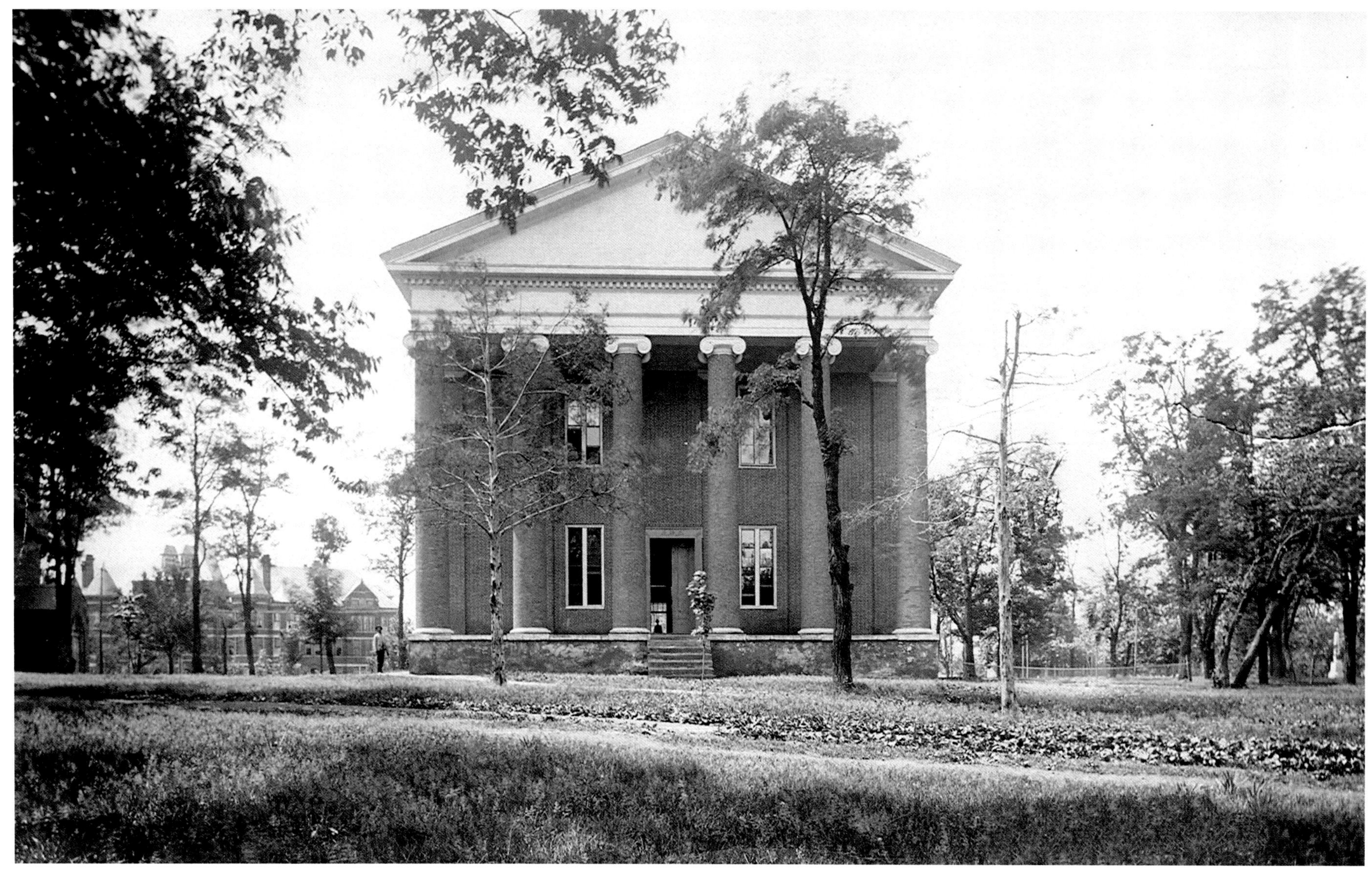

Giddings Hall at Georgetown College in 1901.

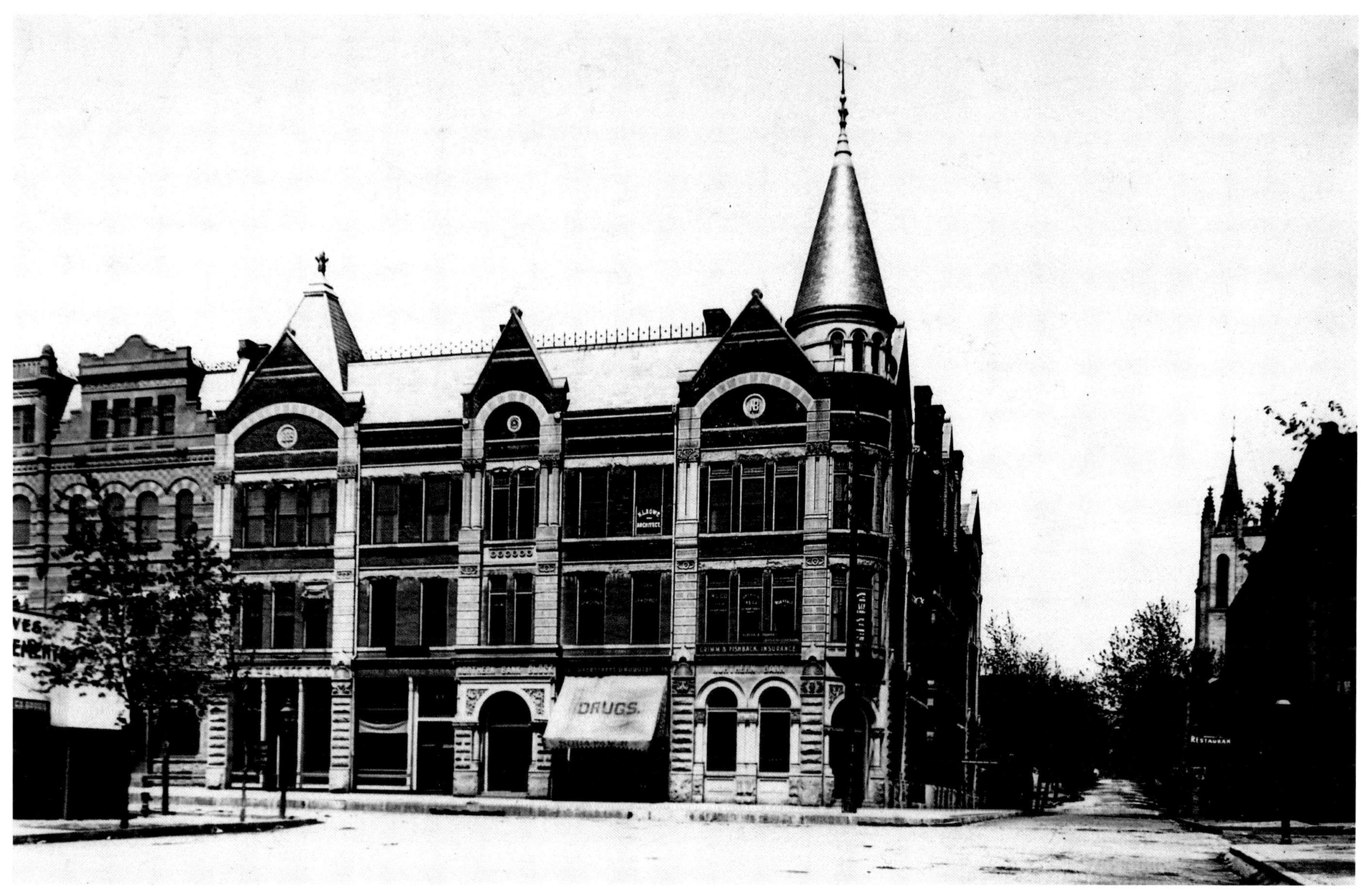

Northern Bank Building (built 1889), at Short and Market streets, as it appeared in the early 1900s.

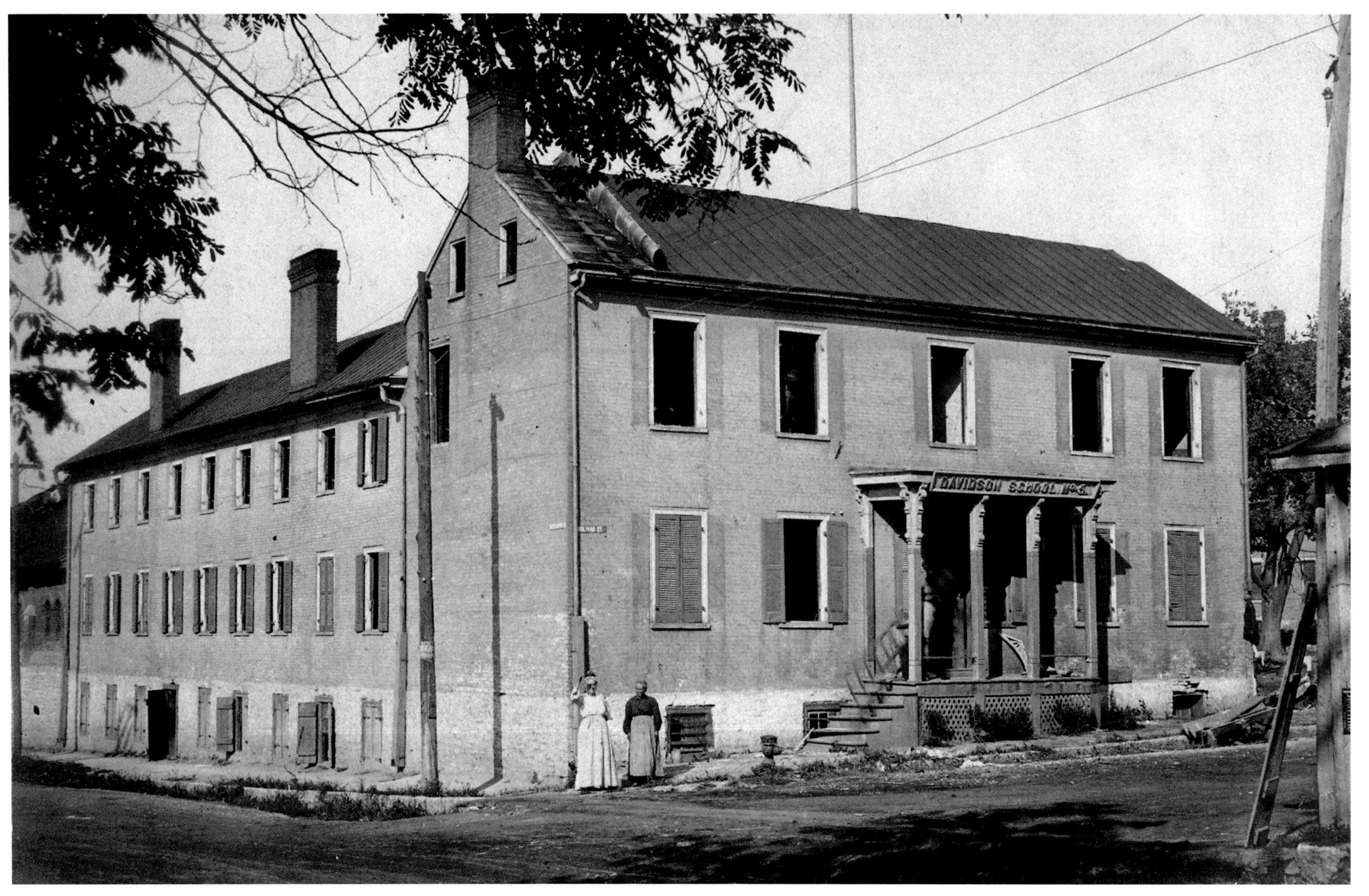

Davidson School (built on the foundation of the old Work House), was demolished around 1903.

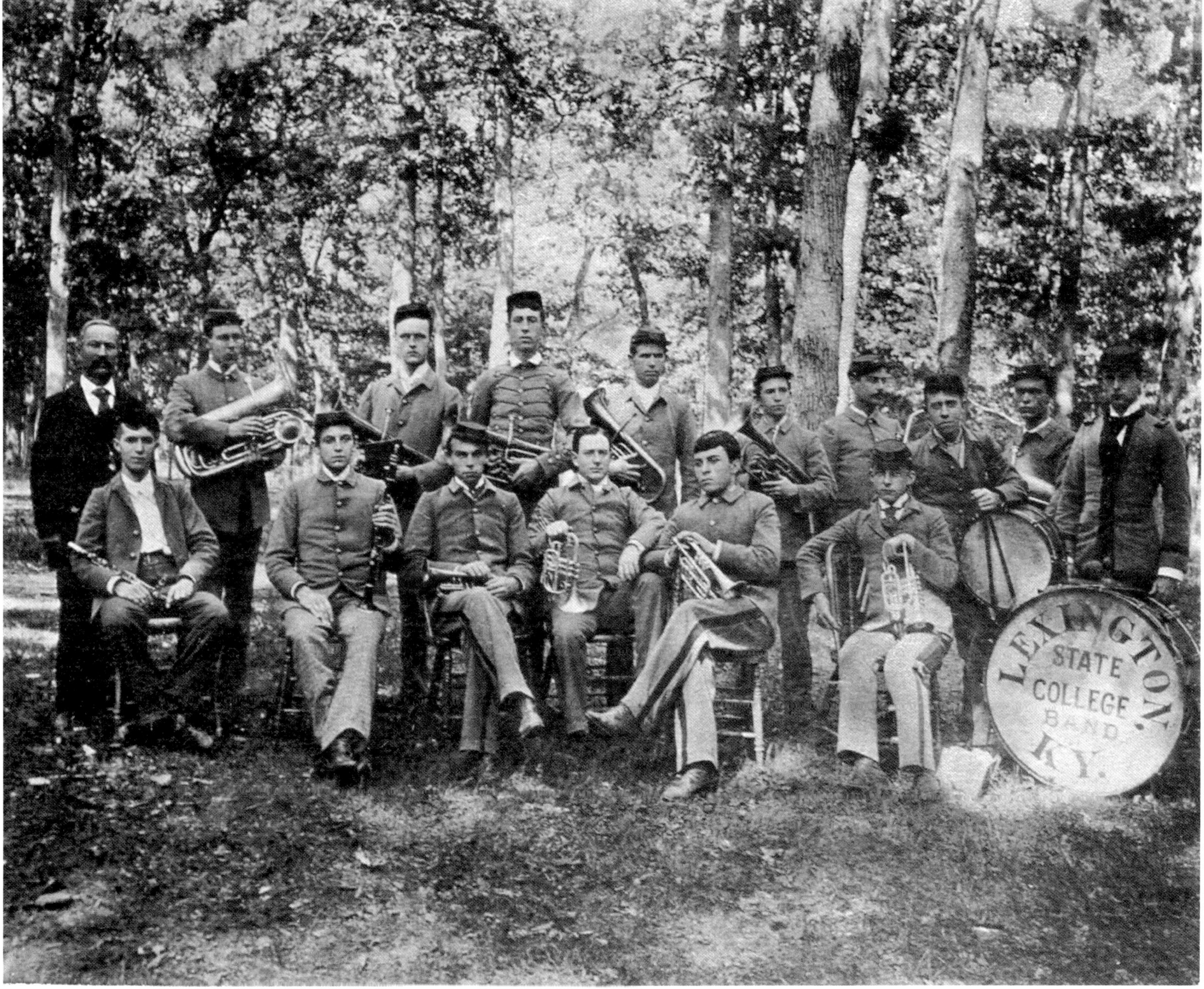

State College Band, ca. 1908.

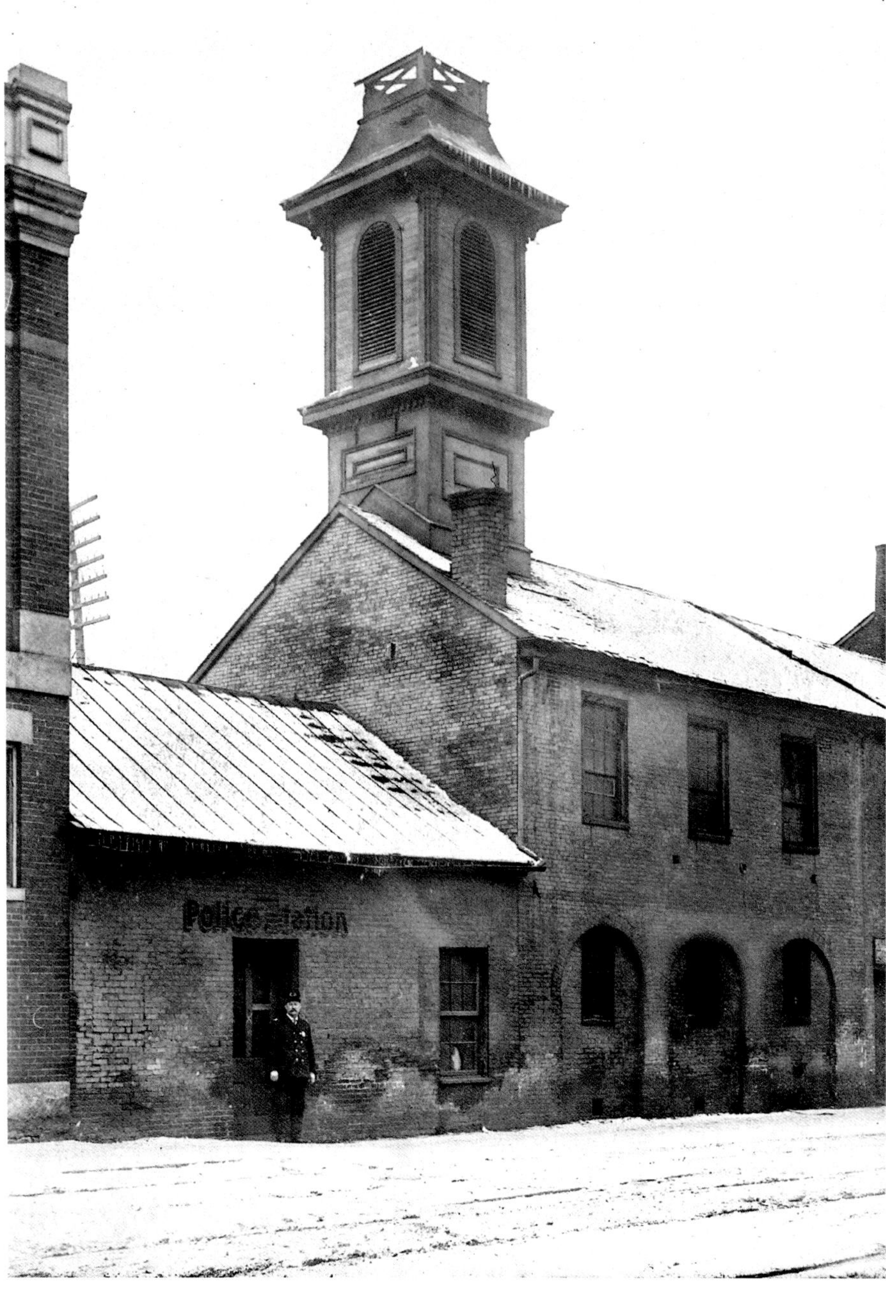

Police station or watch house (formerly a mustard factory), in 1910.

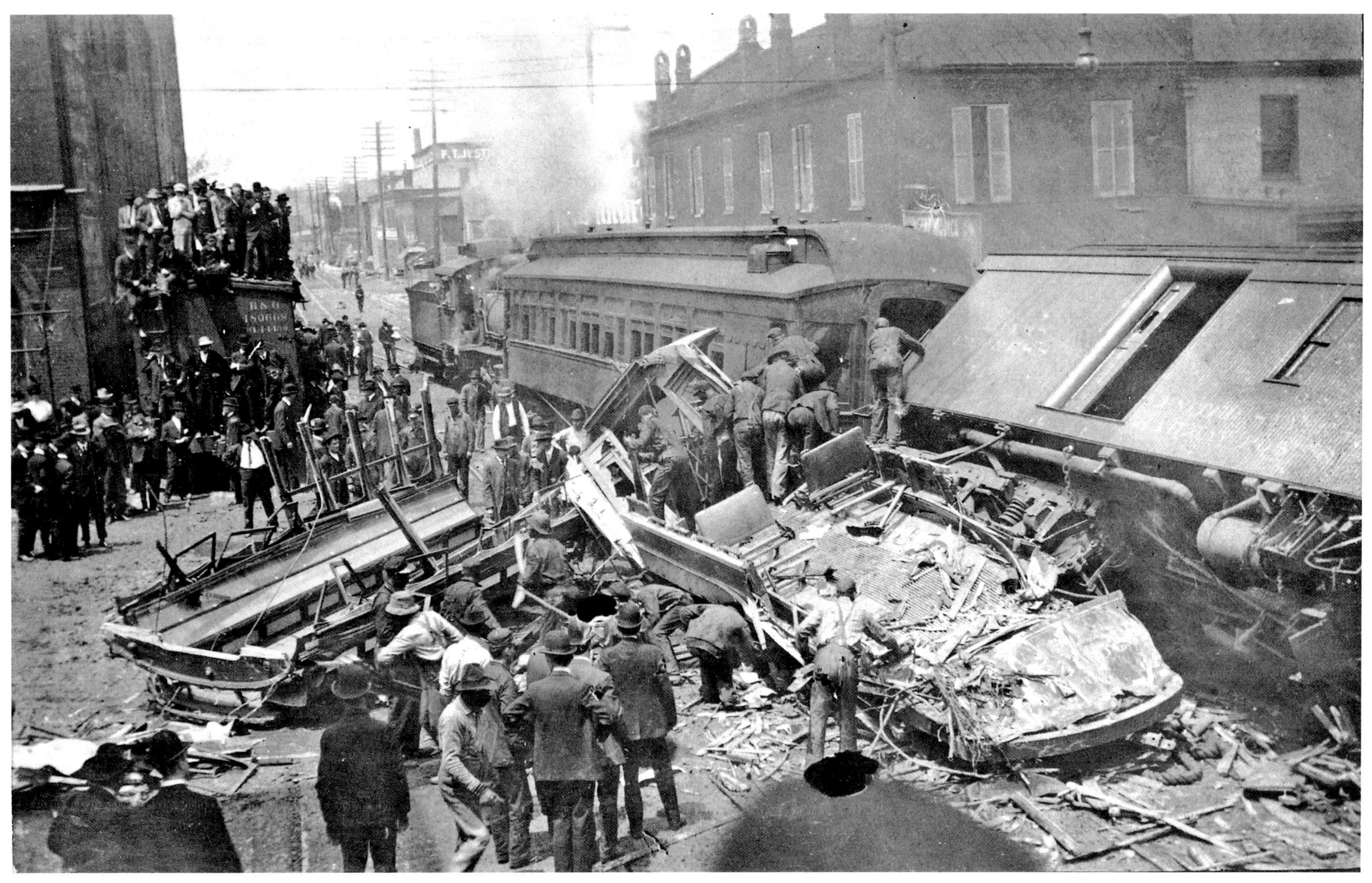

Streetcar and C. & O. train accident, 1907.

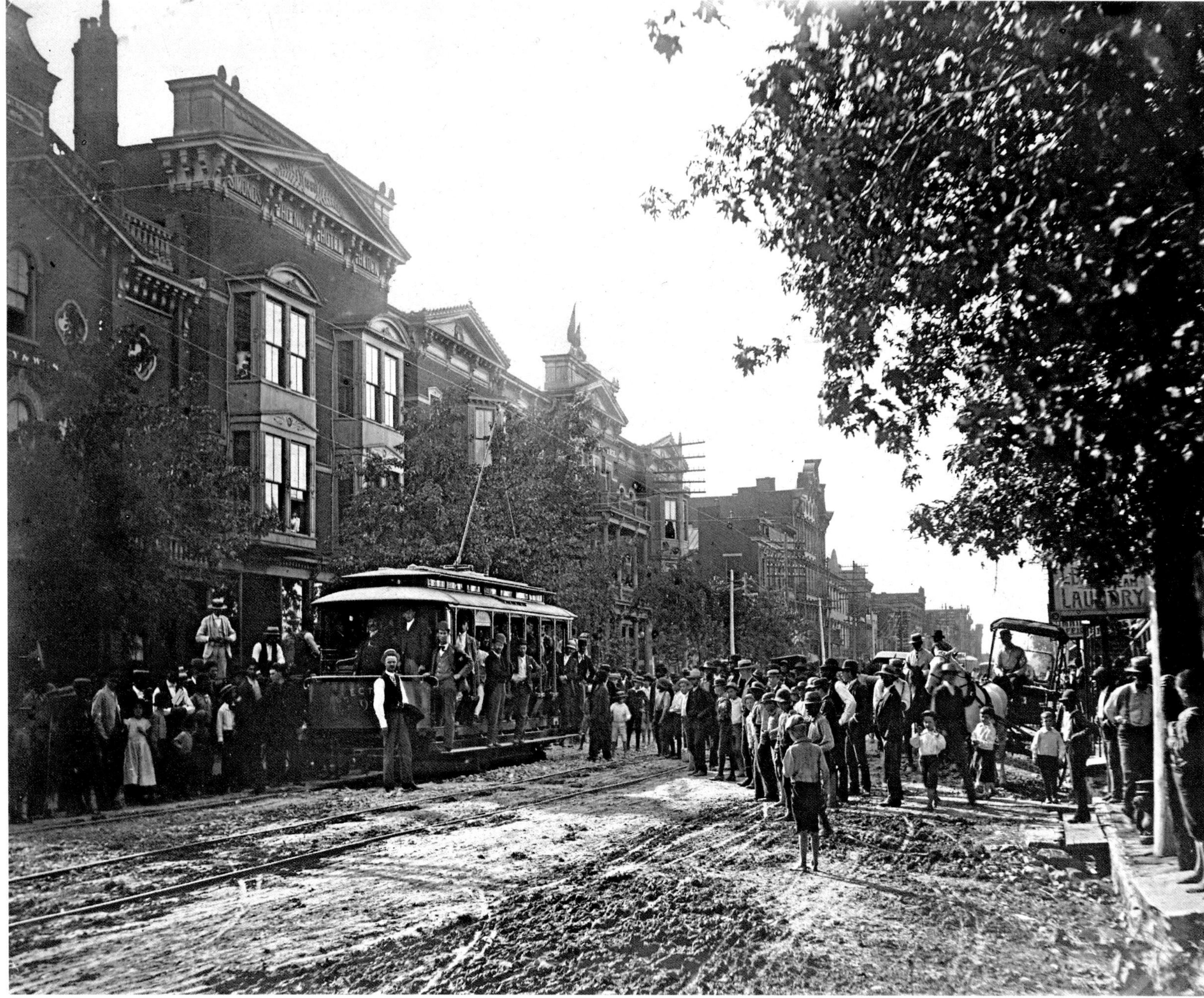

An electric streetcar passes in front of the Phoenix Hotel on Main Street in the early 1900s.

Main and Broadway looking east.

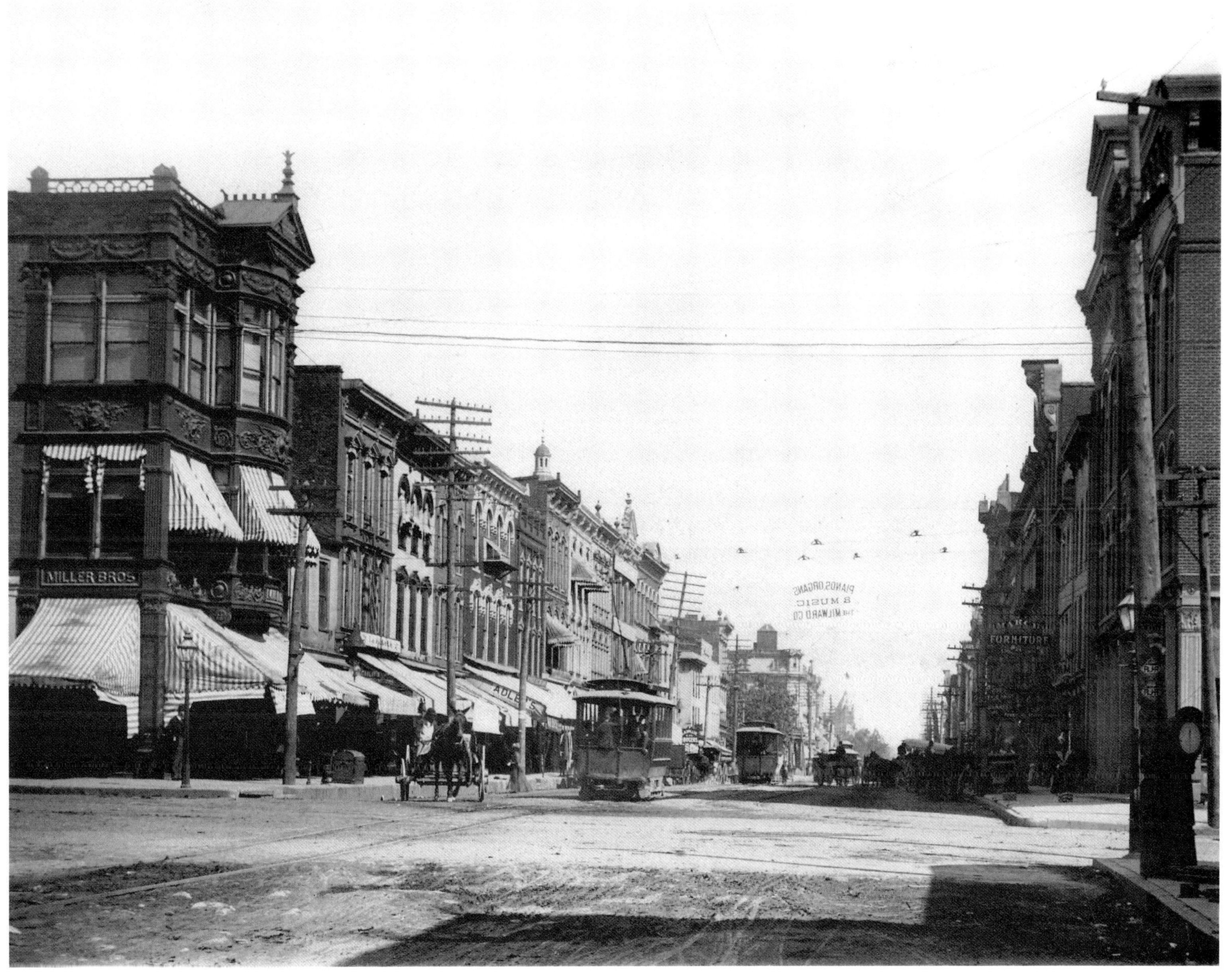

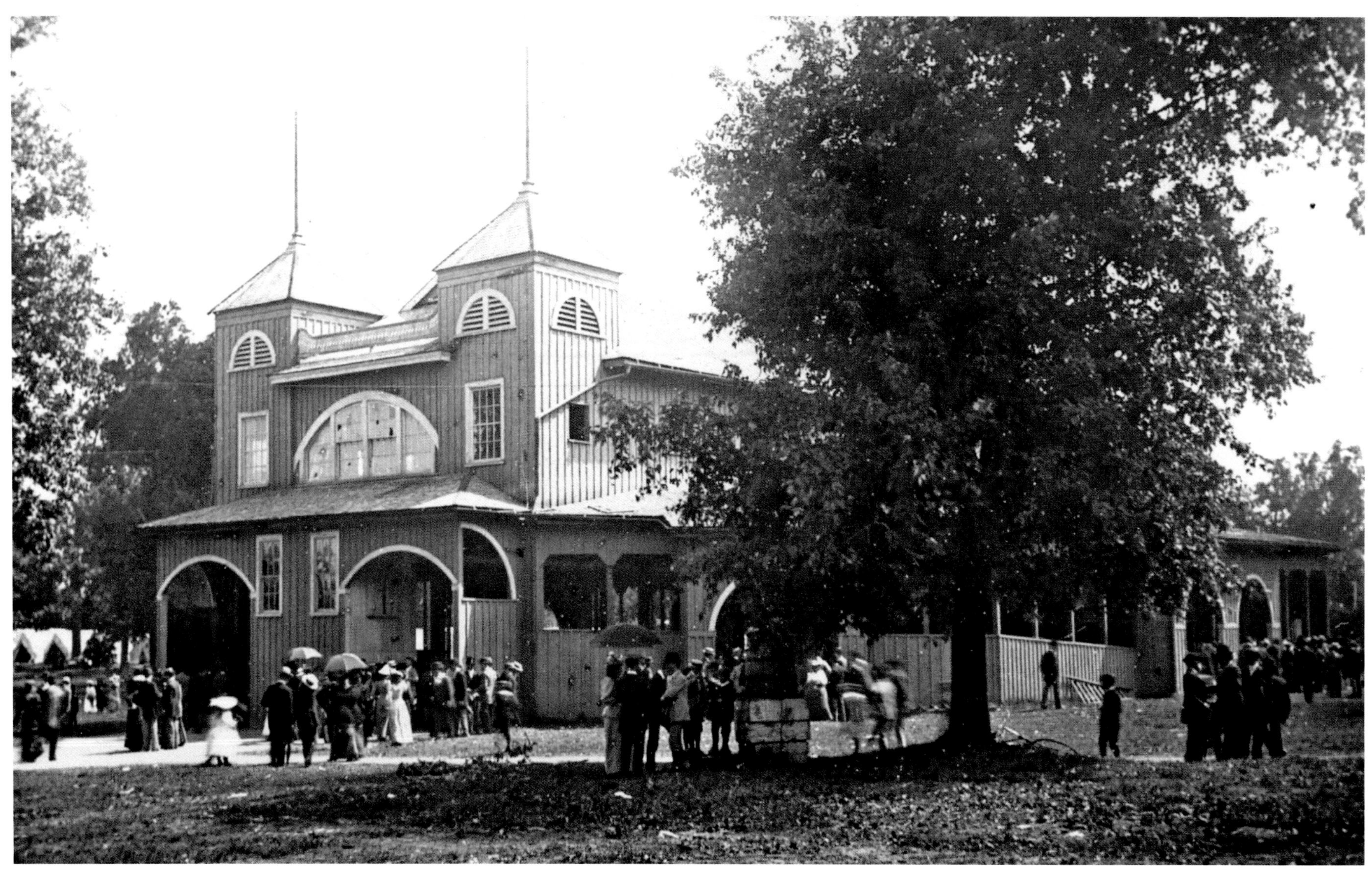

Woodland Park Auditorium, frame construction, moved to Greentree Farm, early twentieth century.

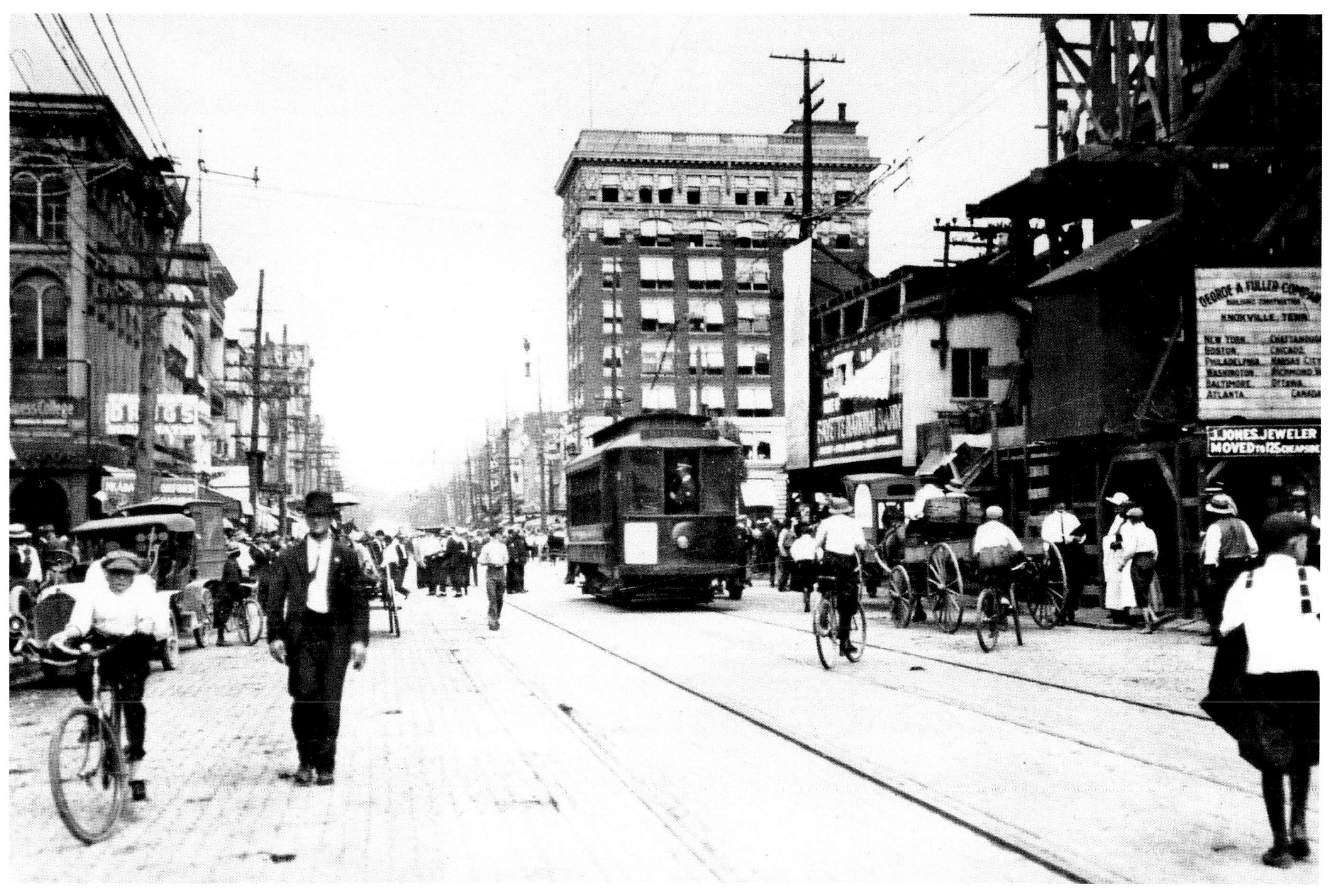

Construction of First National Bank at Main and Upper in 1912. When it was completed two years later, the 15-story building was the tallest building between Cincinnati and Atlanta.

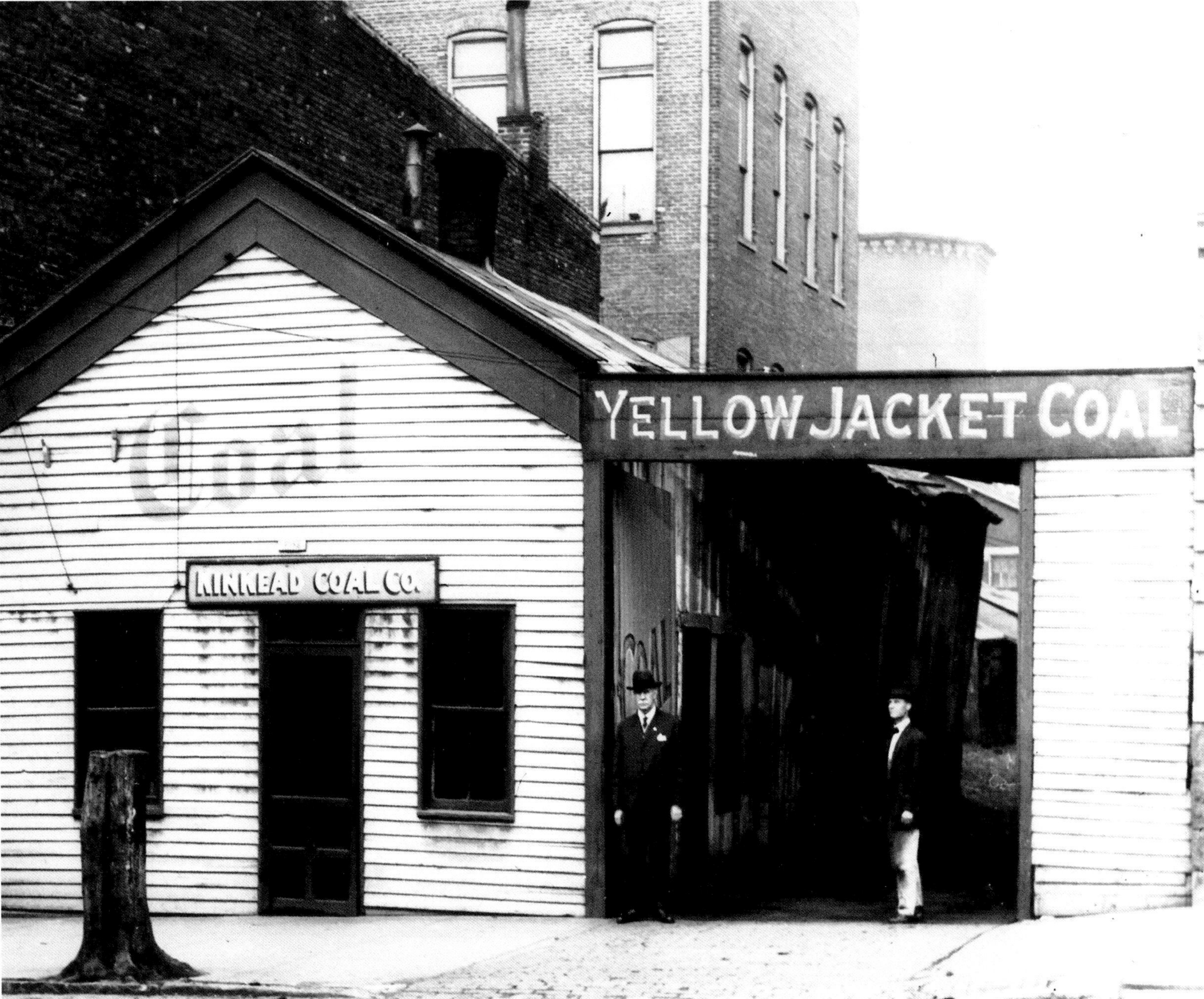

Coal companies on Broadway, early twentieth century.

First Lady Mary Todd Lincoln's girlhood home on West Main was built in 1803-6 as an inn.

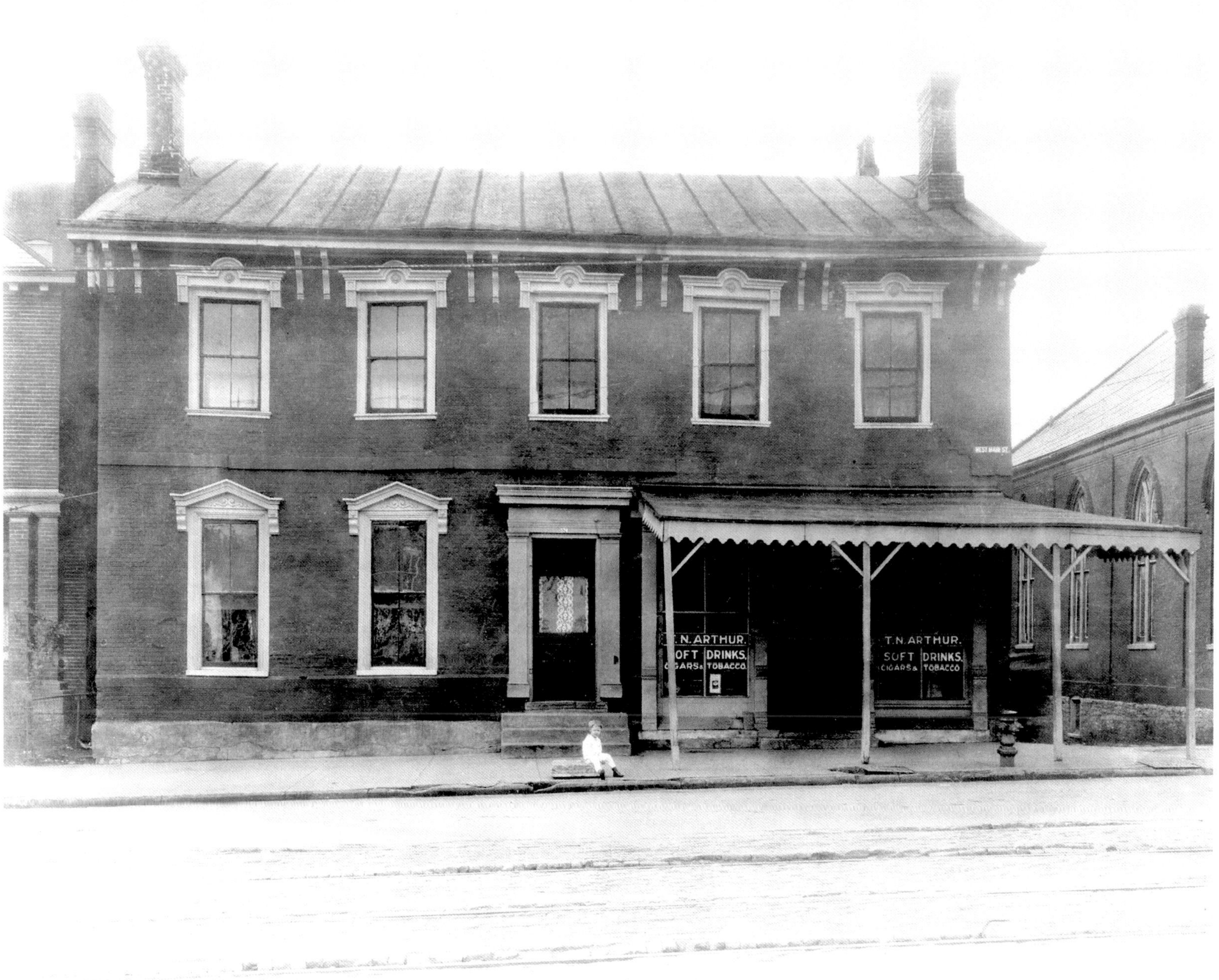

This jail on Short Street (built 1871, razed 1978) is seen here in the early twentieth century.

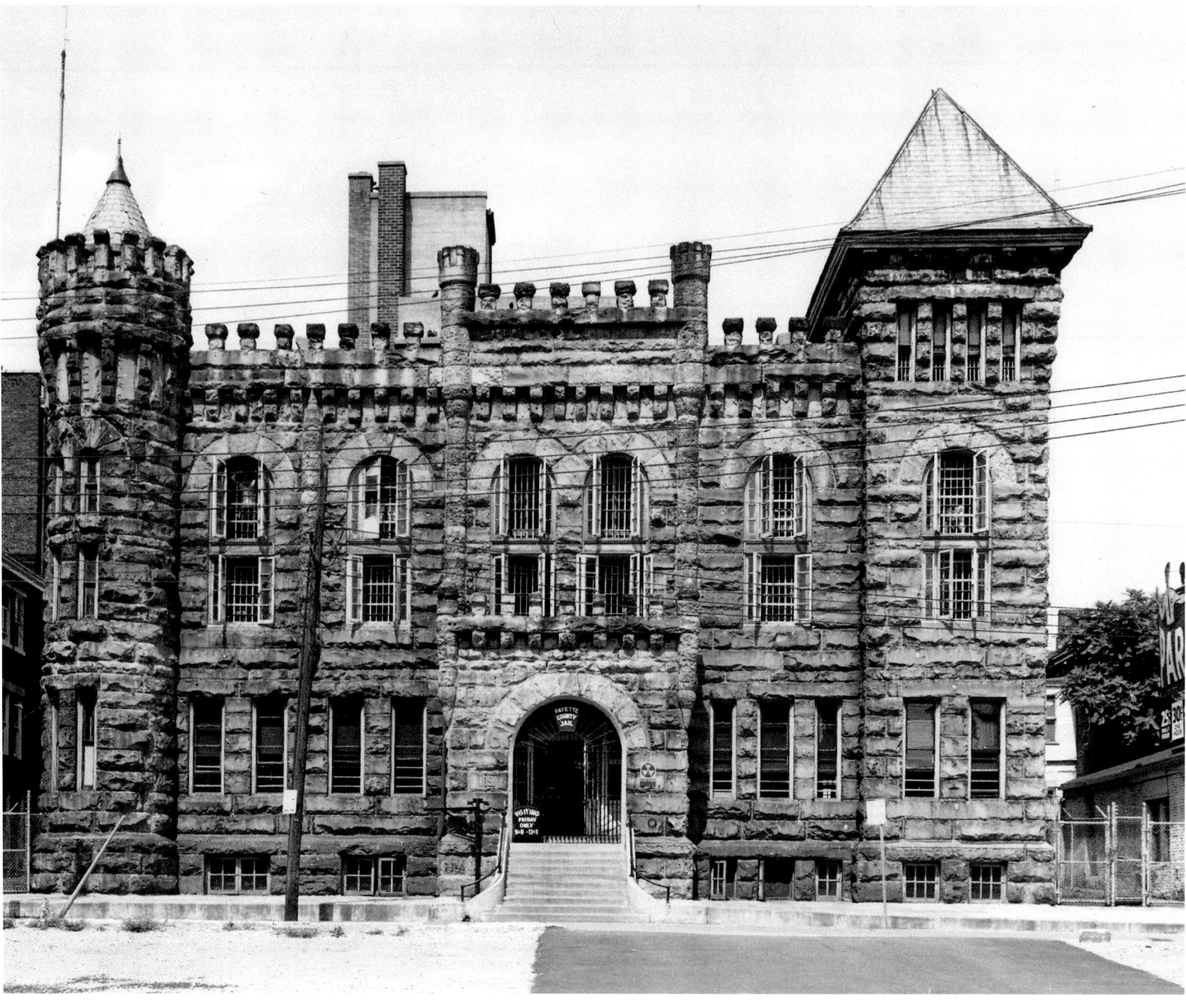

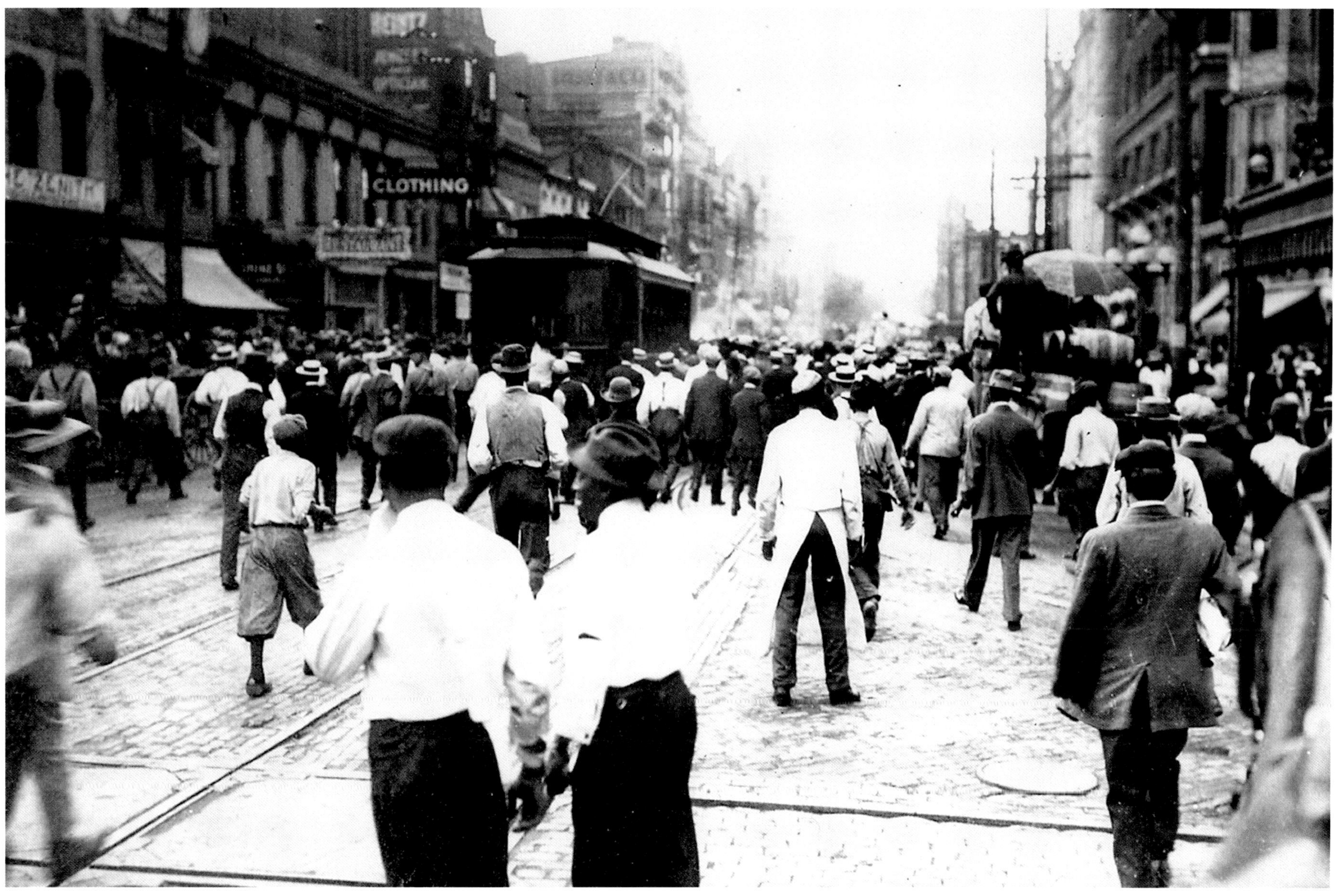

Streetcar strikers on Main Street, 1910.

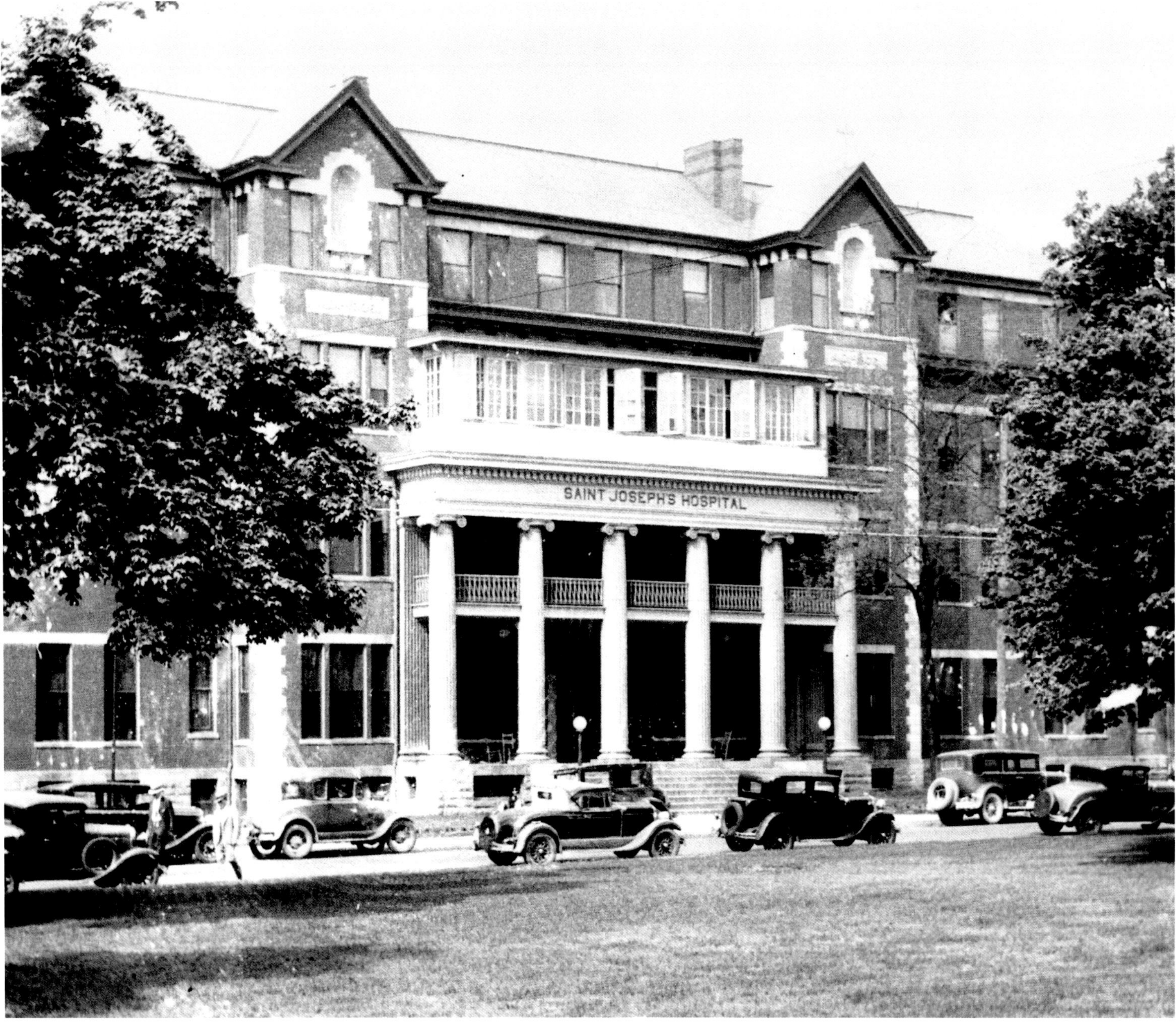

Saint Joseph's Hospital on Second Street (razed 1966), ca. 1910.

The Carty Building, with cast-iron facade, stands at the southwest corner of Main and Mill streets. It was built 1871-72 and razed in 1938.

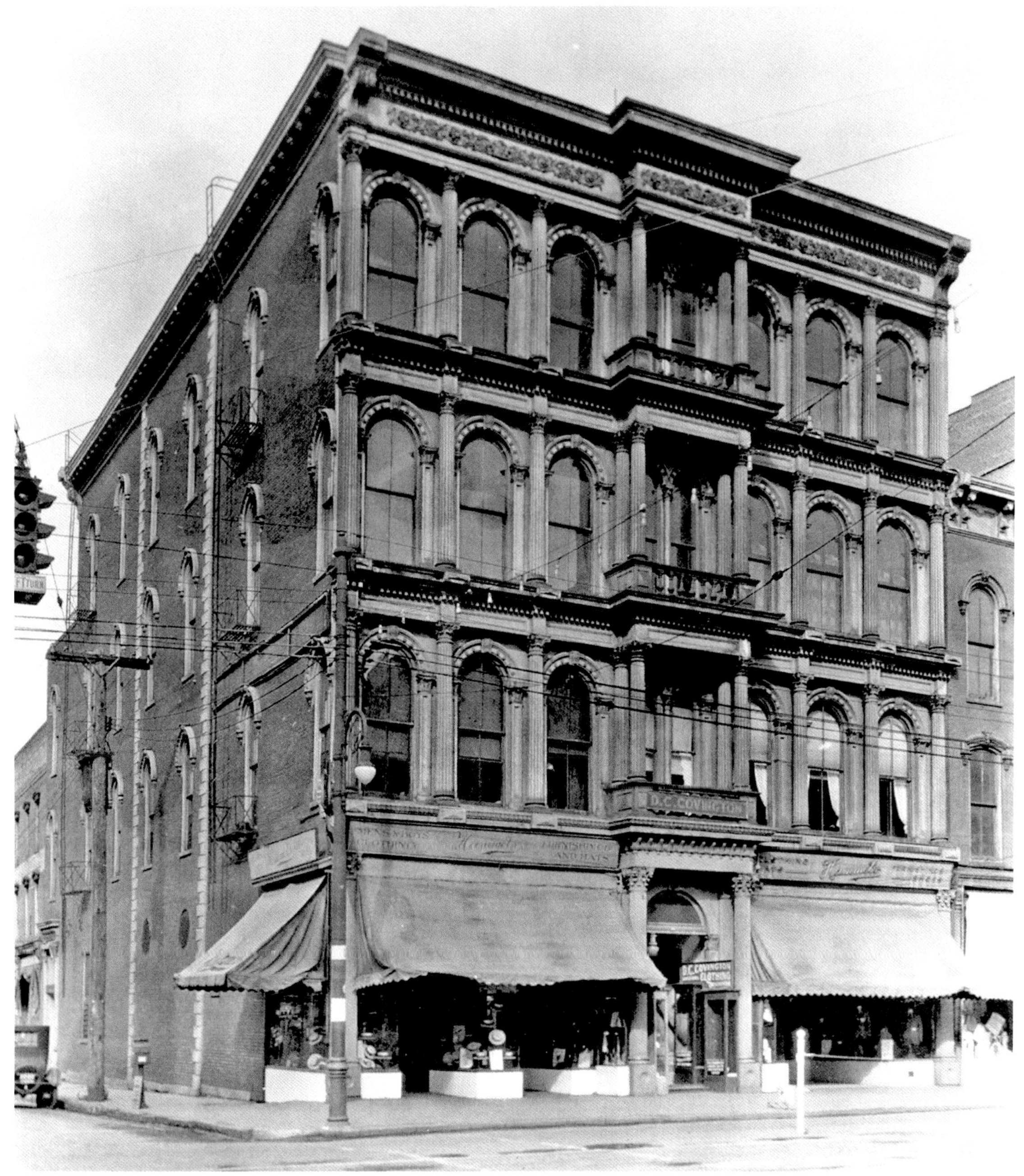

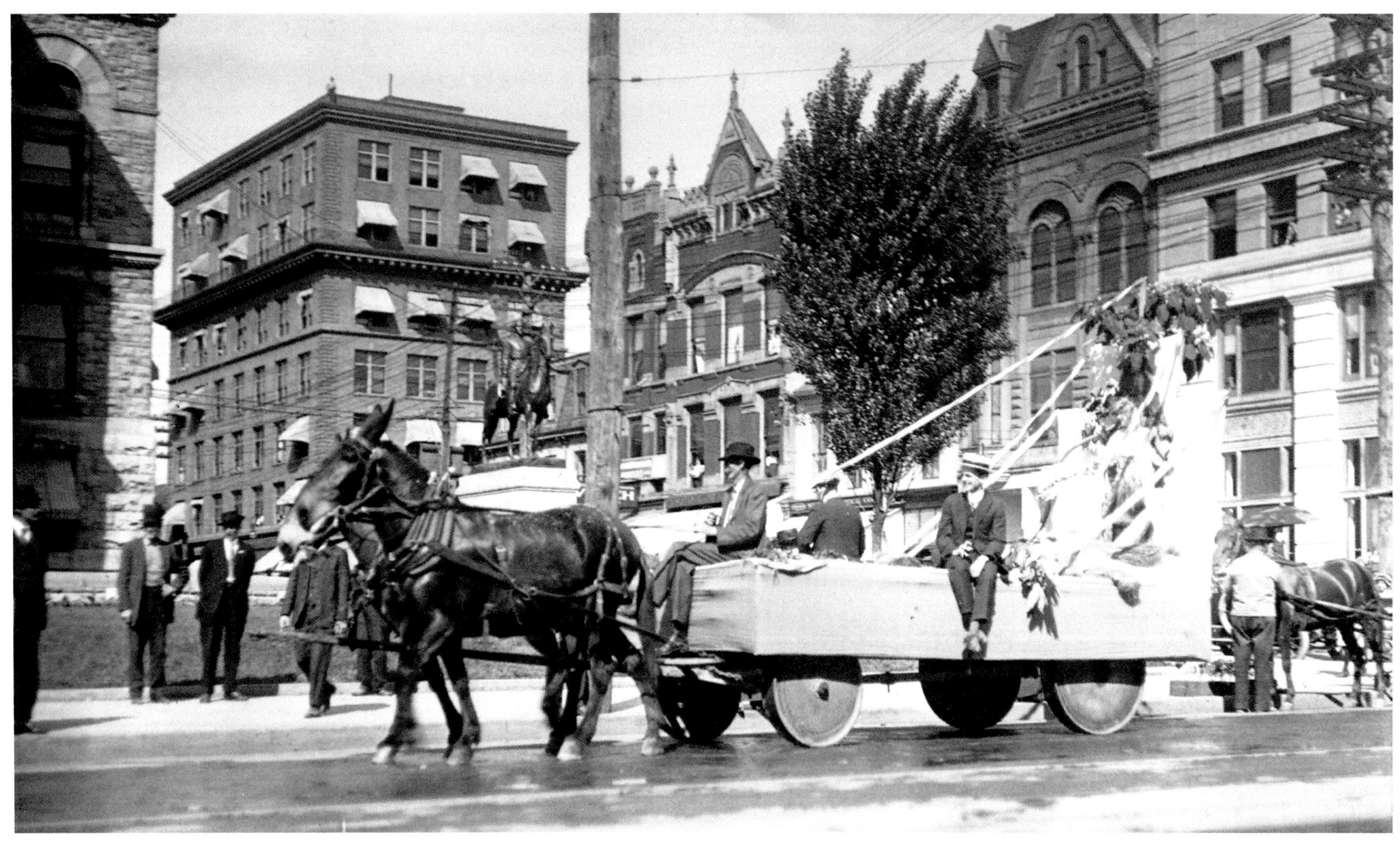

Golden Jubilee Parade at Main and Upper, 1916.

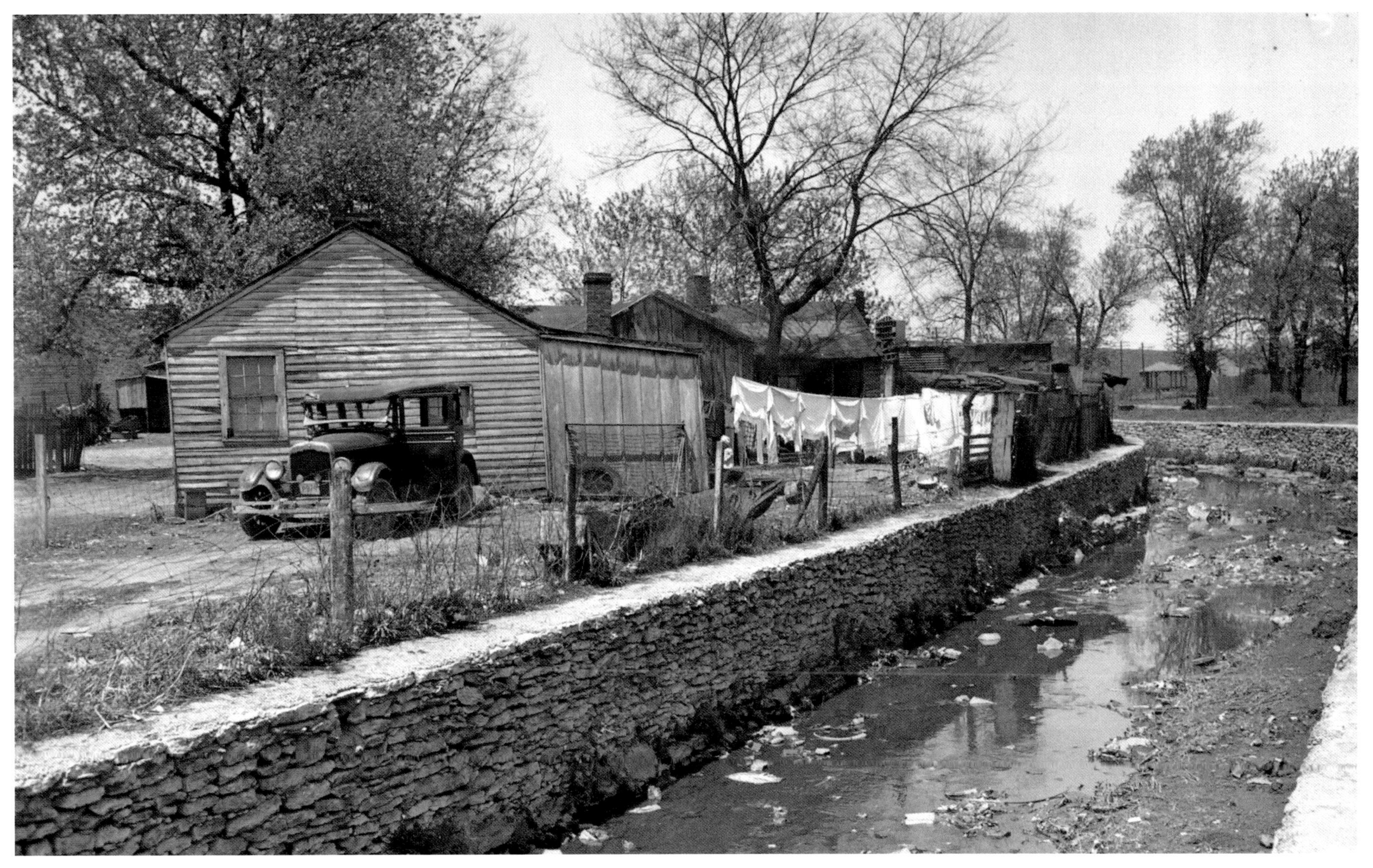

Town branch stream entering the city, early twentieth century.

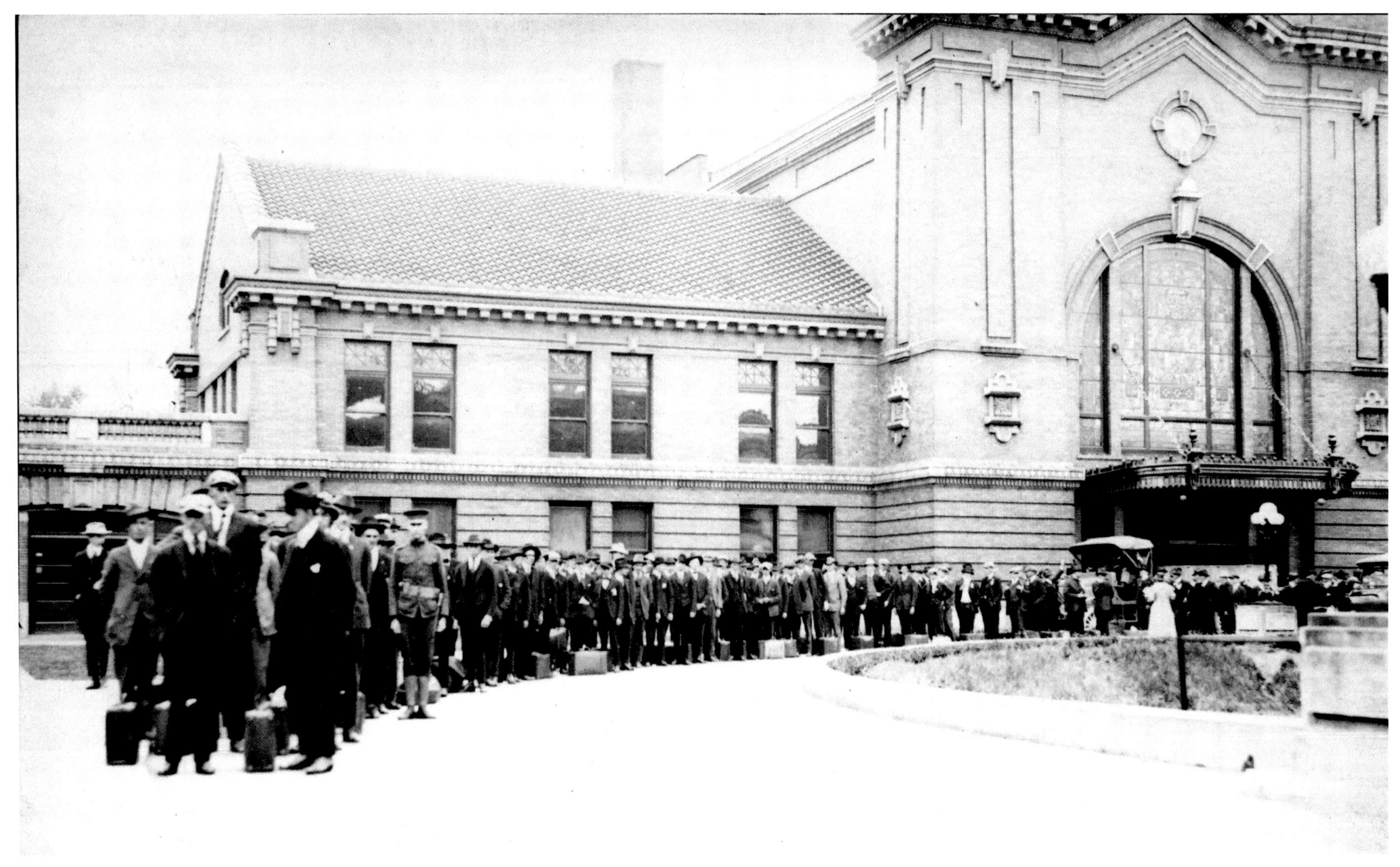

Training recruits arrive at Union Station, May 7, 1918, for military technical training at the University of Kentucky.

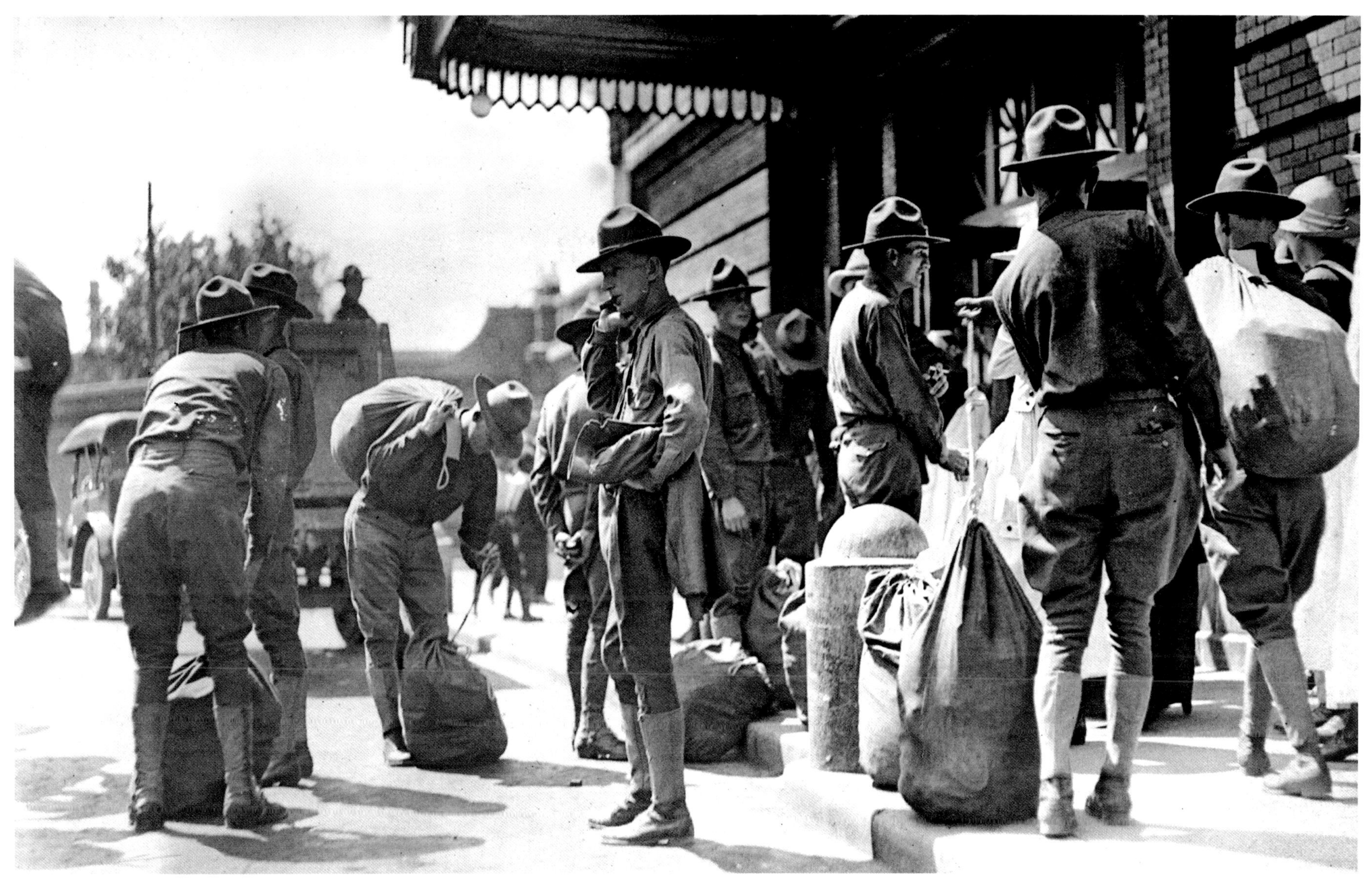

Soldiers arrive at Union Station on Main Street in July 1918 for military technical training at the University of Kentucky.

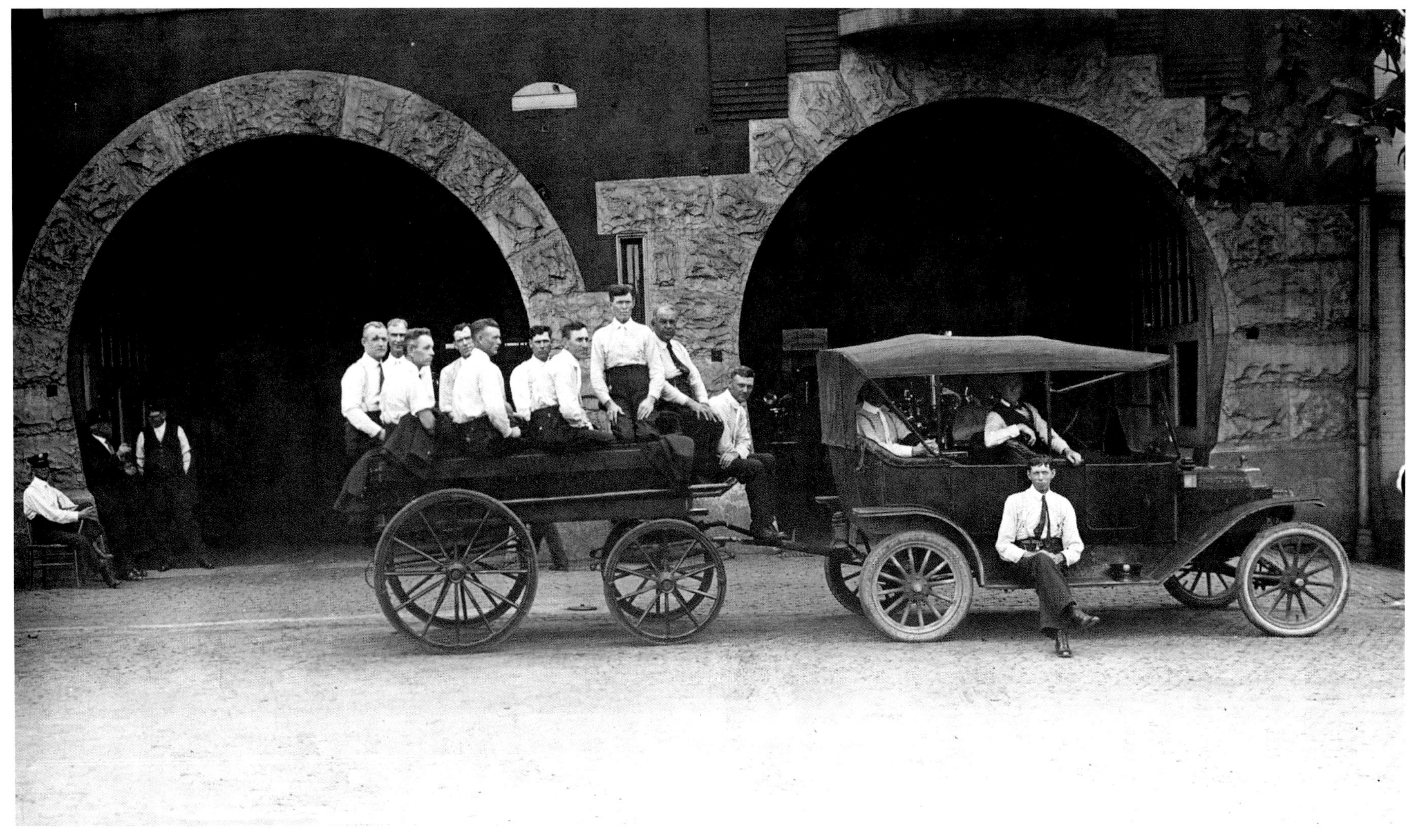

Fire Department volunteers who helped with the hemp and wheat harvest during World War I, ca. 1918.

Life Between the Wars

(1920–1940)

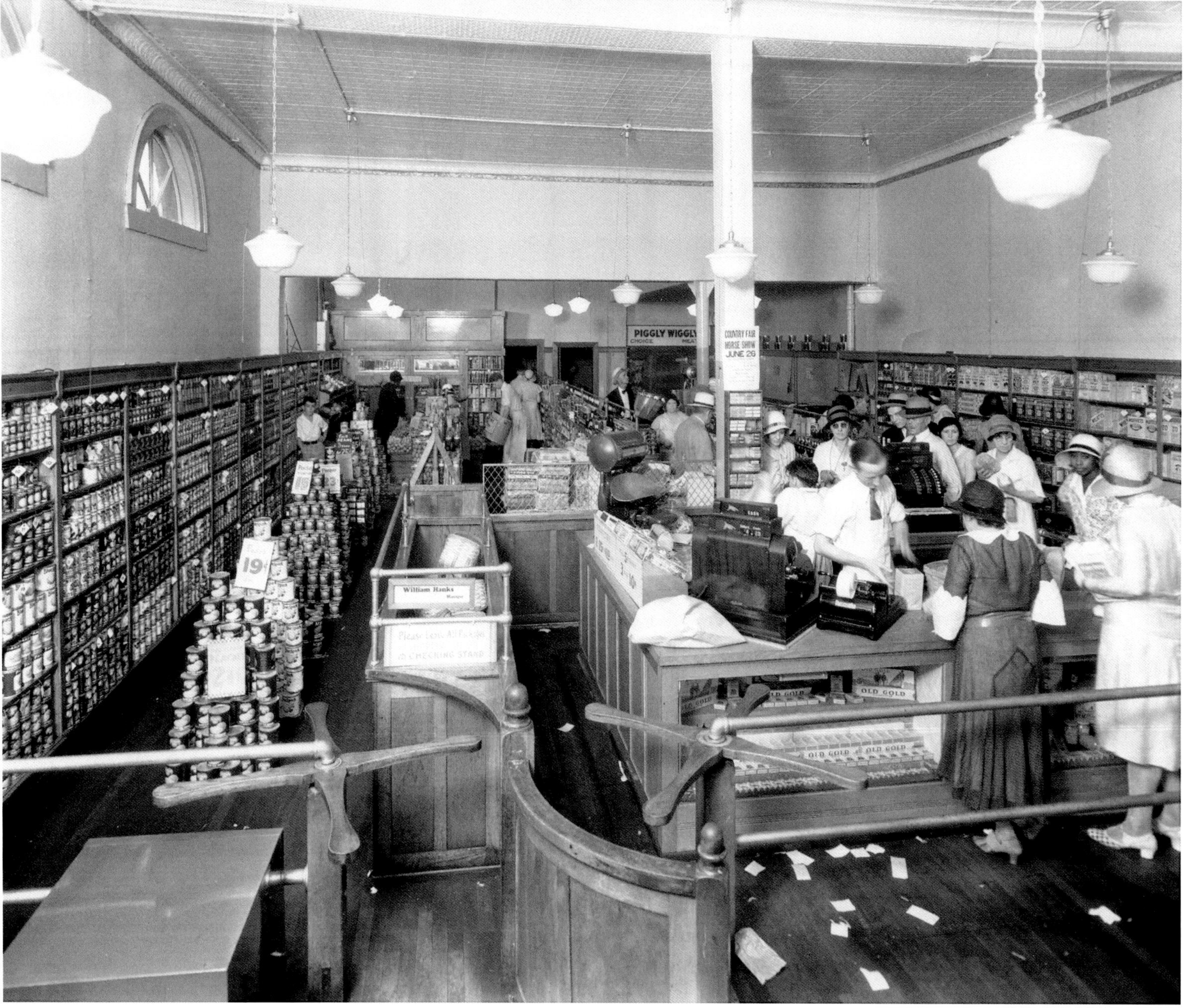

Piggly Wiggly new "self-service" grocery store at Broadway and Short Street, 1920.

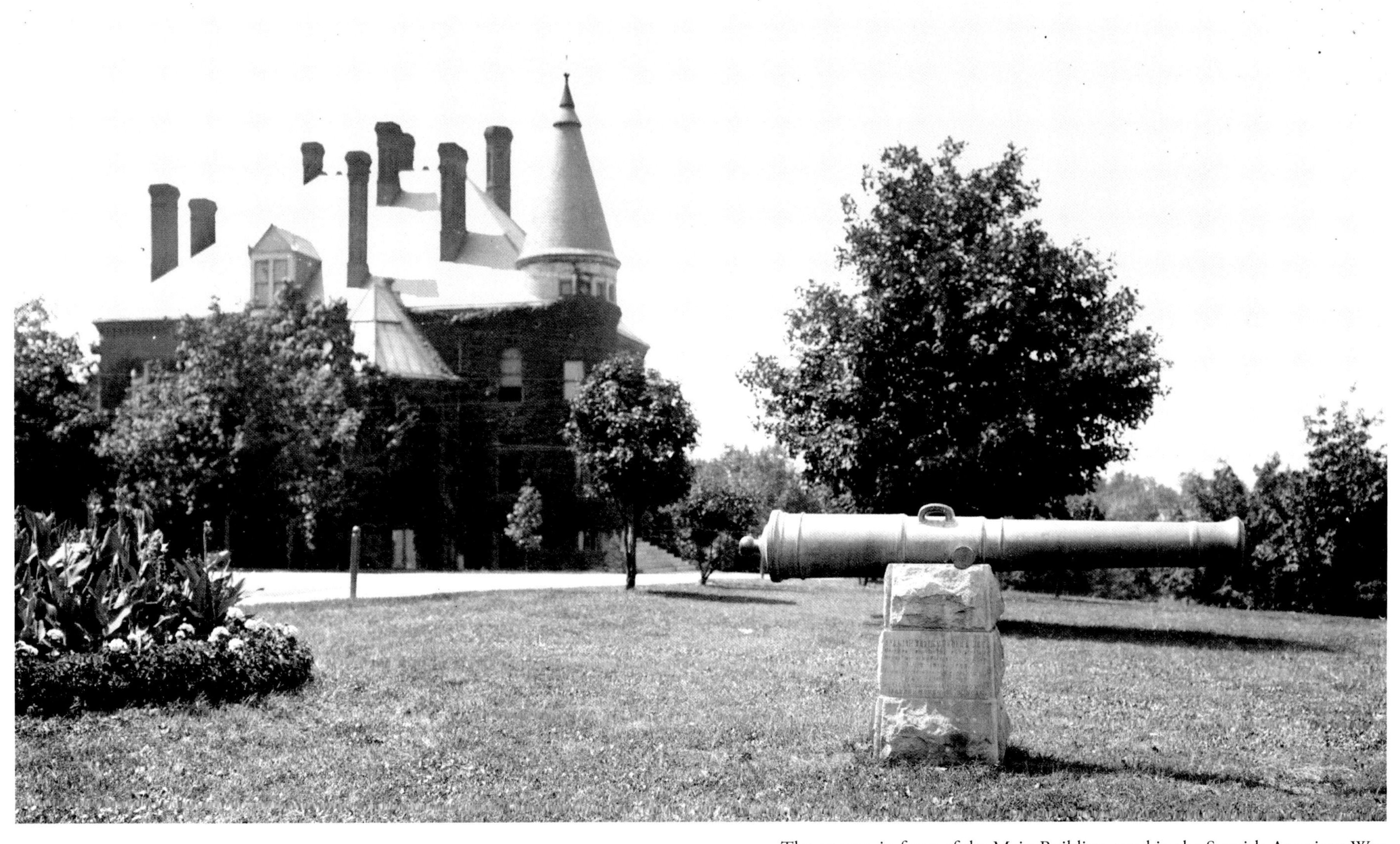

The cannon in front of the Main Building, used in the Spanish-American War.

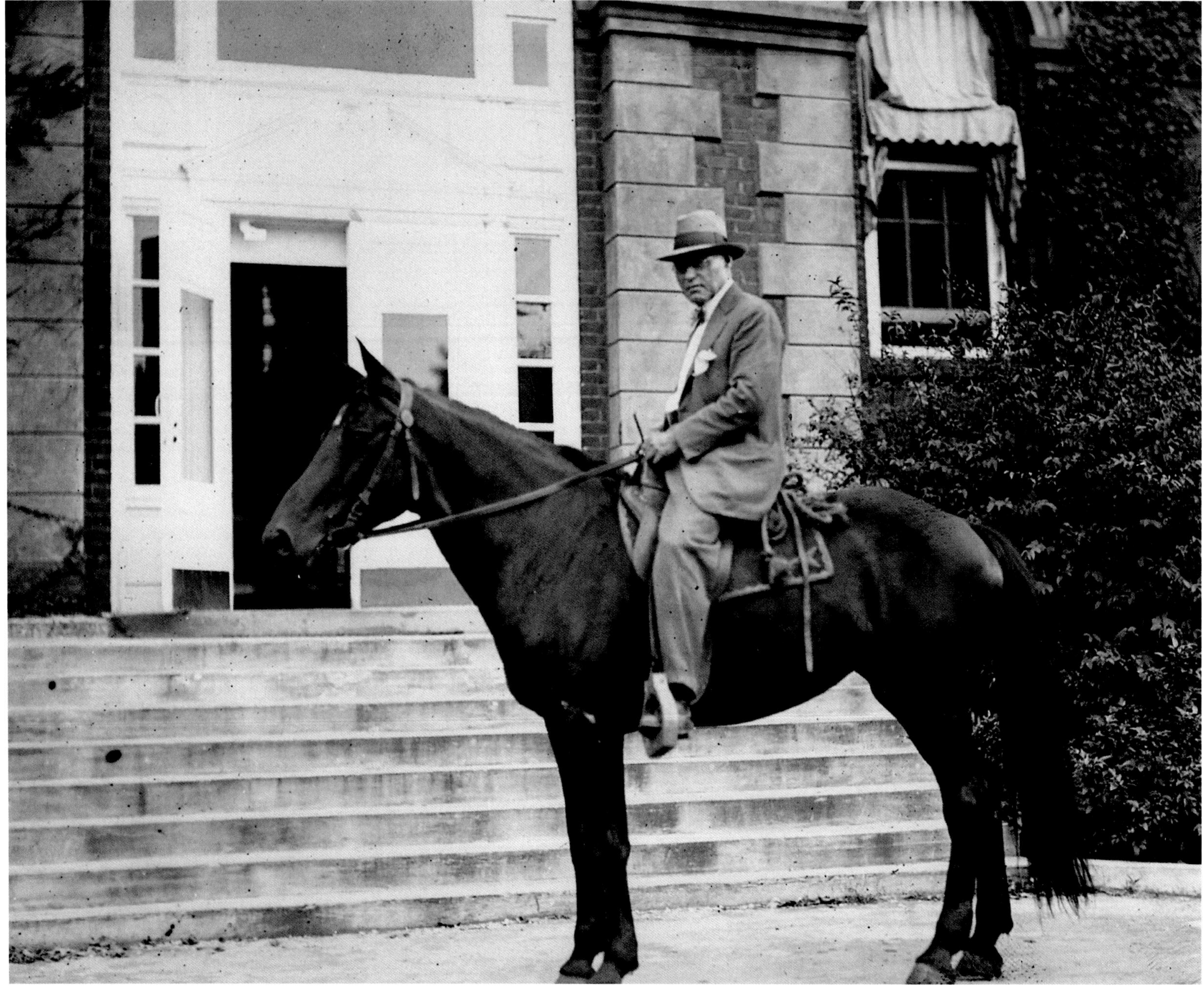

Professor Granville Terrel and his horse Katy arrive at the University of Kentucky after a 610-mile ride, 1927.

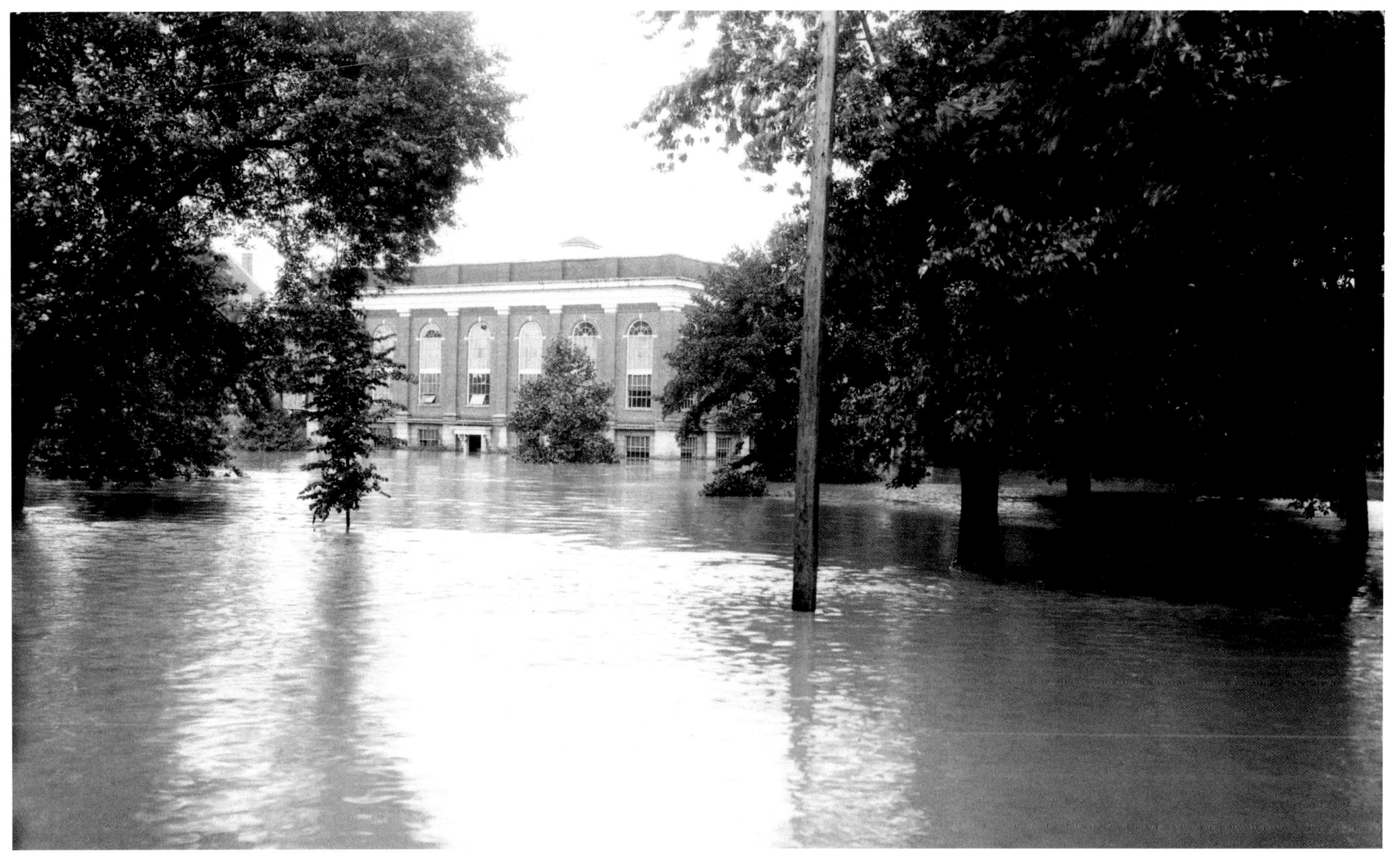

Flooded Alumni Gymnasium at the University of Kentucky, 1928.

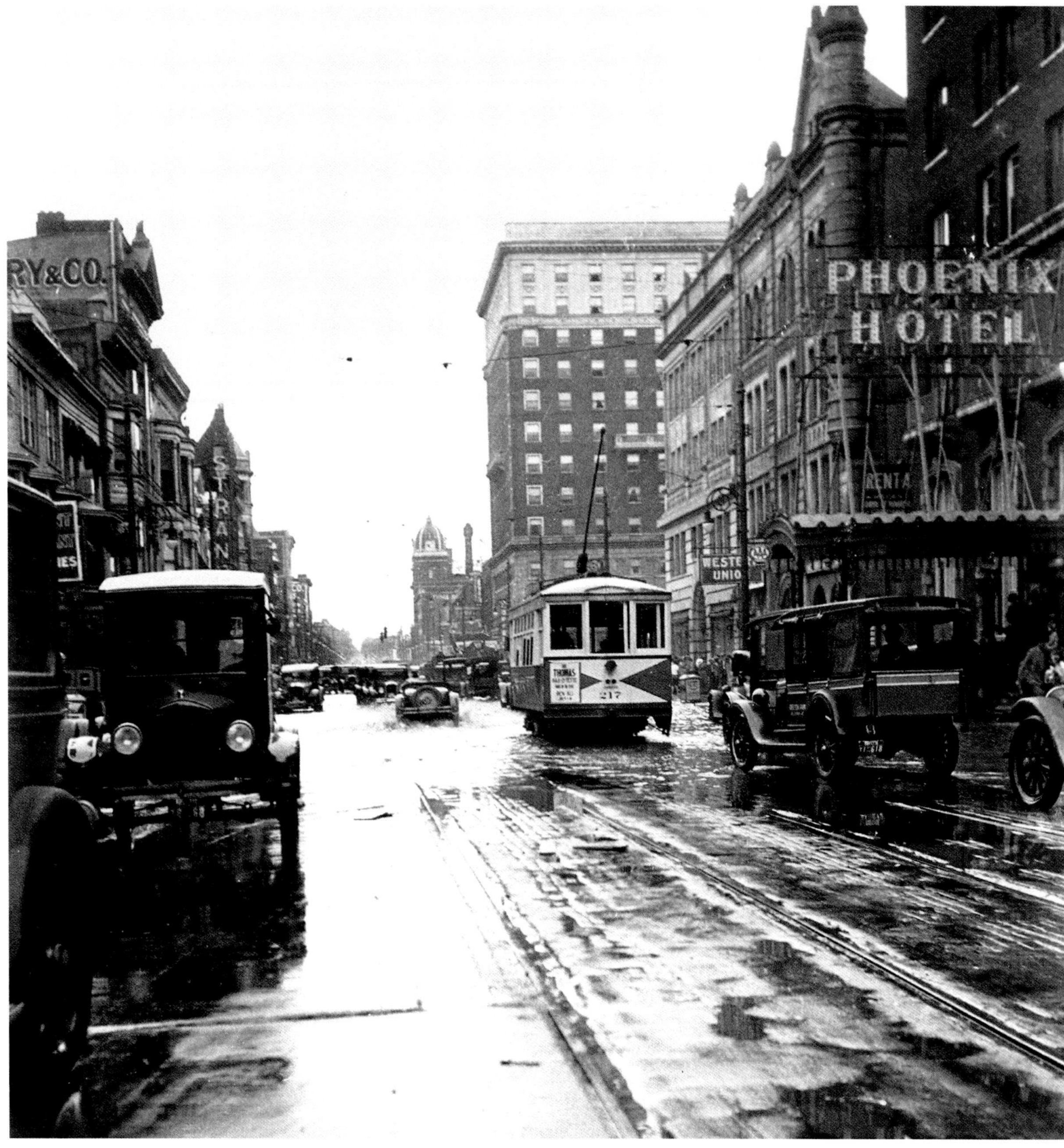

Main Street flooded, 1928.

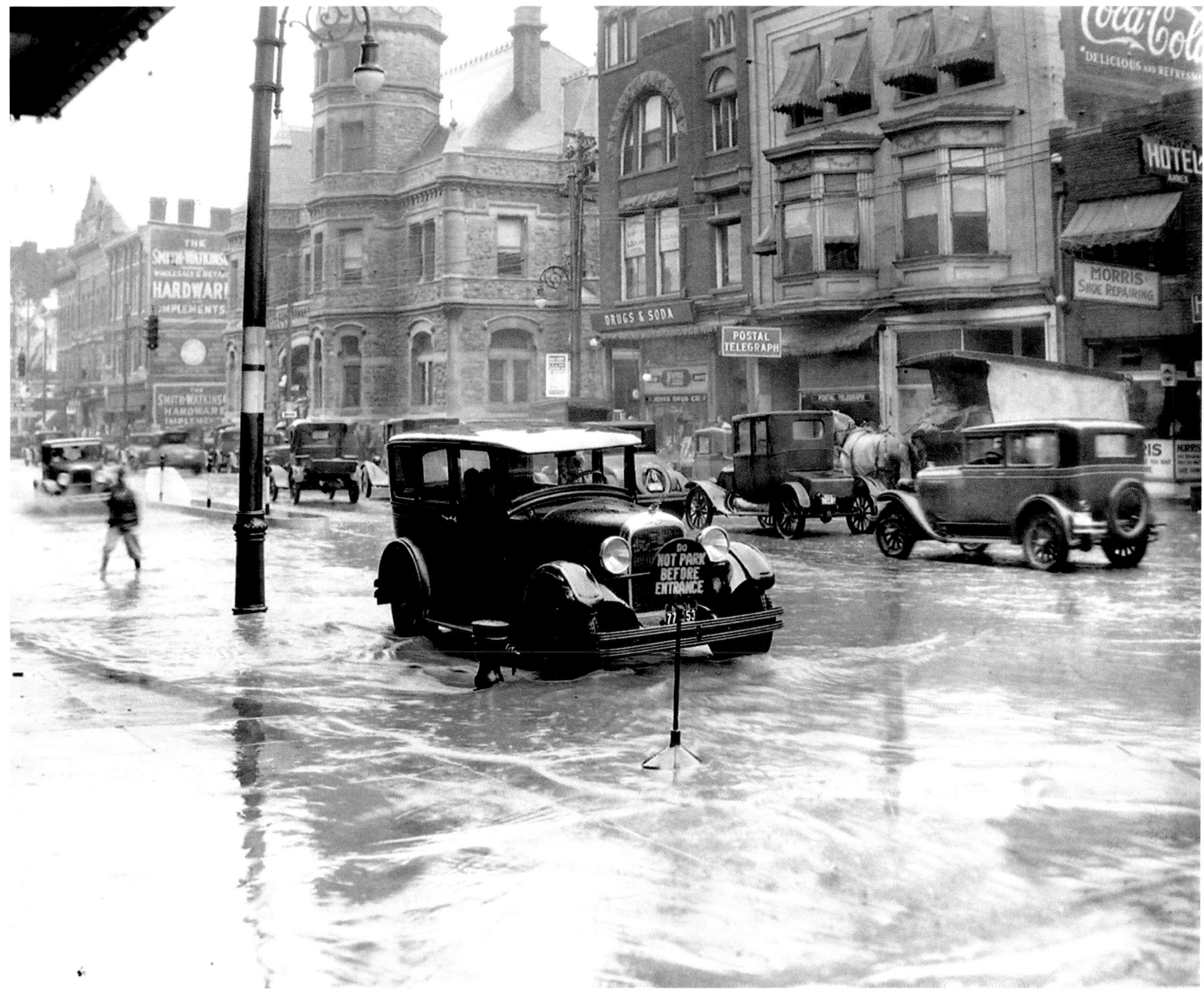

Another view of flooded Main Street, 1928.

Ice Plant of Kentucky Utilities on Loudoun Avenue, 1929.

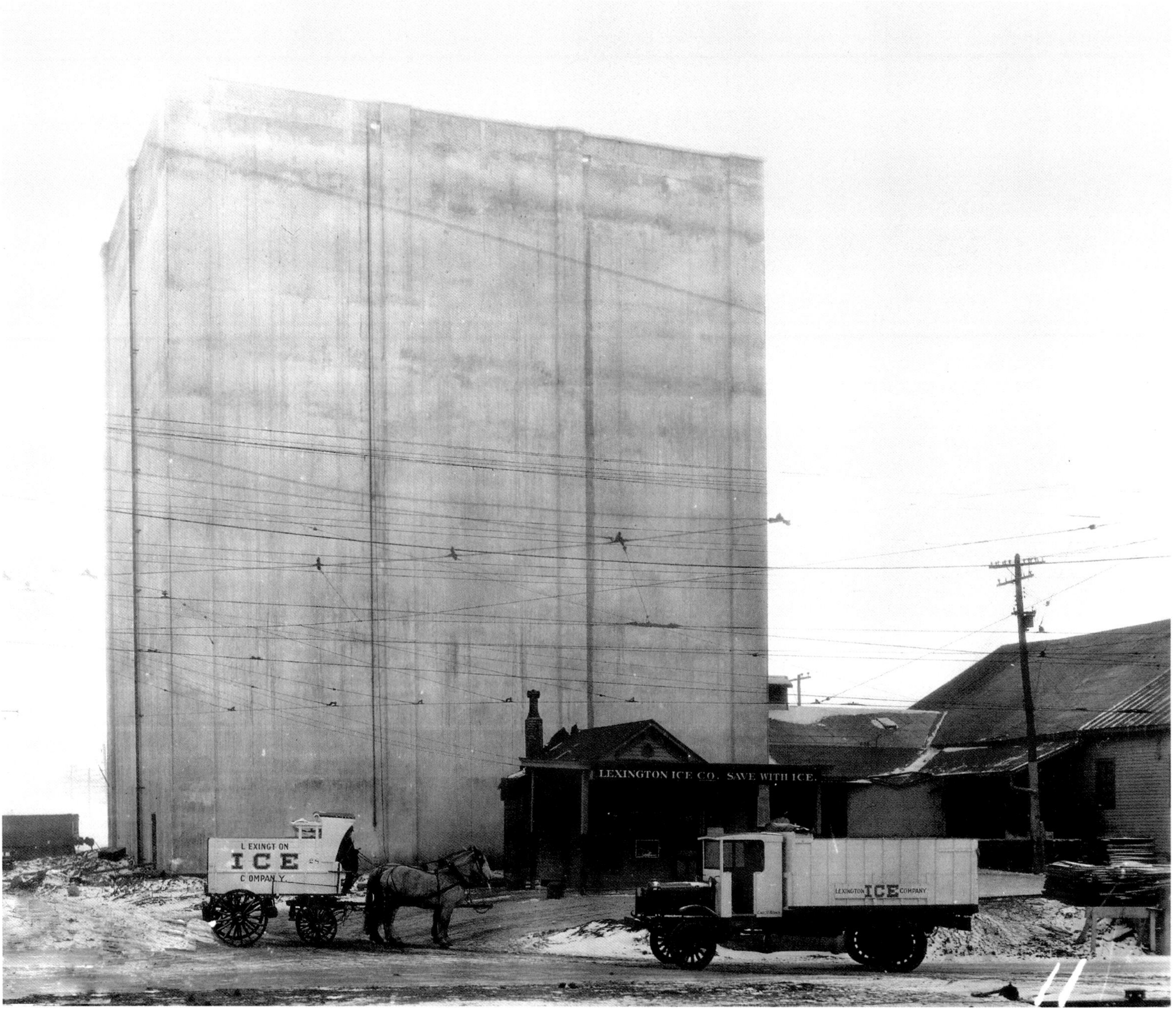

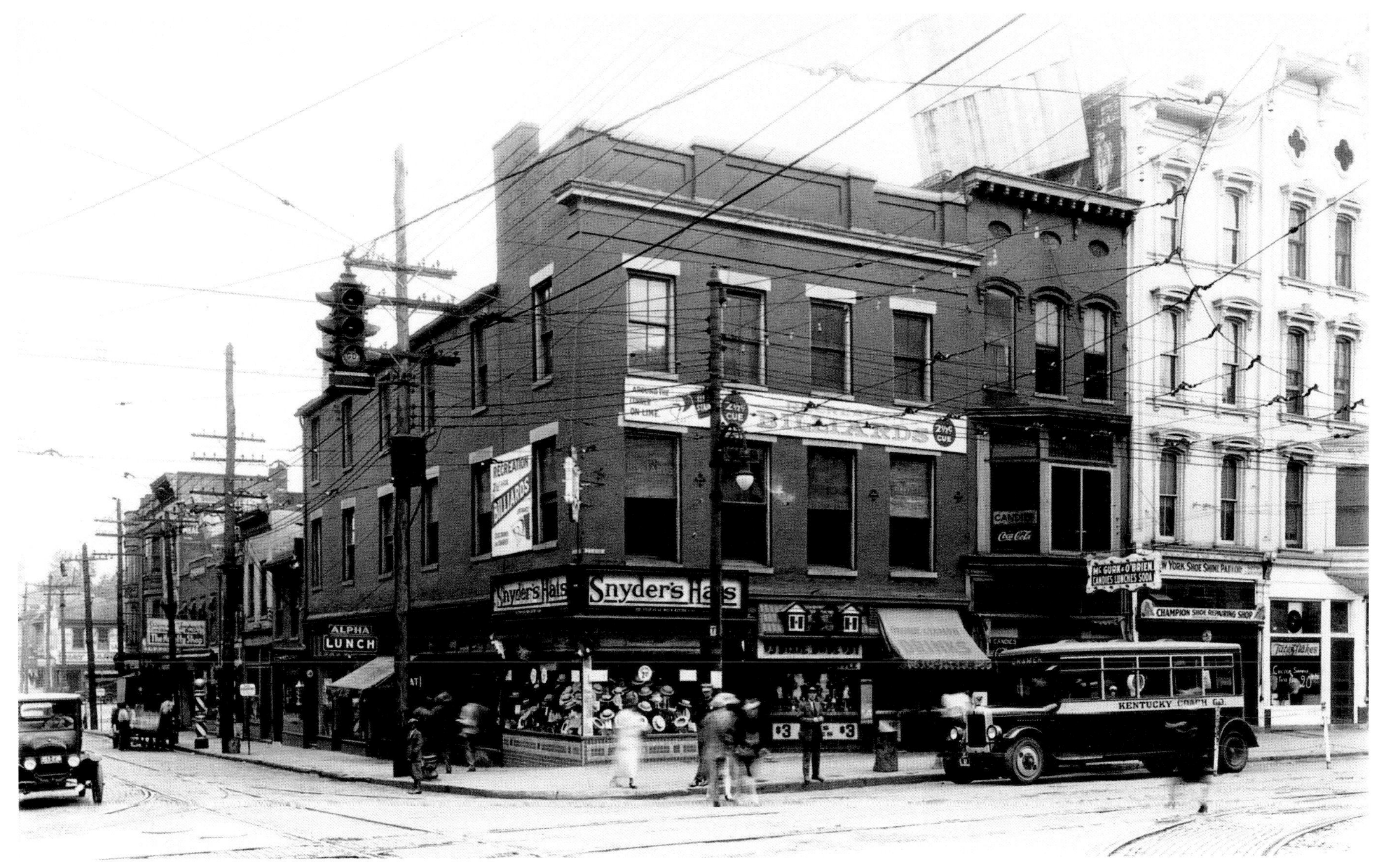

Urban vitality at the southwest corner of Main and Limestone streets with early Crower bus, ca. 1930.

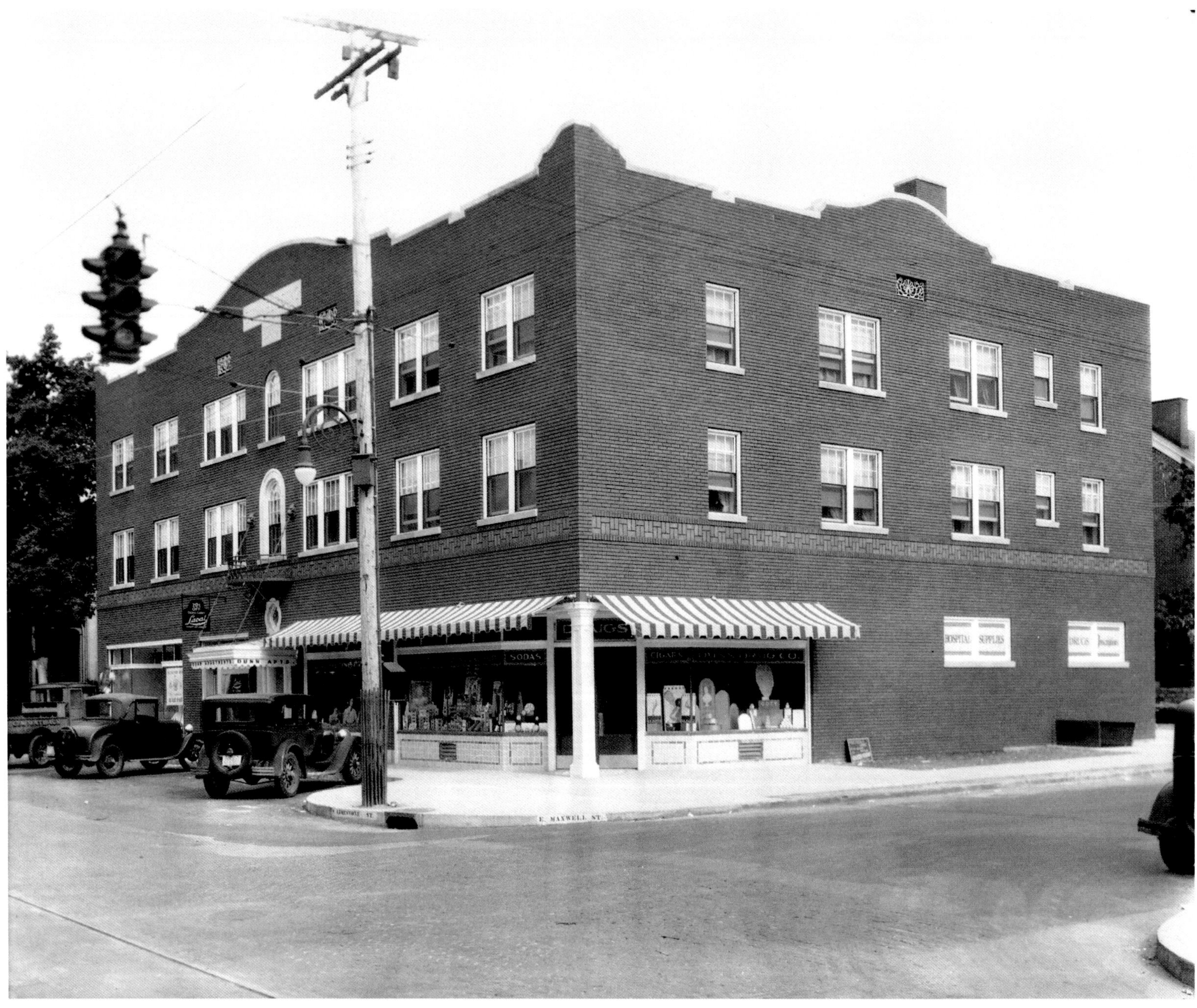

Dunn's Drug Store on South Limestone Street.

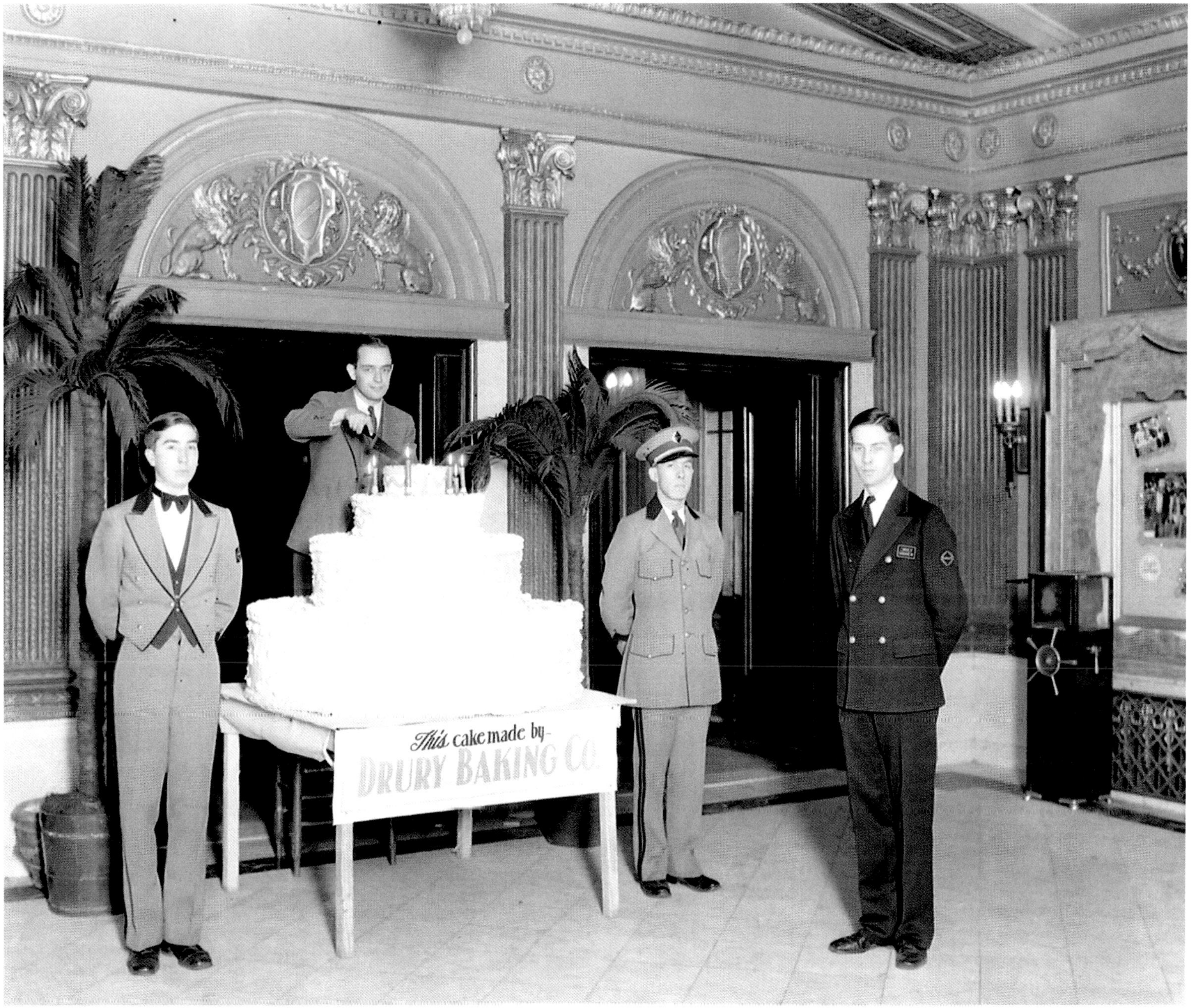

Celebration at the Kentucky Theater, 1930.

Printing at Spotswood Specialty Company, 1930.

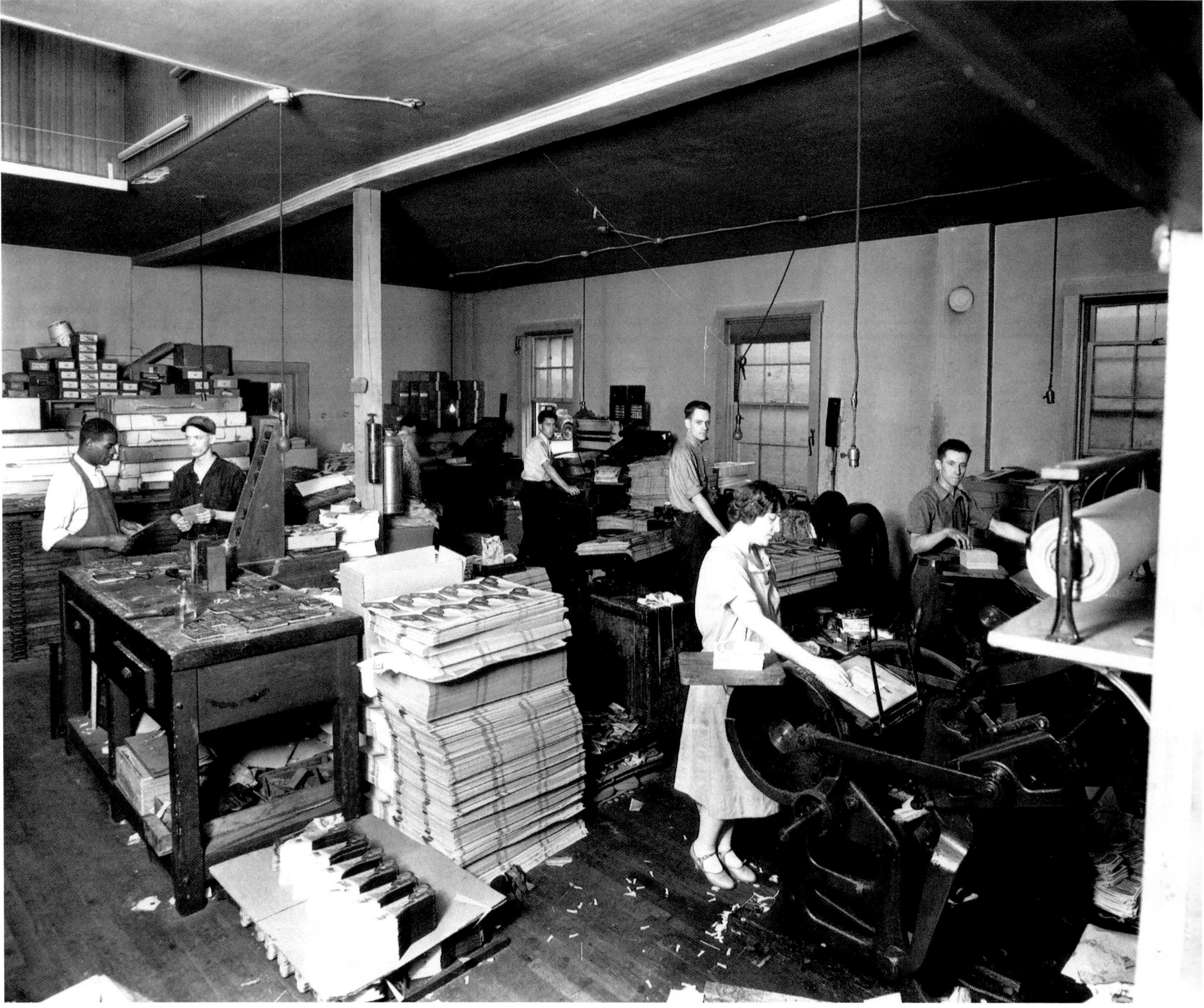

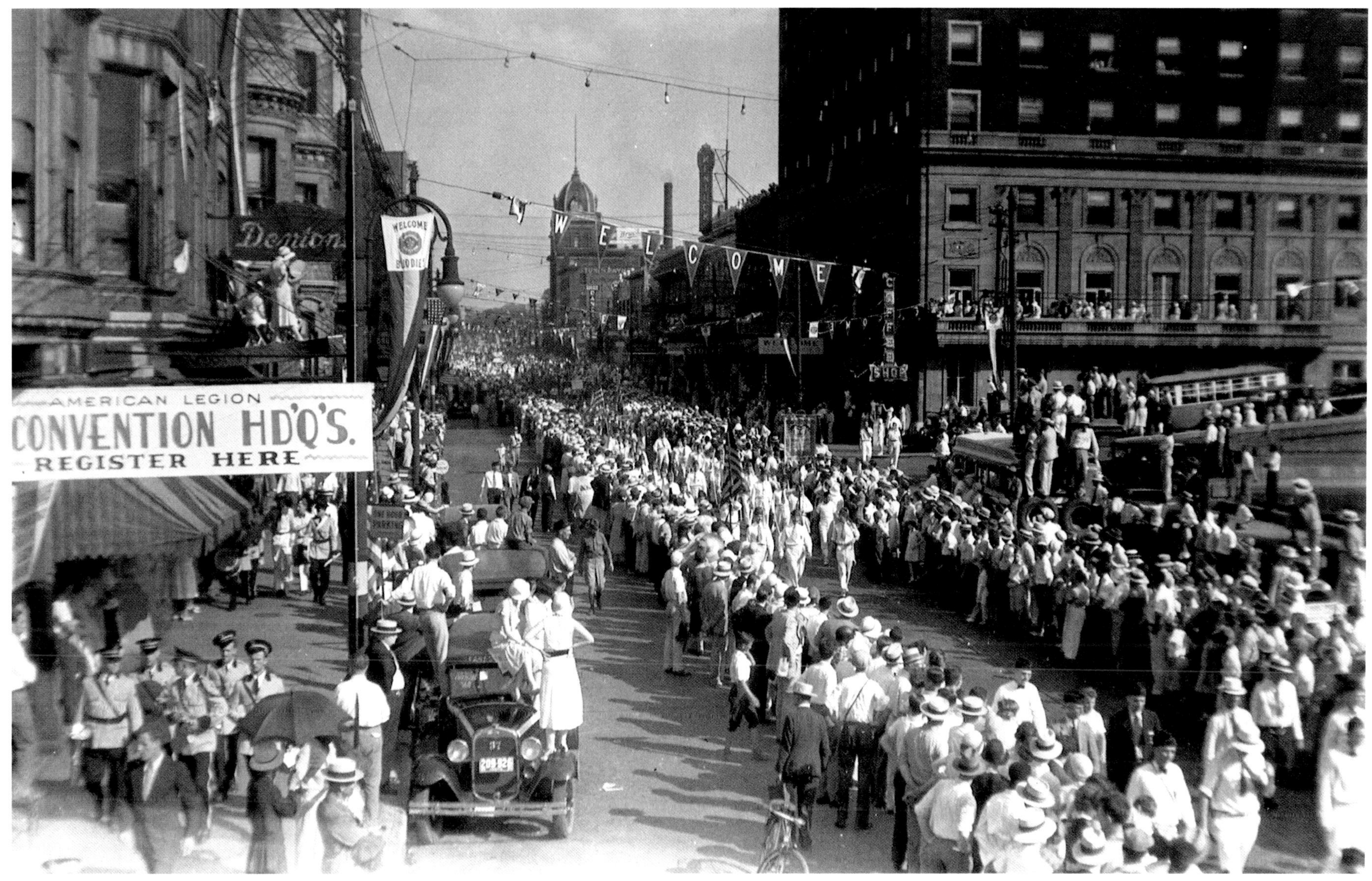

American Legion Parade on Main Street, 1931.

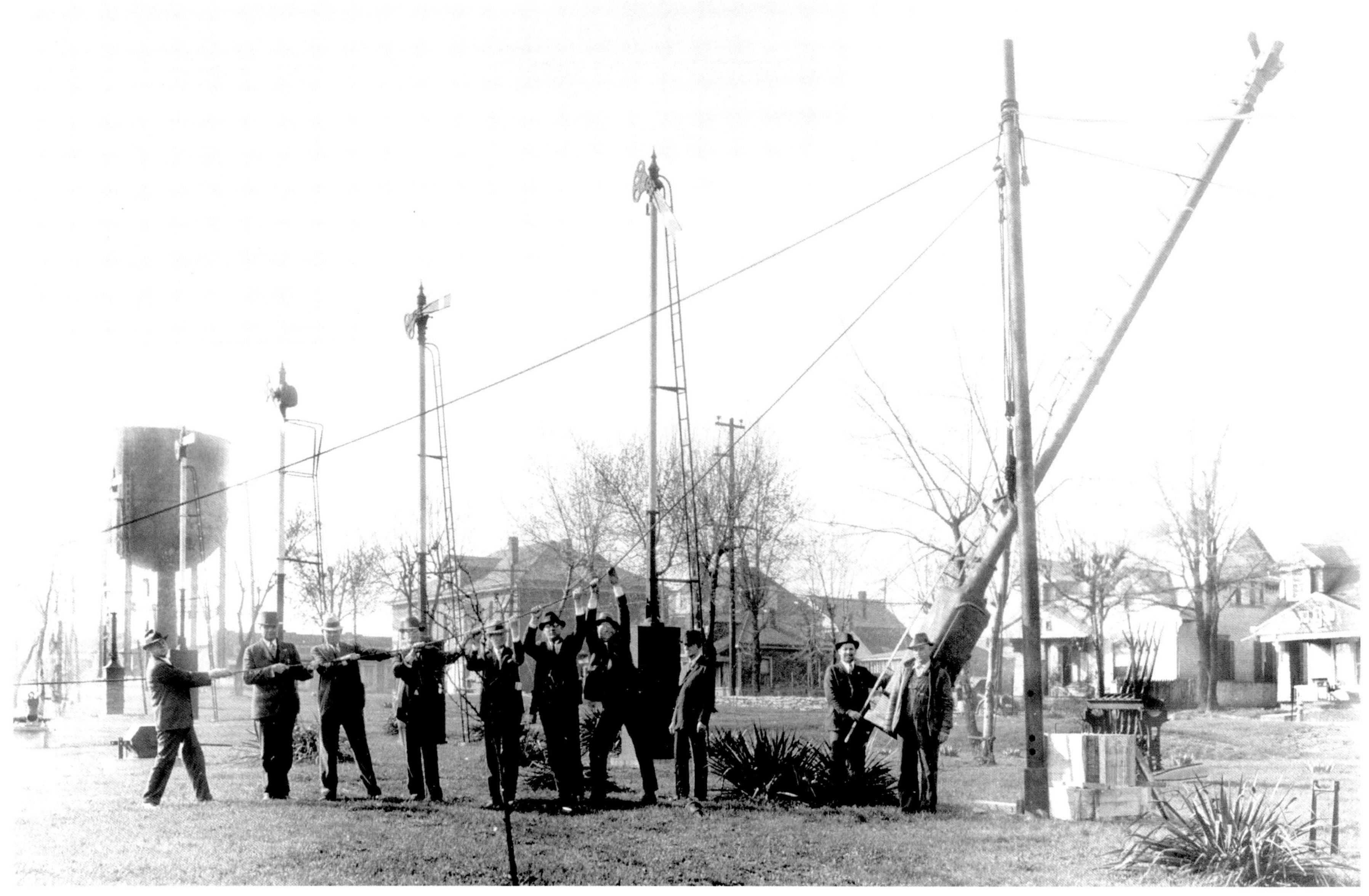

Hoisting a signal near Southern Station in Lexington in the 1930s.

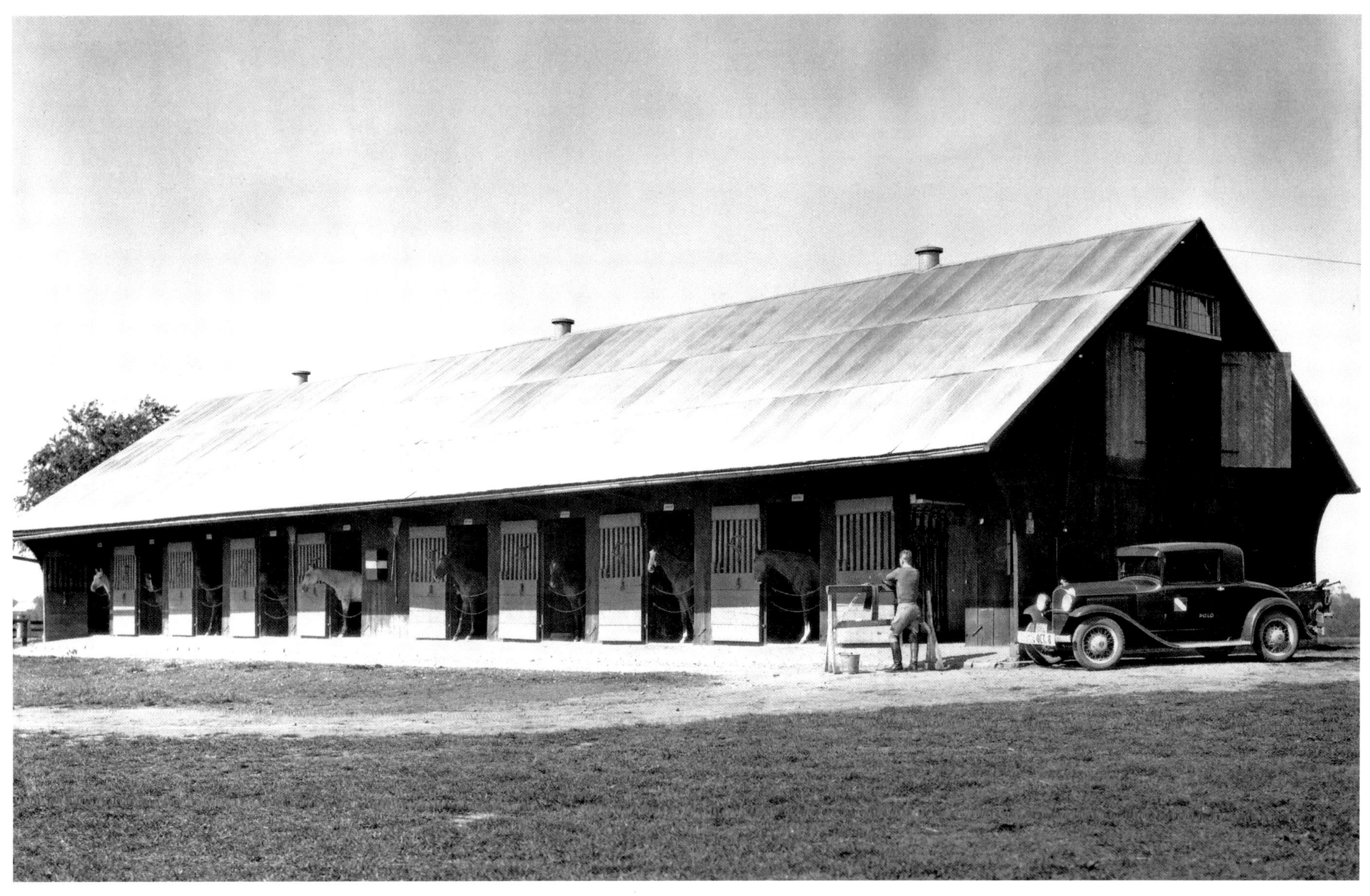

Barn at Hamburg Place, 1932.

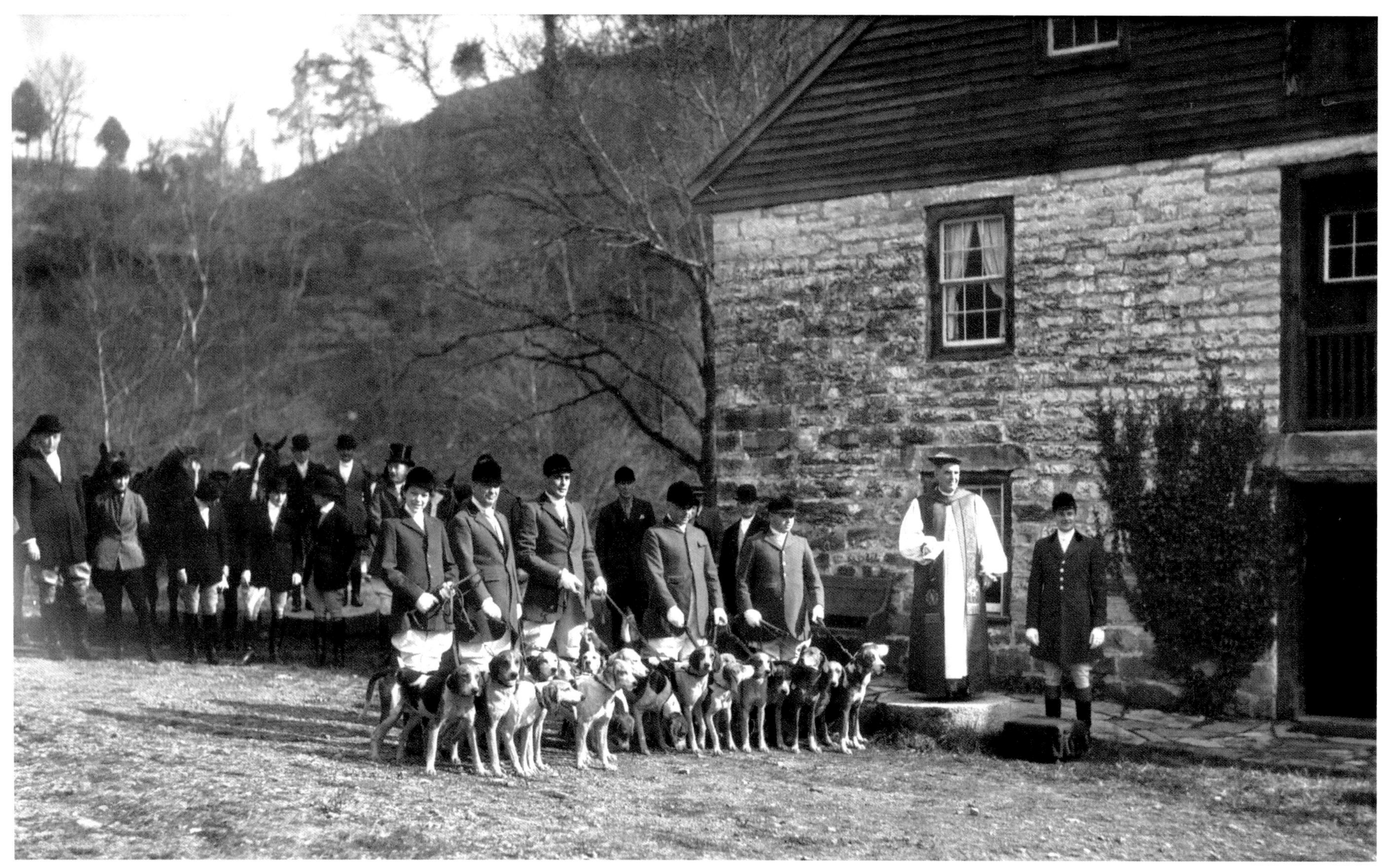

Bishop Abbott officiates at the Iroquois Hunt Club's second Blessing of the Hounds, 1933.

Mayor O'Brien and lion cub promote a film from the steps of City Hall, 1931.

Kelley's Liquor store on Main Street, 1934.

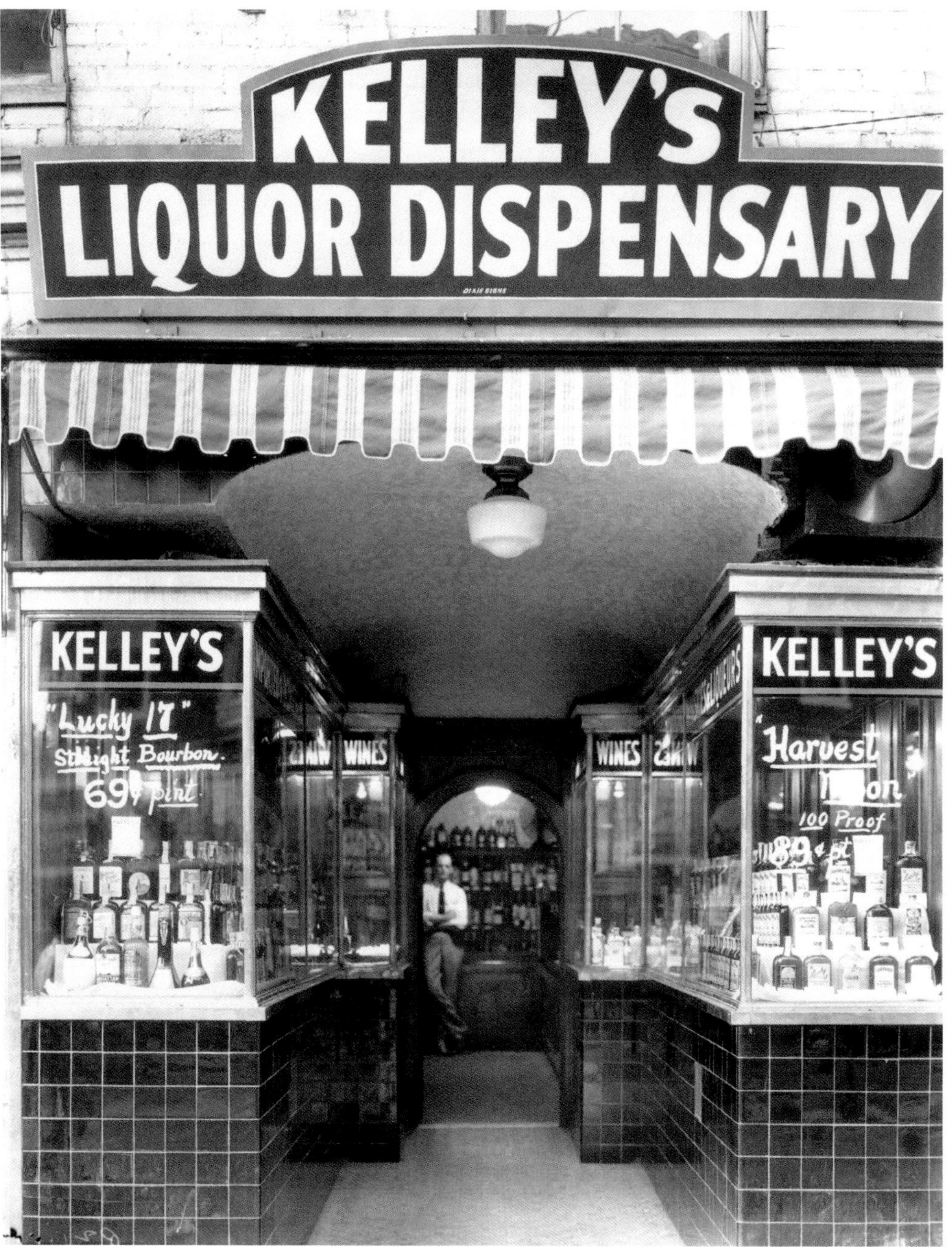

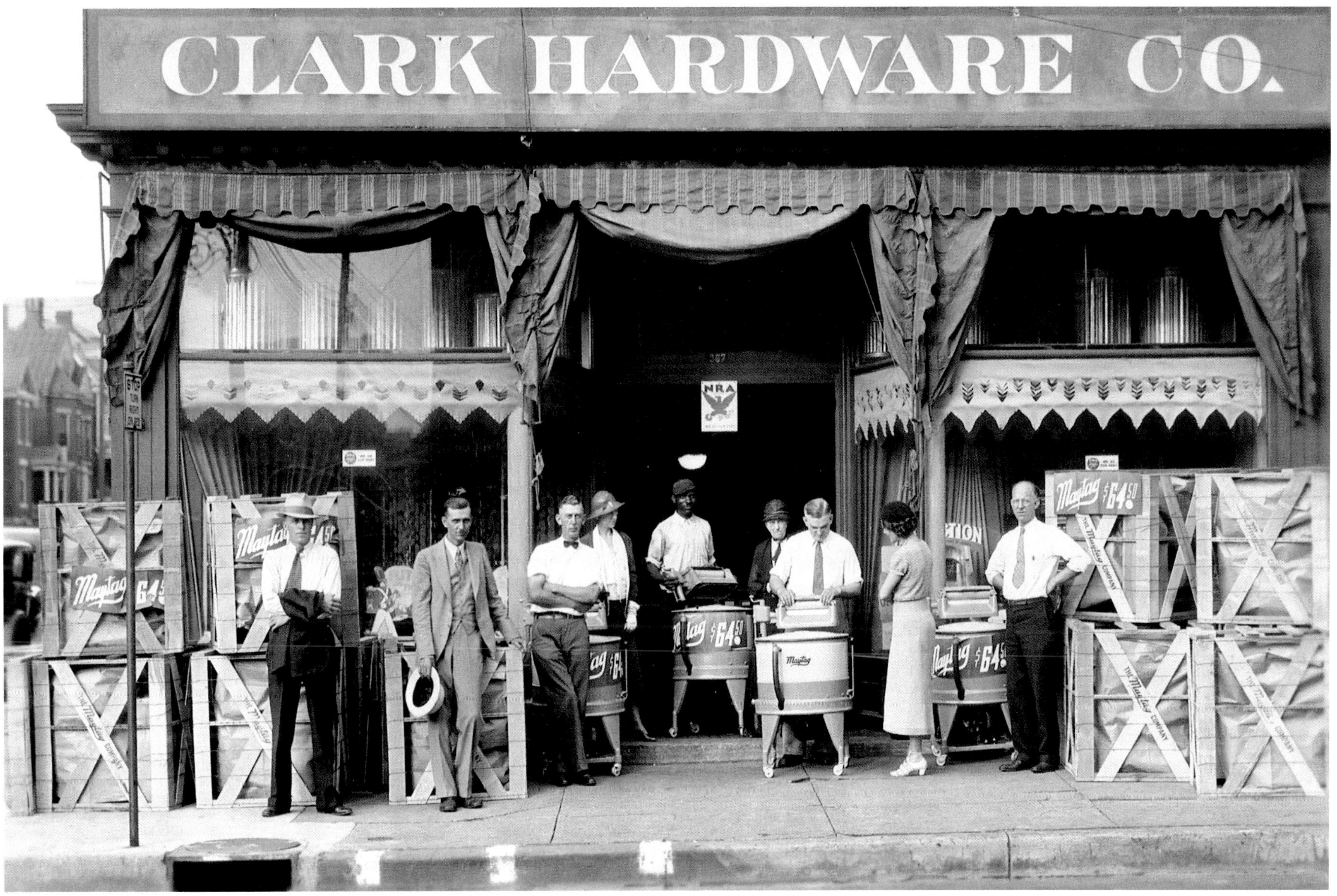

Clark's Hardware Store in 1933 after the arrival of a new shipment of Maytag washers.

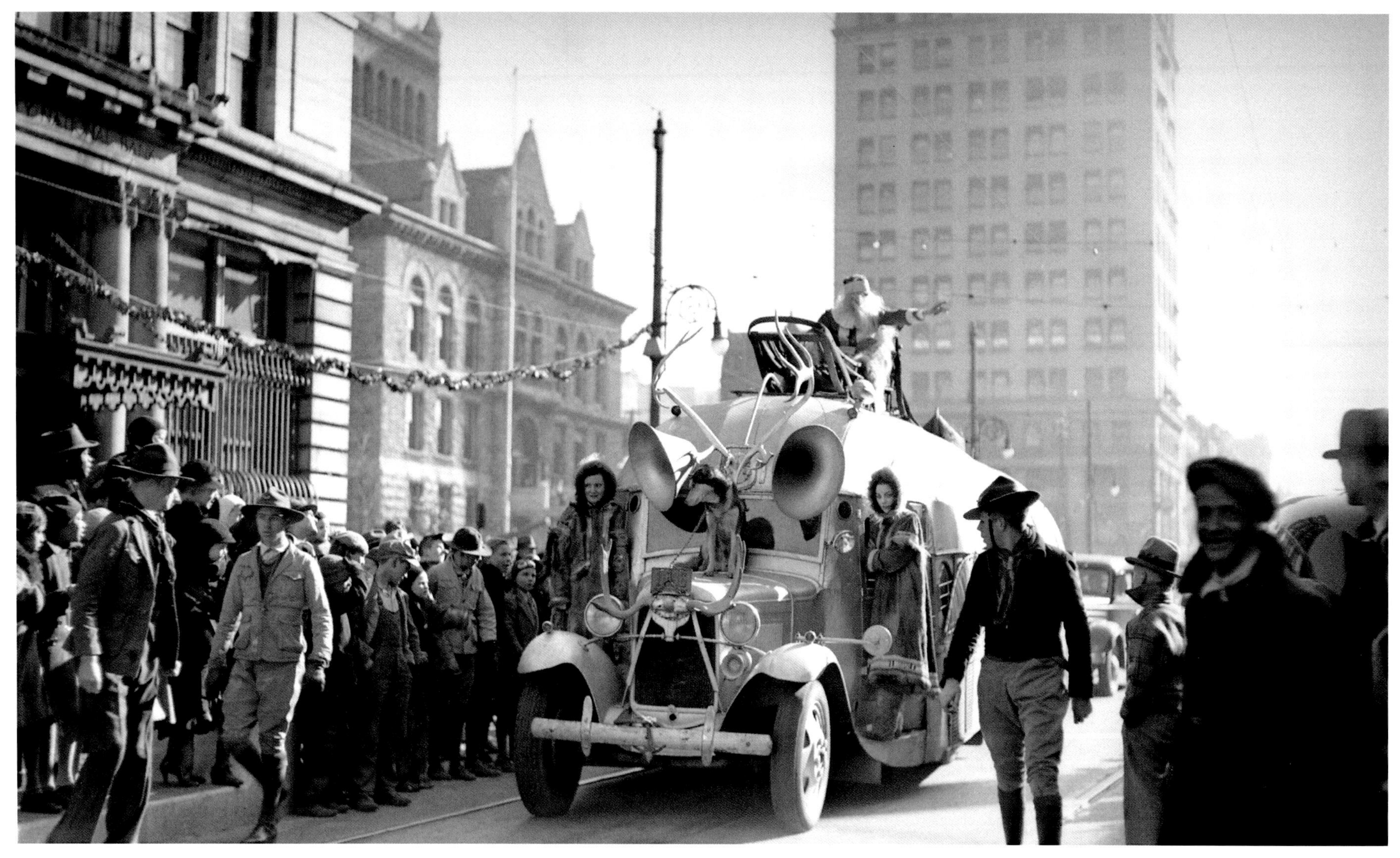

Christmas Parade on Main Street, 1935.

Golfer Marion Miley and Mayor Thompson, 1935.

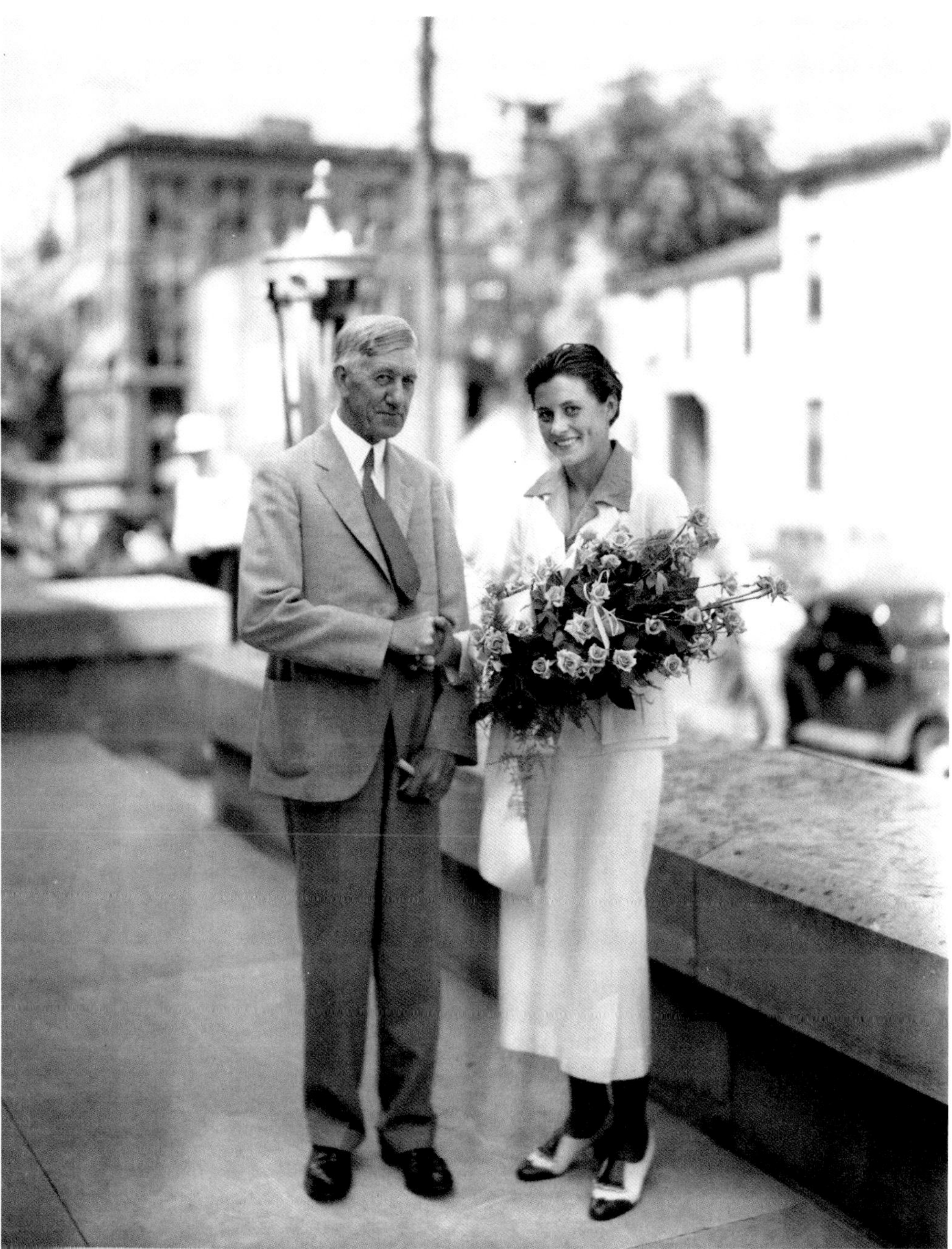

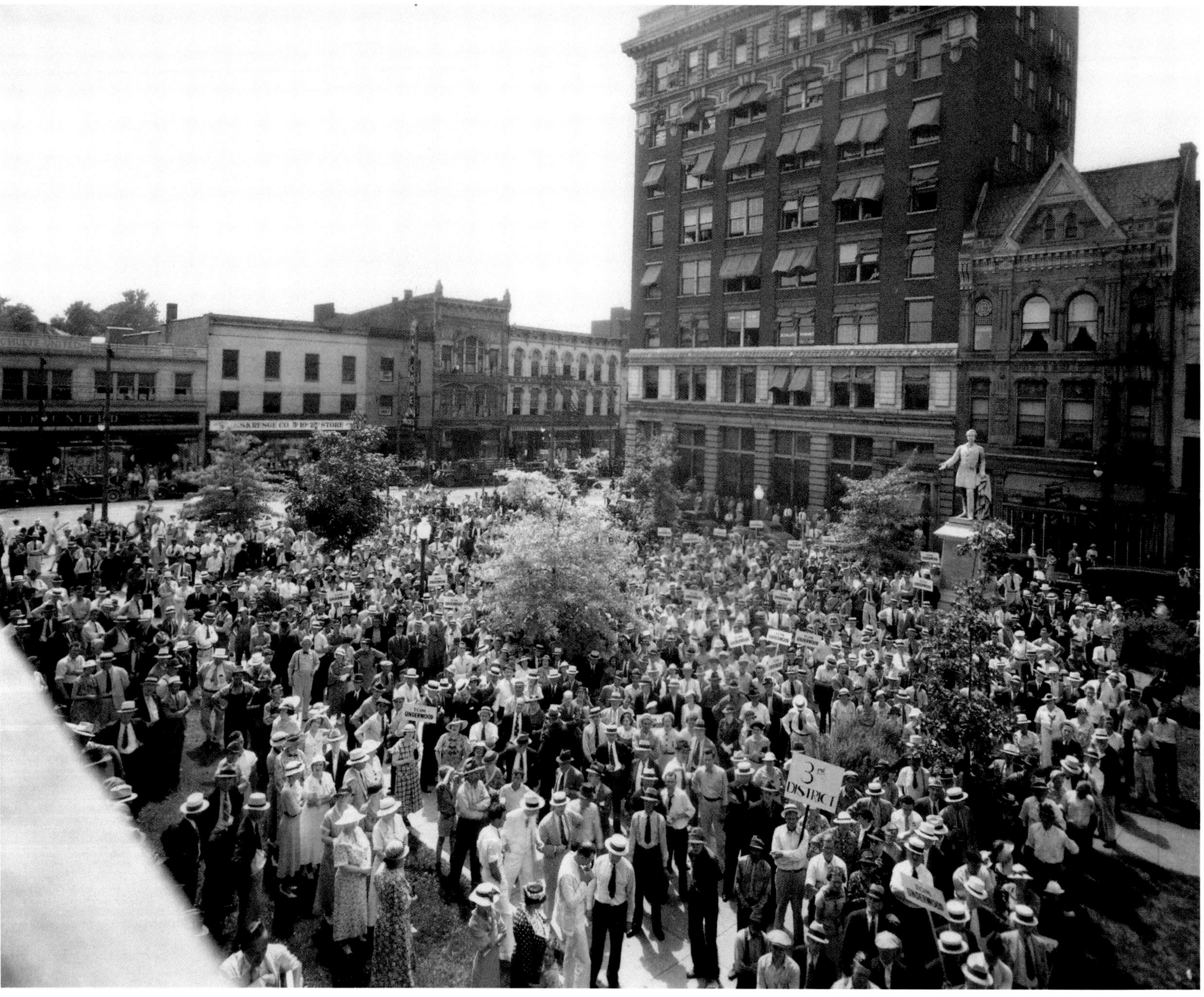

"Split" Democratic Convention on Cheapside, 1936.

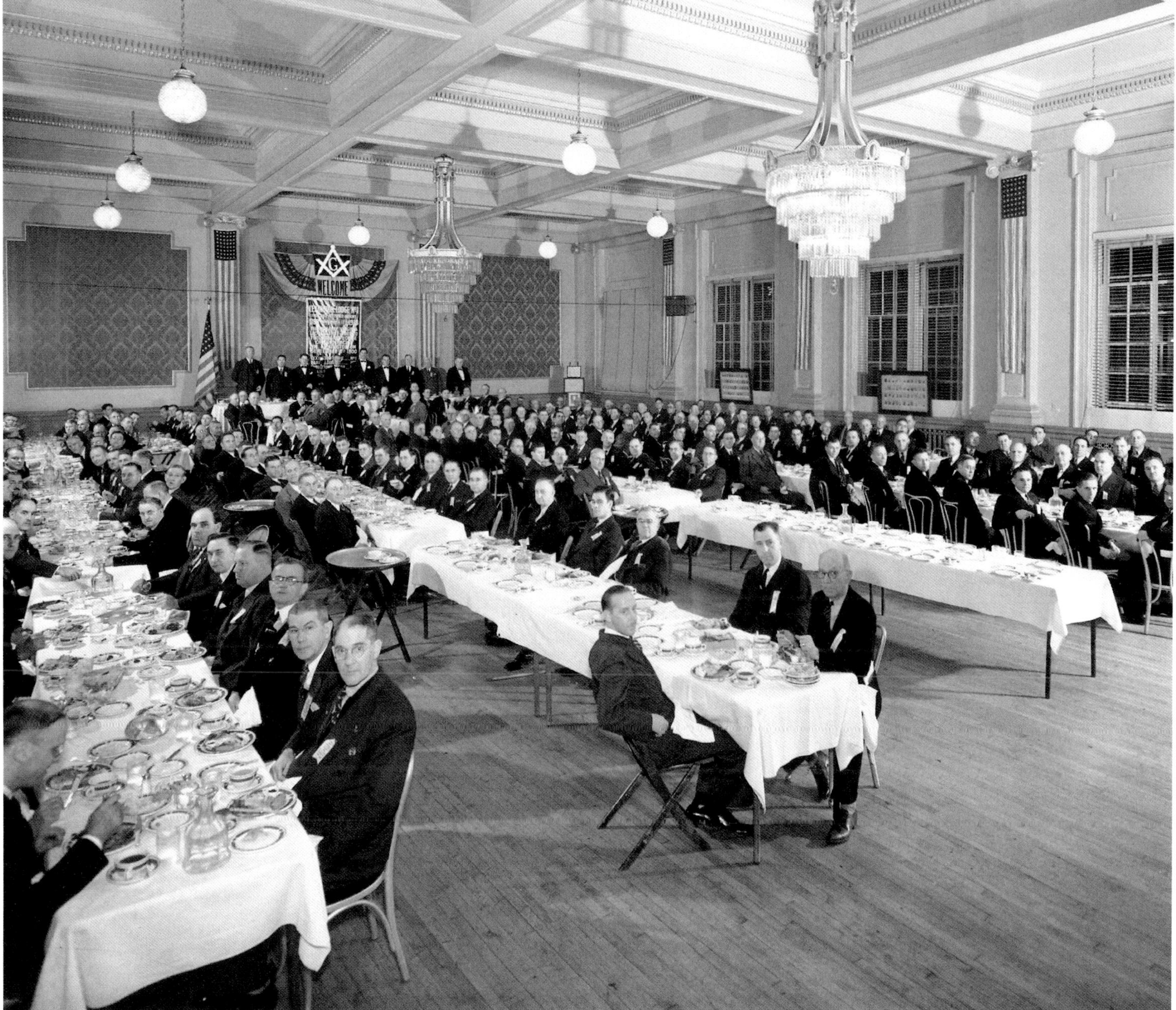

Banquet at the Phoenix Hotel, 1938.

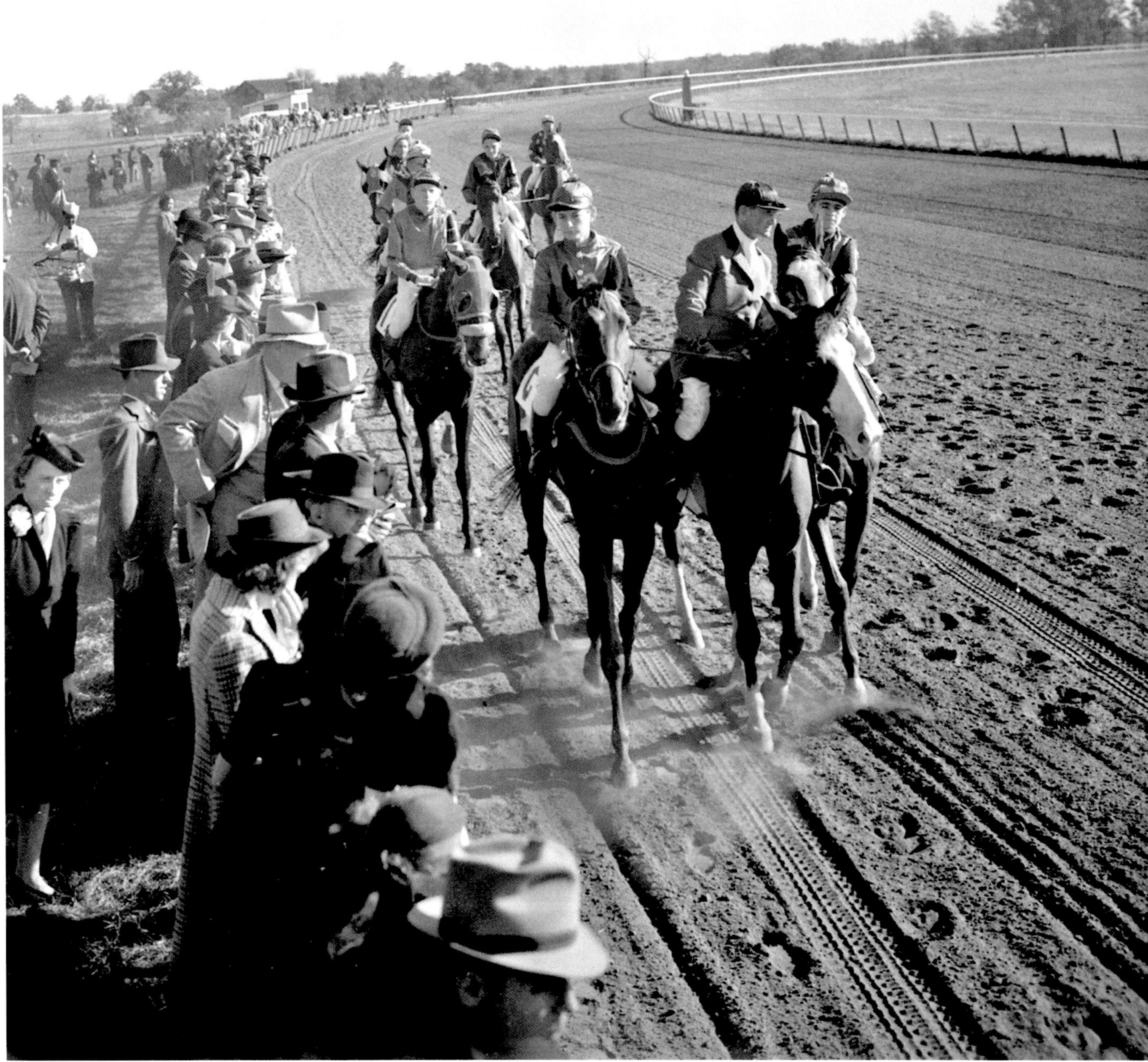

Racehorses and jockeys walk the track prior to a race at Keeneland, 1939.

Man O'War and his groom Will Harbut are visited by singer-actress Jeannette McDonald, 1939.

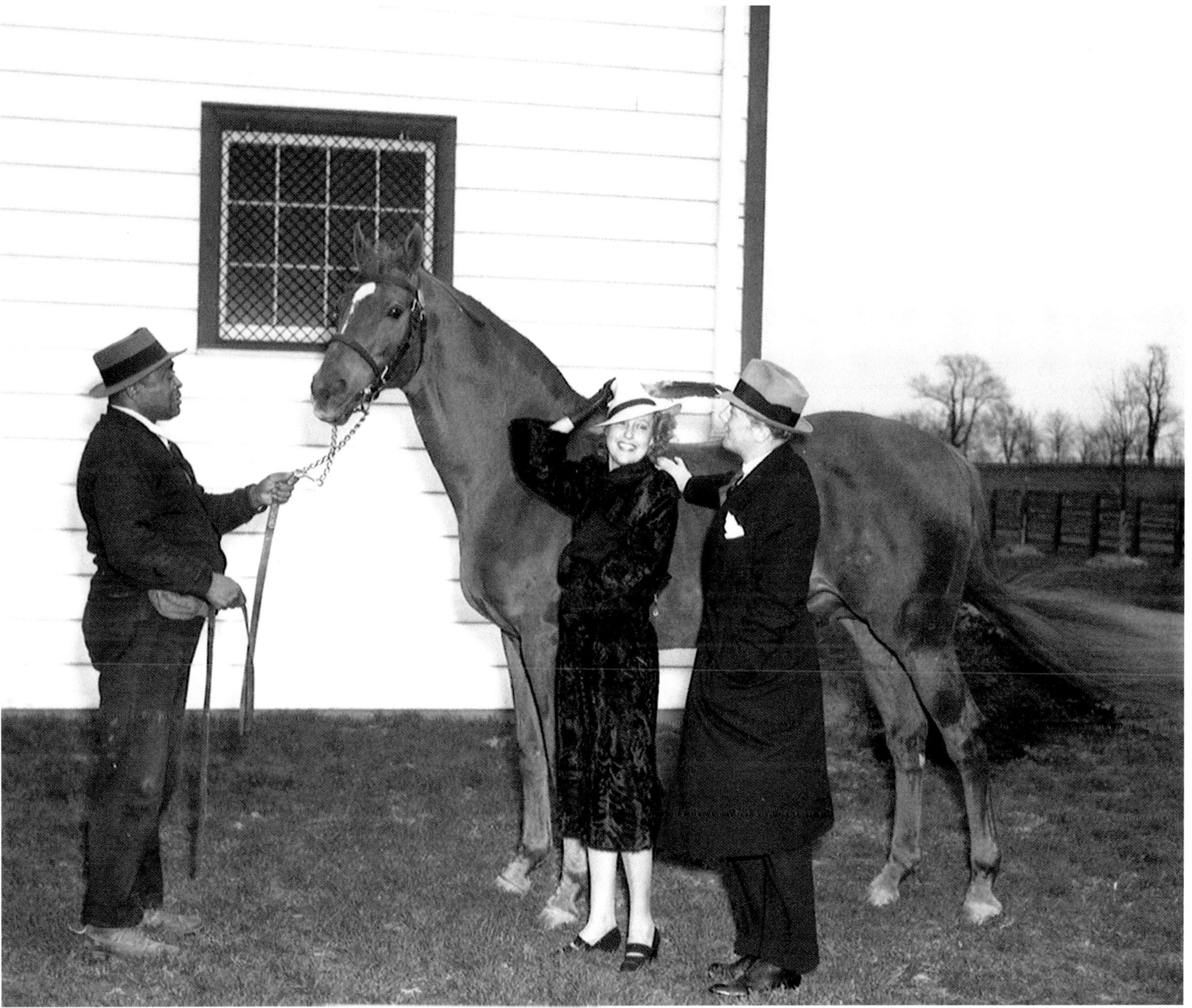

A jockey weighs out at Keeneland, 1939.

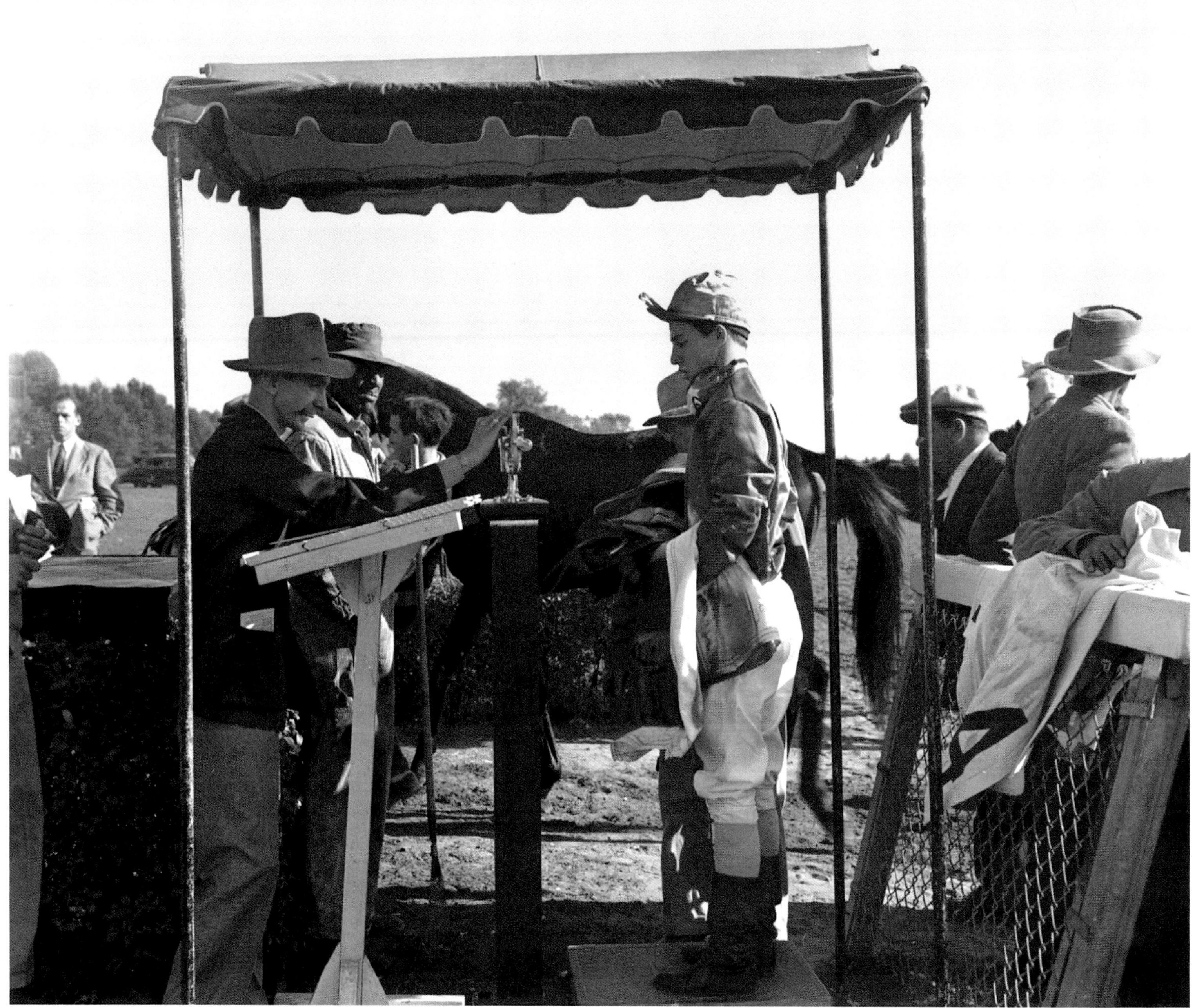

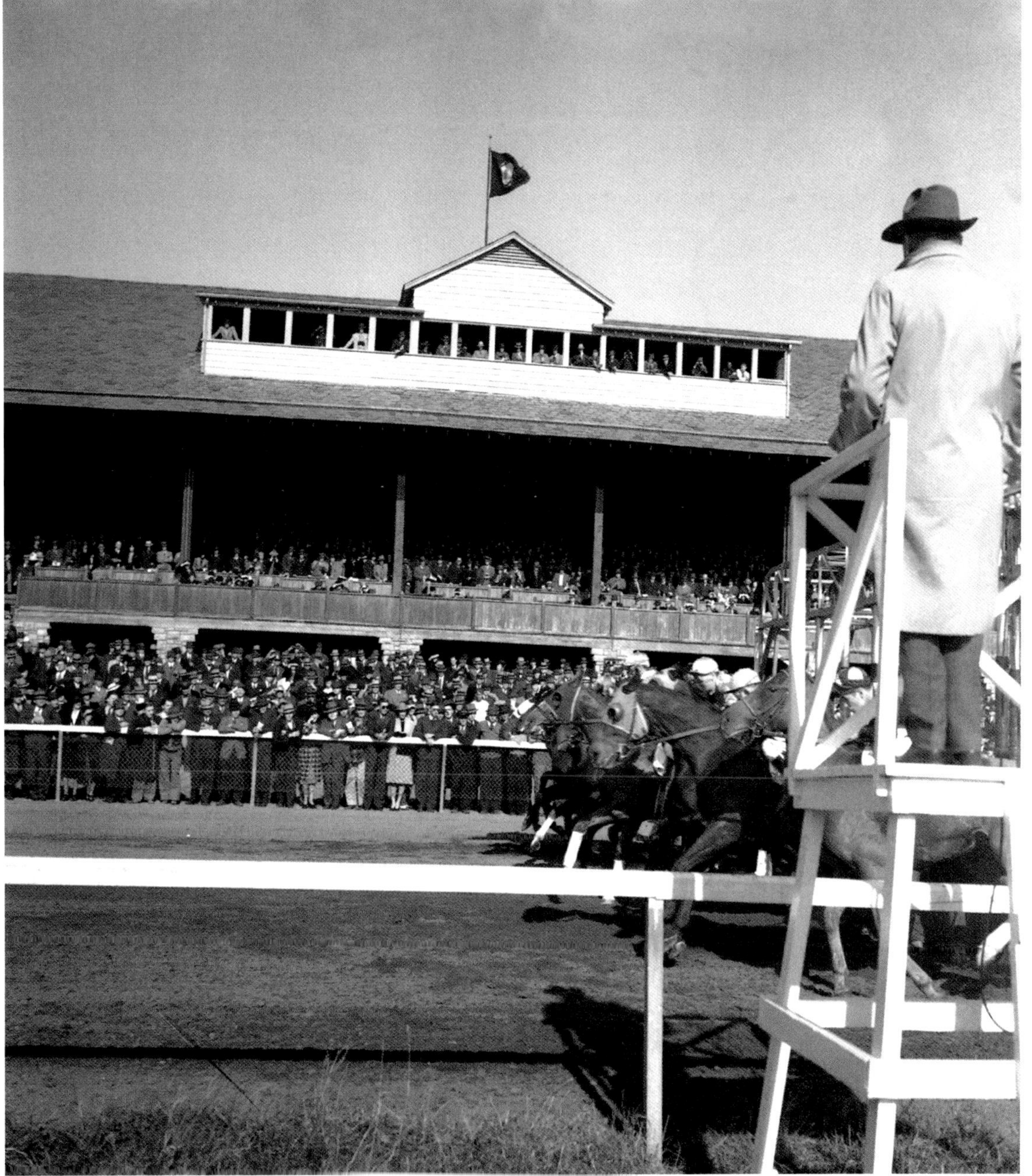

And they're off! The start of a race at Keeneland, 1939.

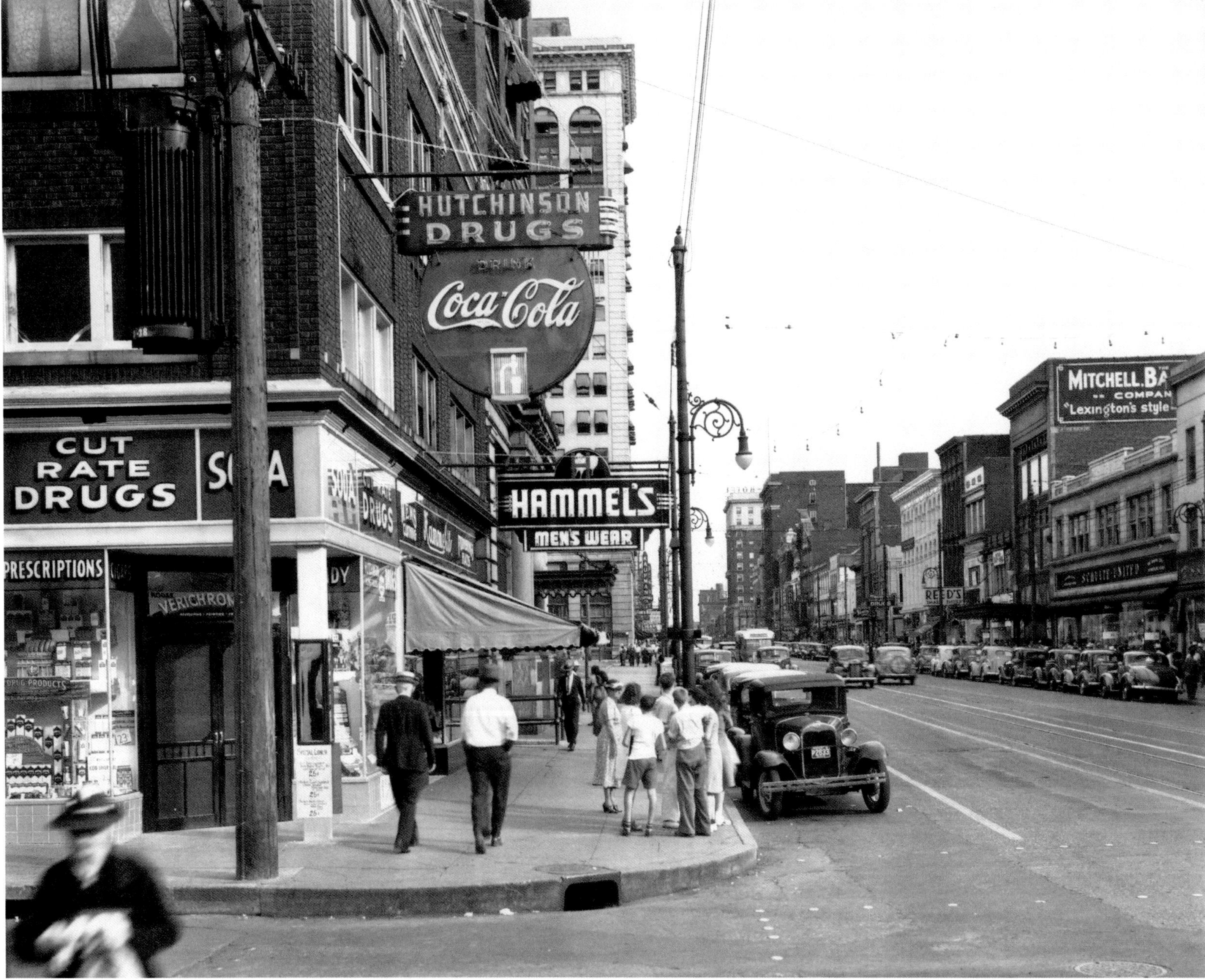

Hutchinson Drugs' West Main Street store (they had another store on East Main) with the Lafayette and new Phoenix hotels in the distance, 1939.

Toward the Second Century

(1941–1975)

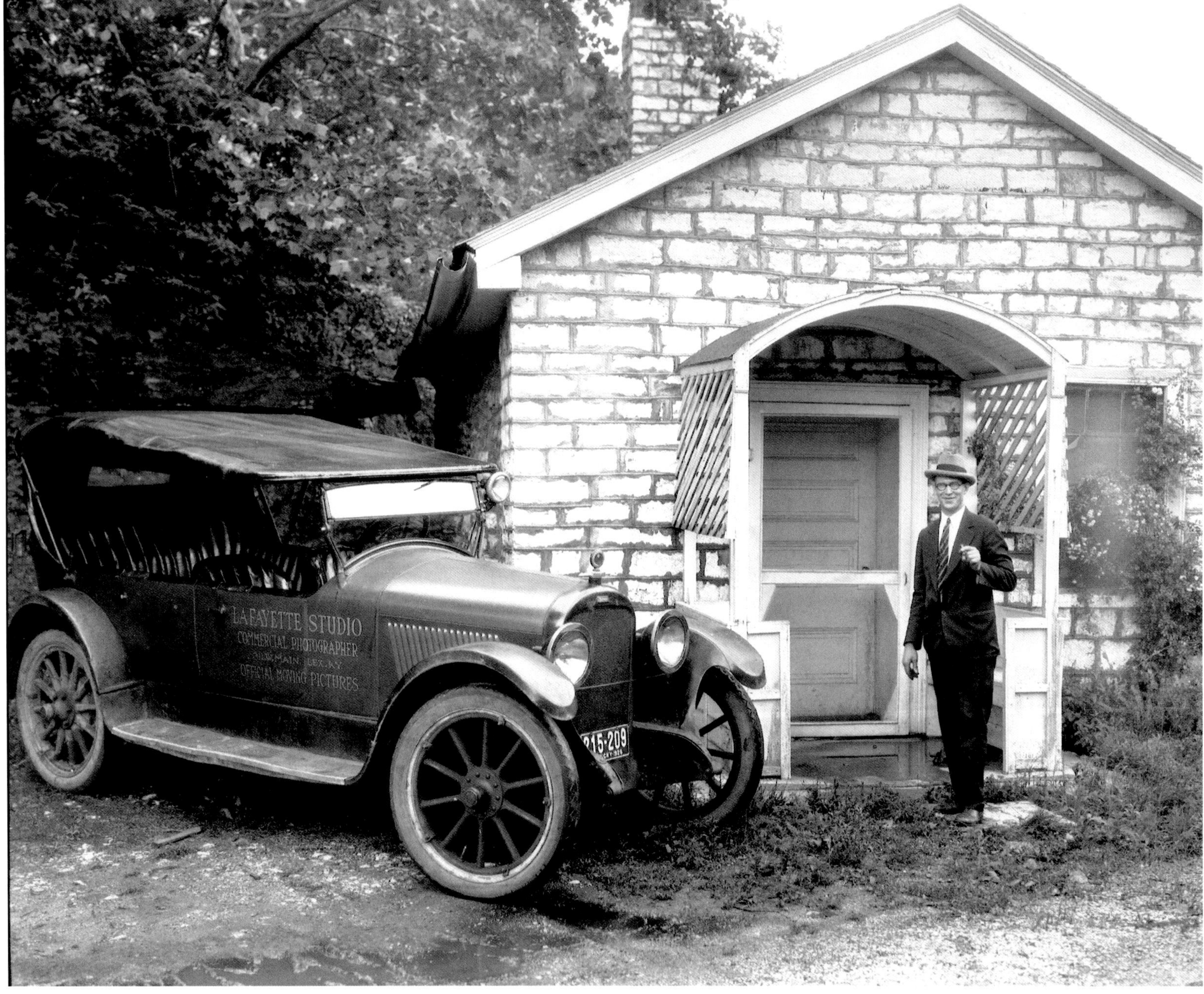

Photographer Robert J. Long stands next to a Lexington Minute Man Six automobile, manufactured in the early 1900s on West Main Street.

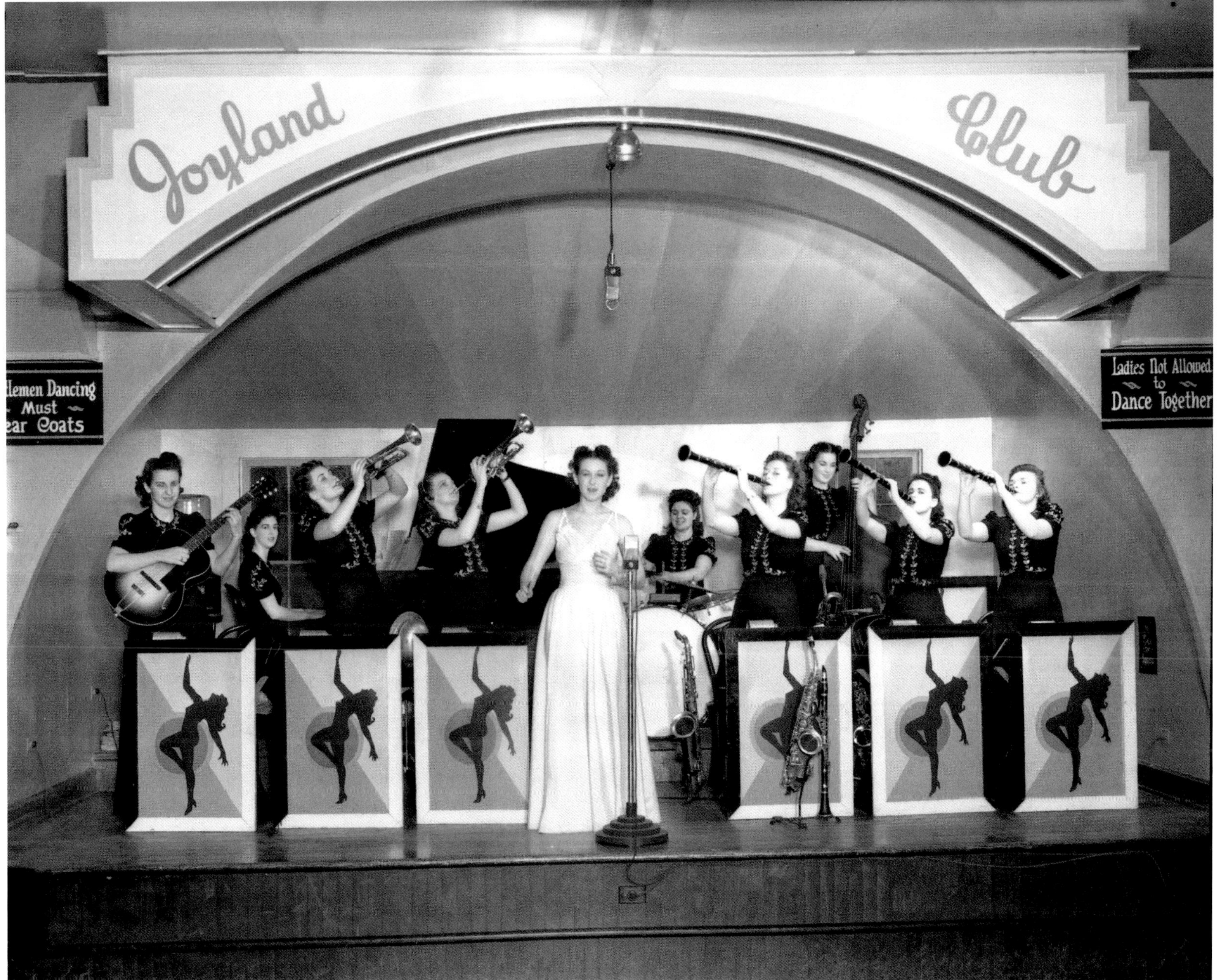

Locals Betty Coed and the Debs perform at Joyland Park's dance casino on Paris Pike, 1940. National acts appeared there from time to time in the summer season.

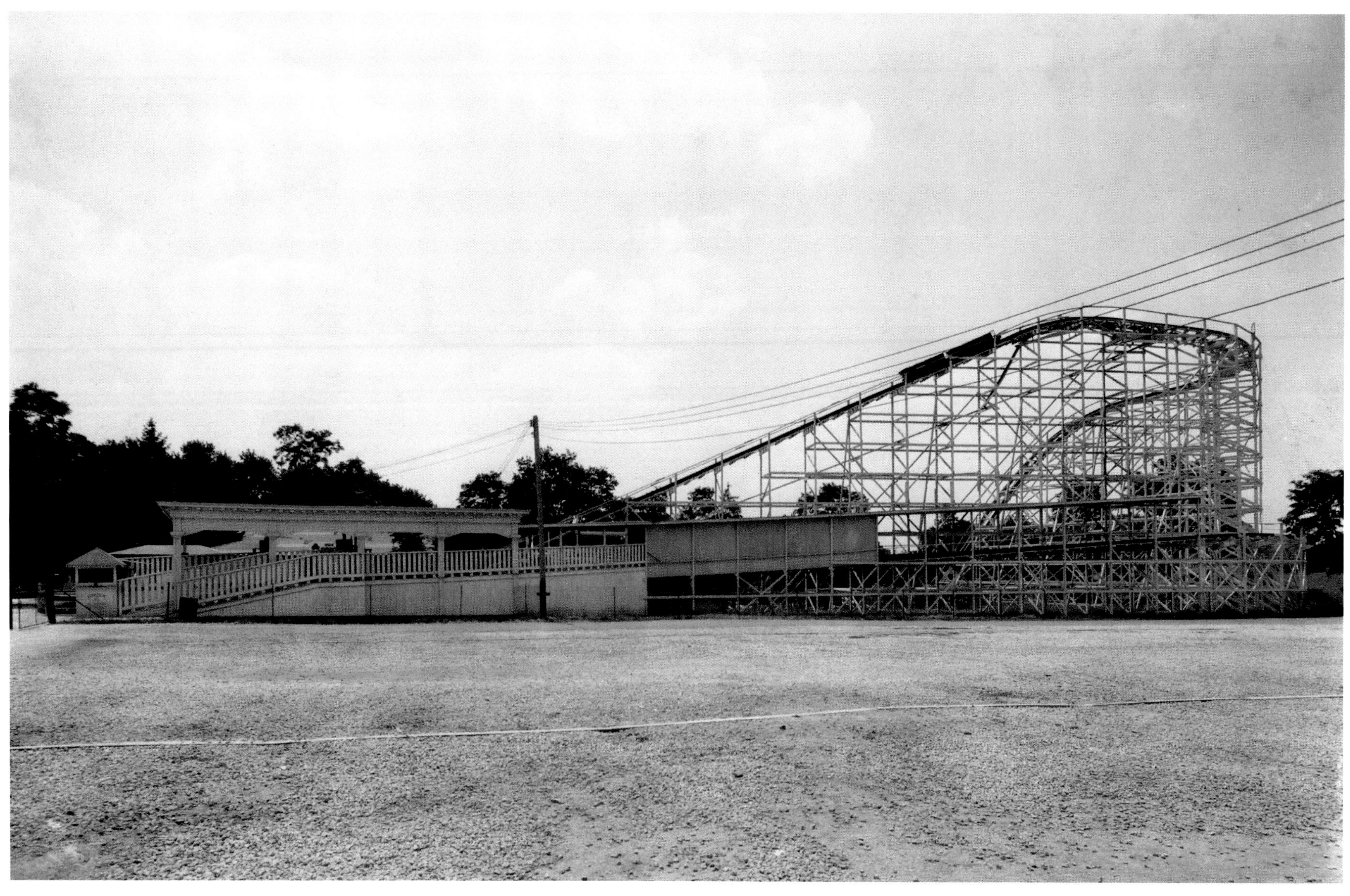

Roller coaster at Joyland Park, 1940.

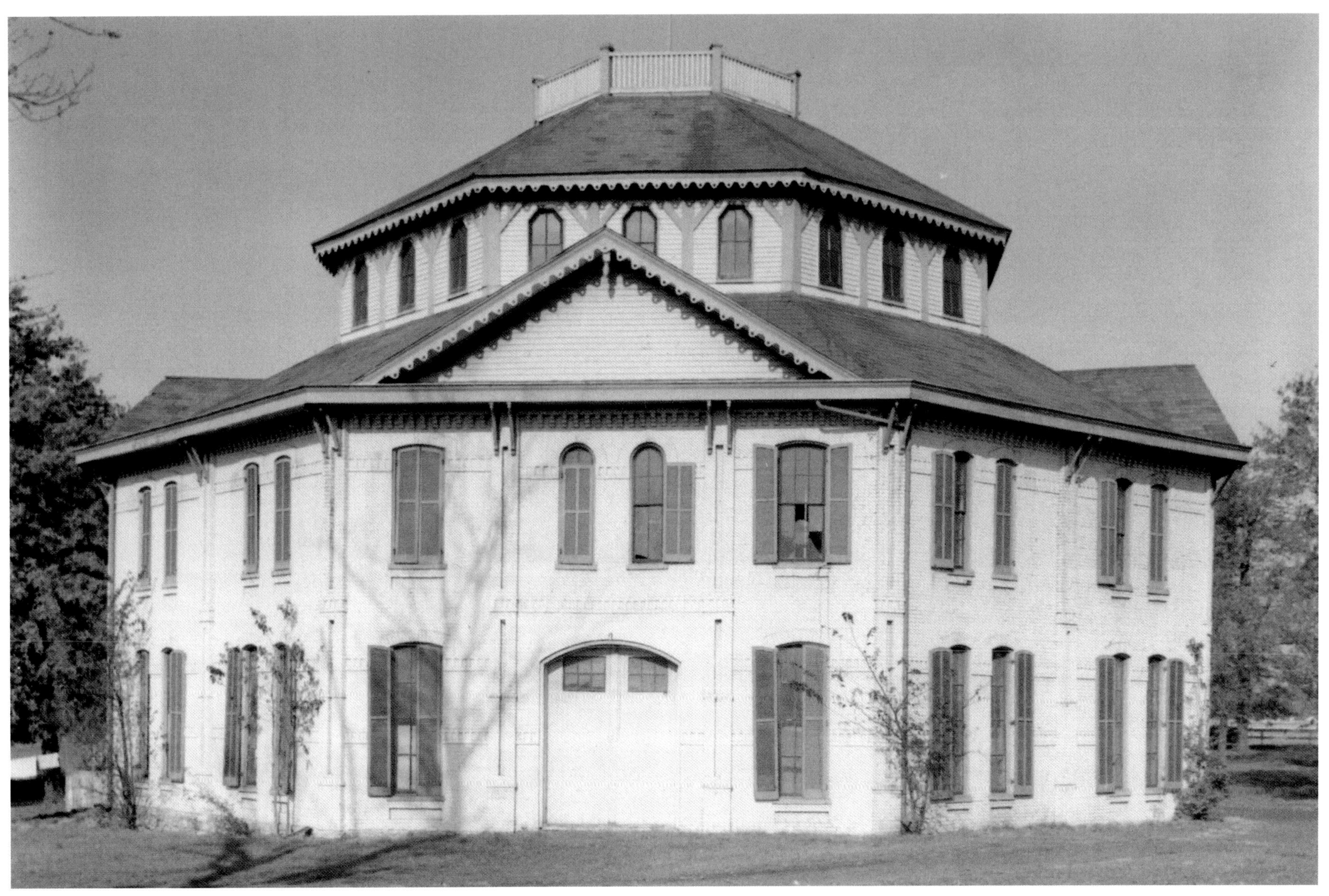

"Floral Hall" at the entrance to Red Mile after renovation and removal of cupola.

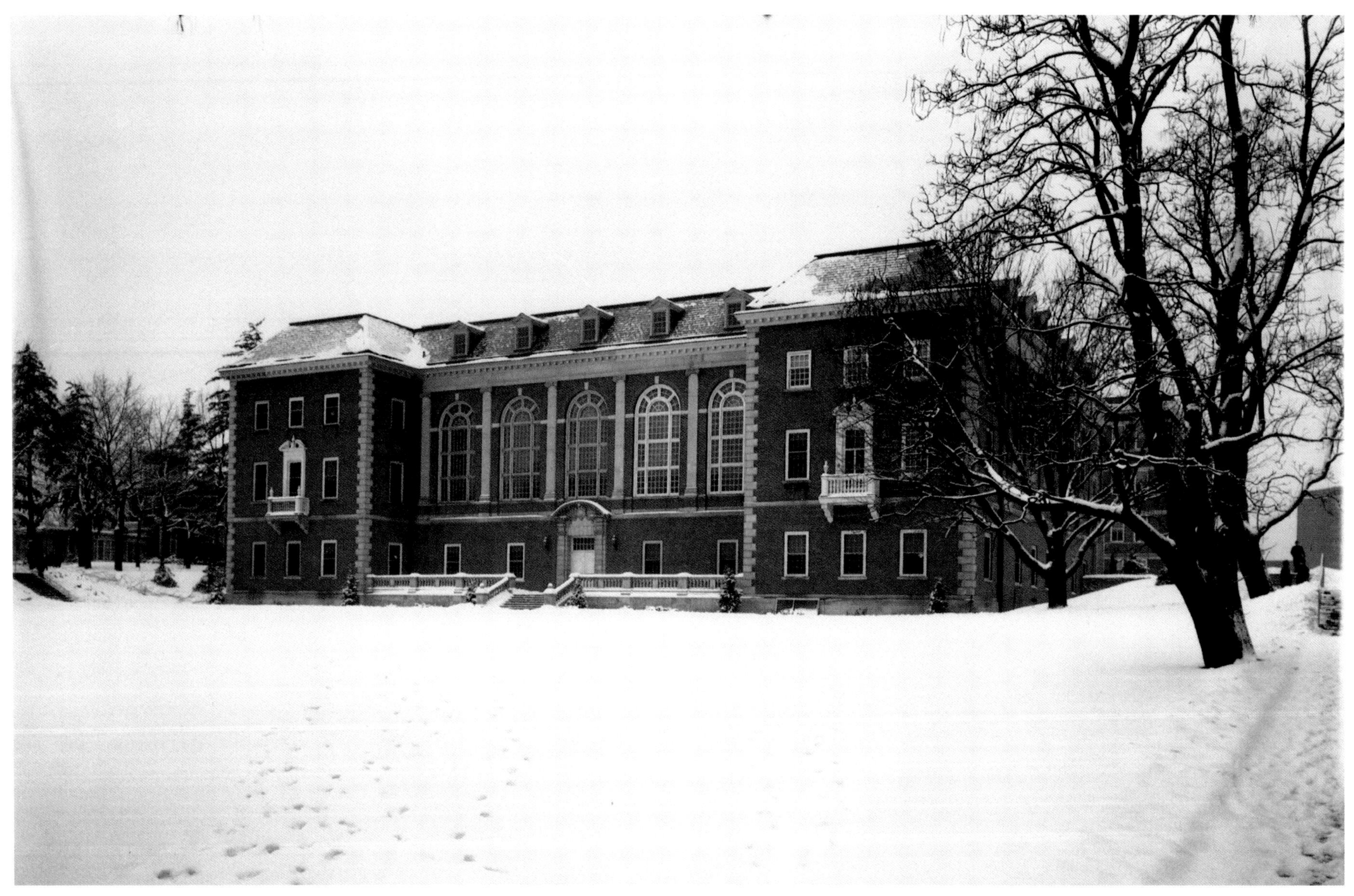

Margaret I. King Library at the University of Kentucky (dedicated in 1931), as it appeared in 1940.

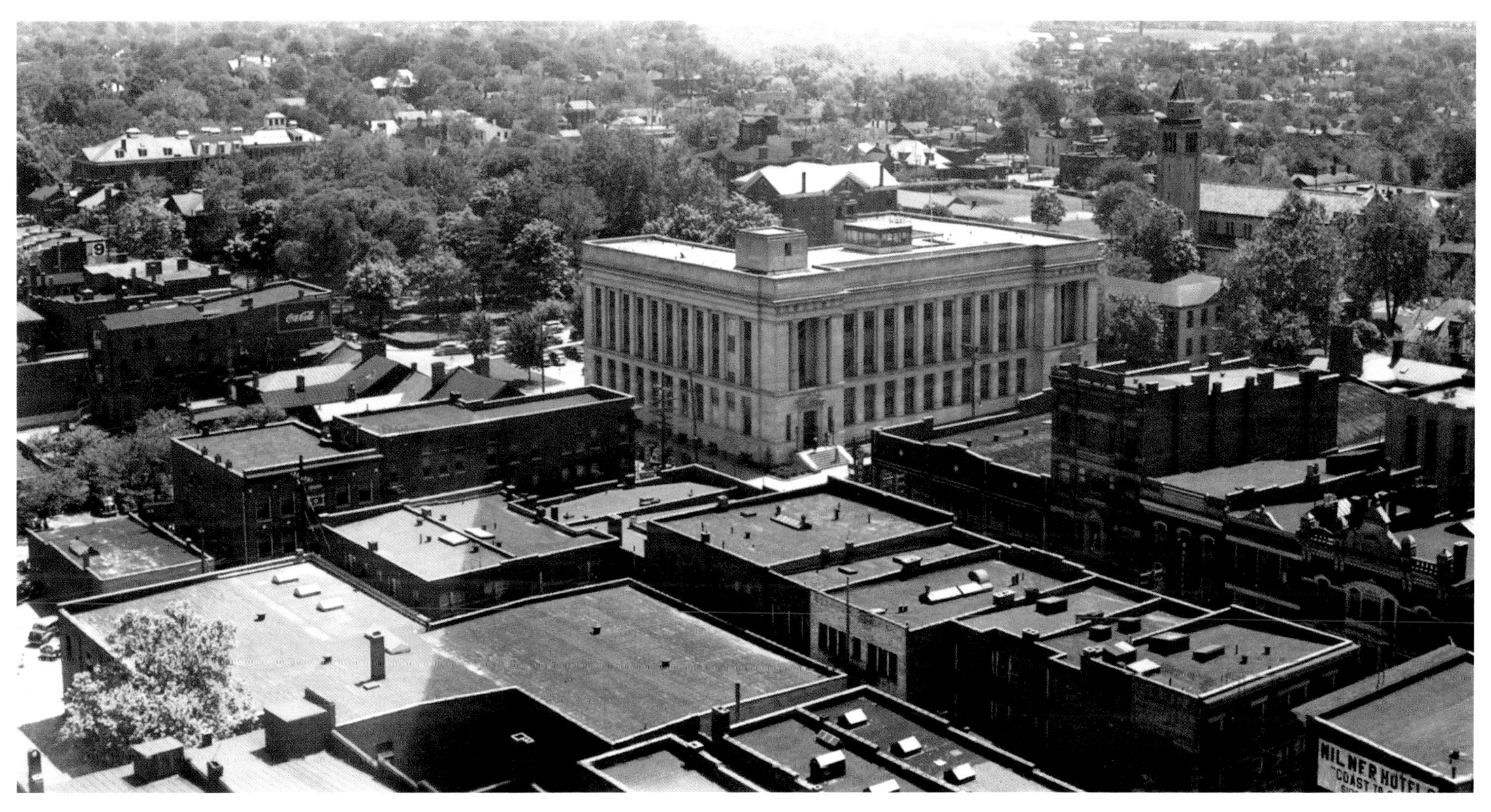

New Federal Post Office on Barr Street, 1941.

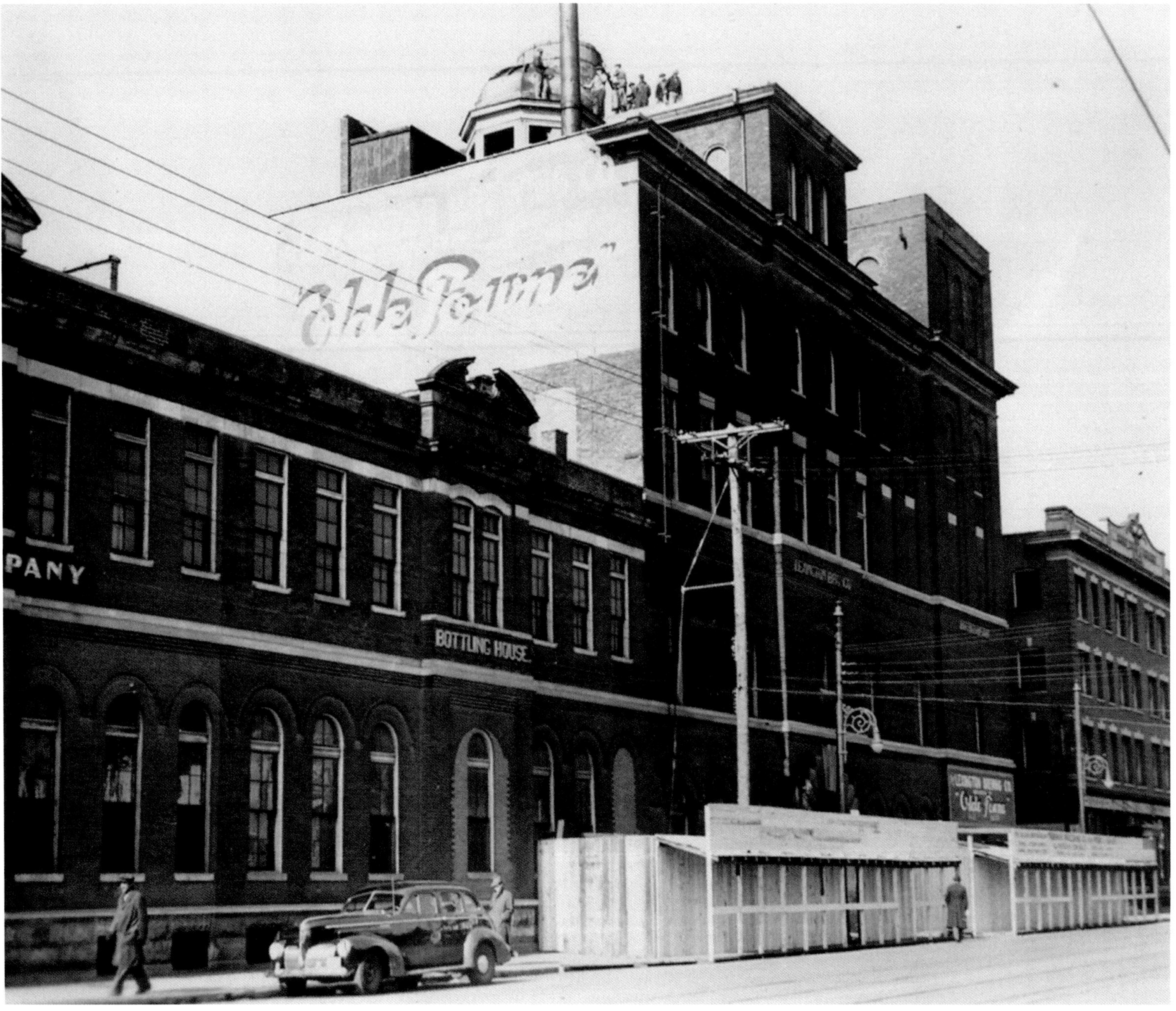

Lexington Brewery (built 1897) on East Main Street near Rose Street.

Goodwin Brothers automobile dealership on Main Street, 1941.

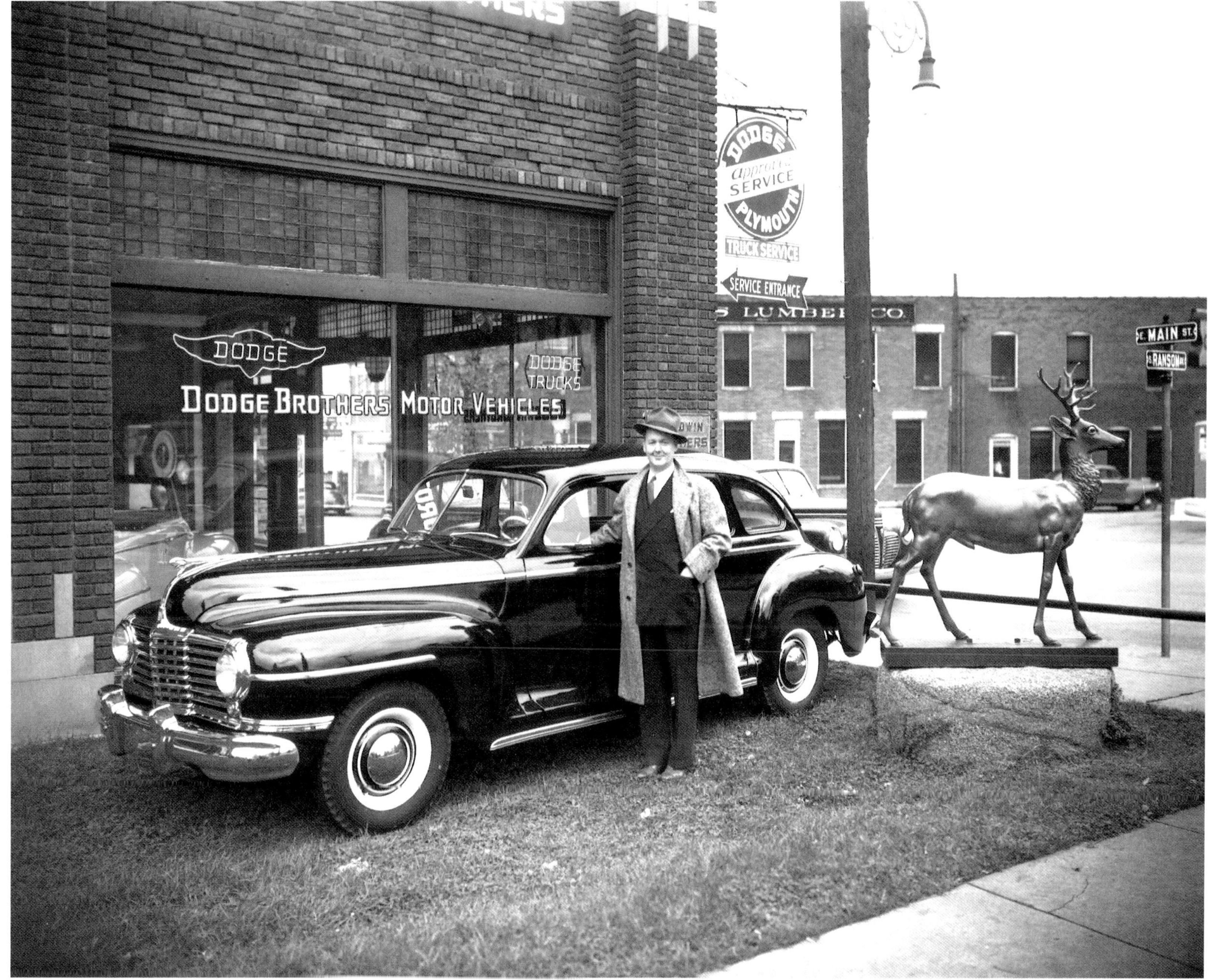

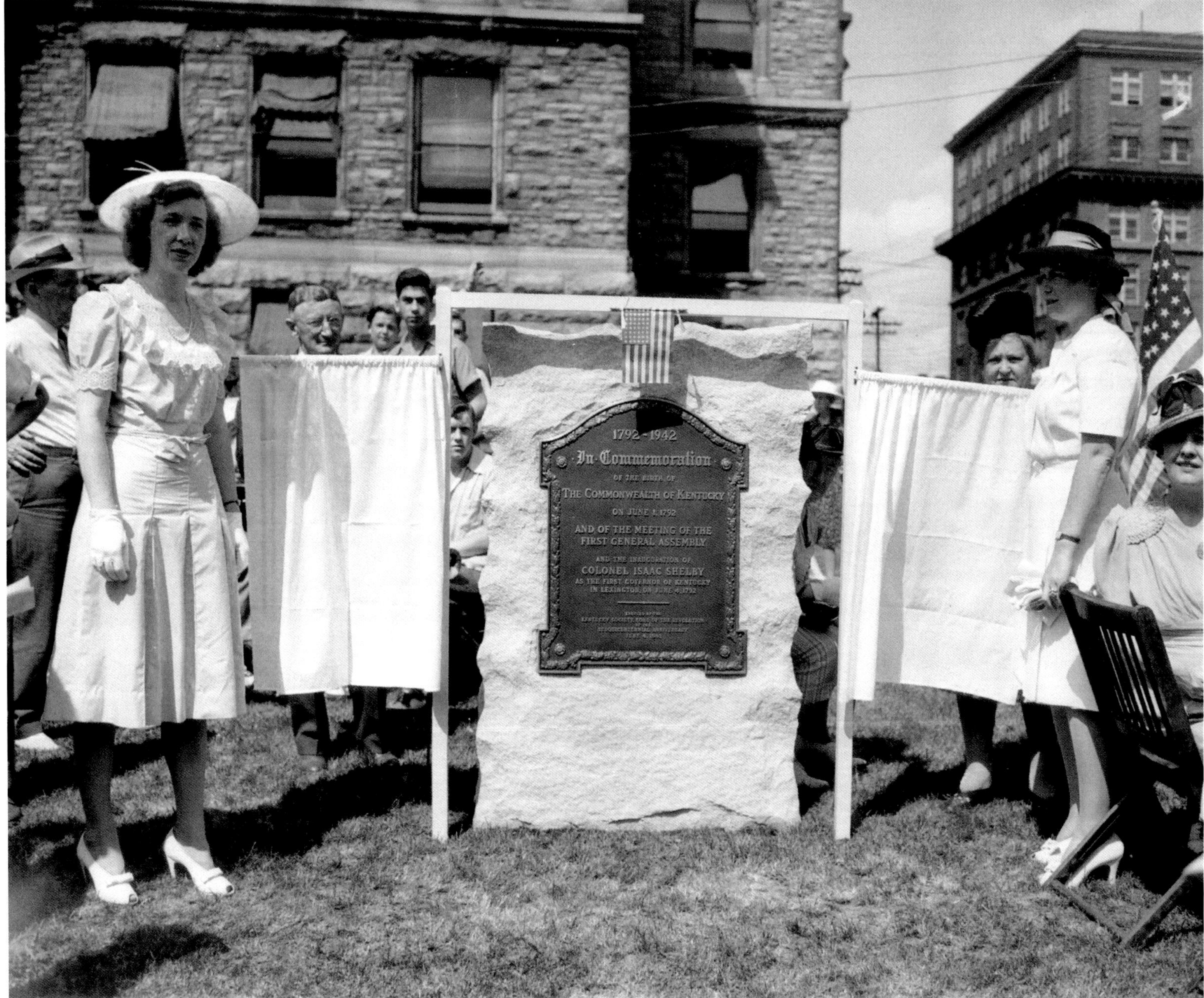

The monument celebrating Lexington's sesquicentennial reads: 1792–1942: In Commemoration of the Birth of the Commonwealth of Kentucky on June 1, 1792.

John G. Epping
Bottling Works,
March 1942.

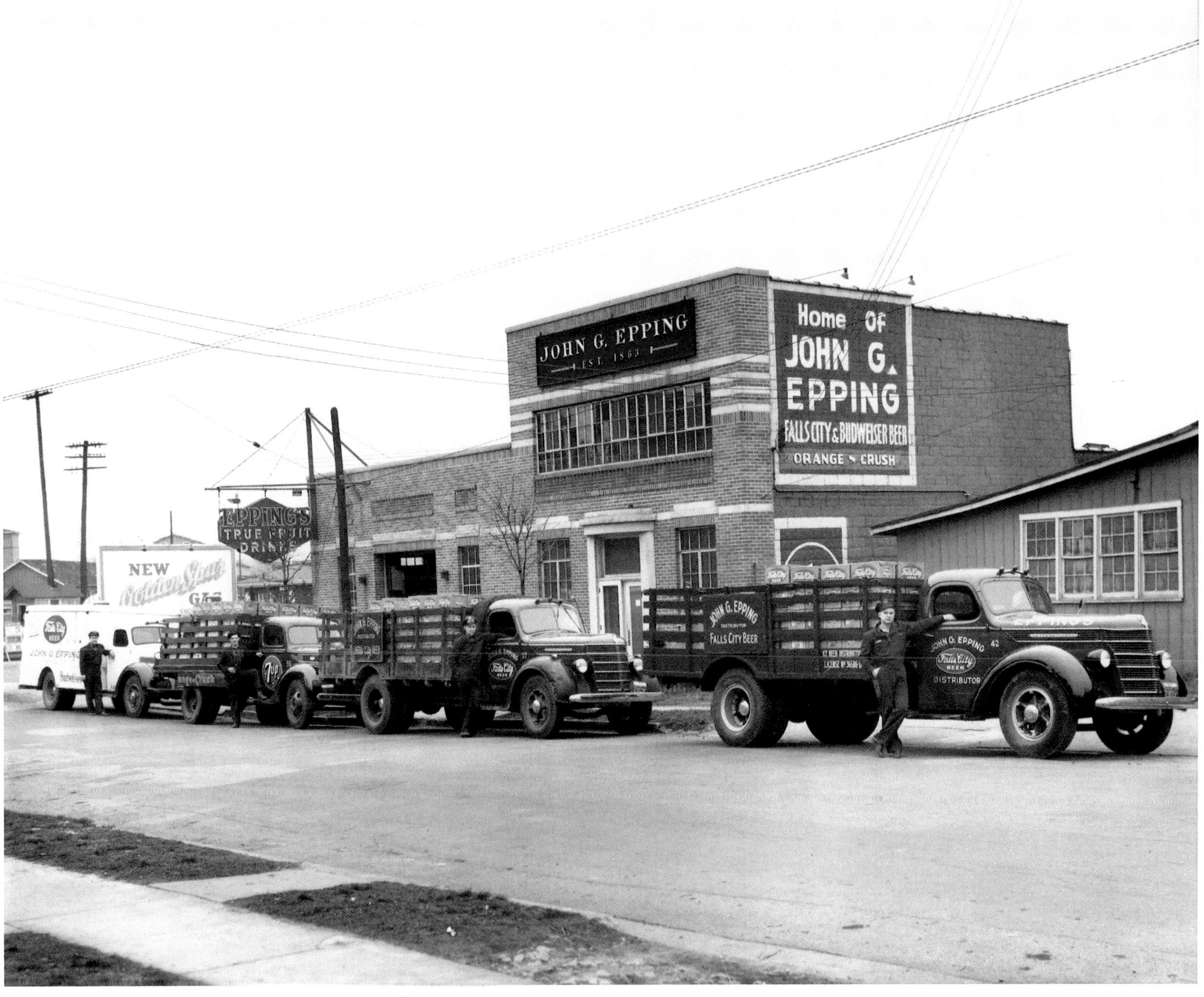

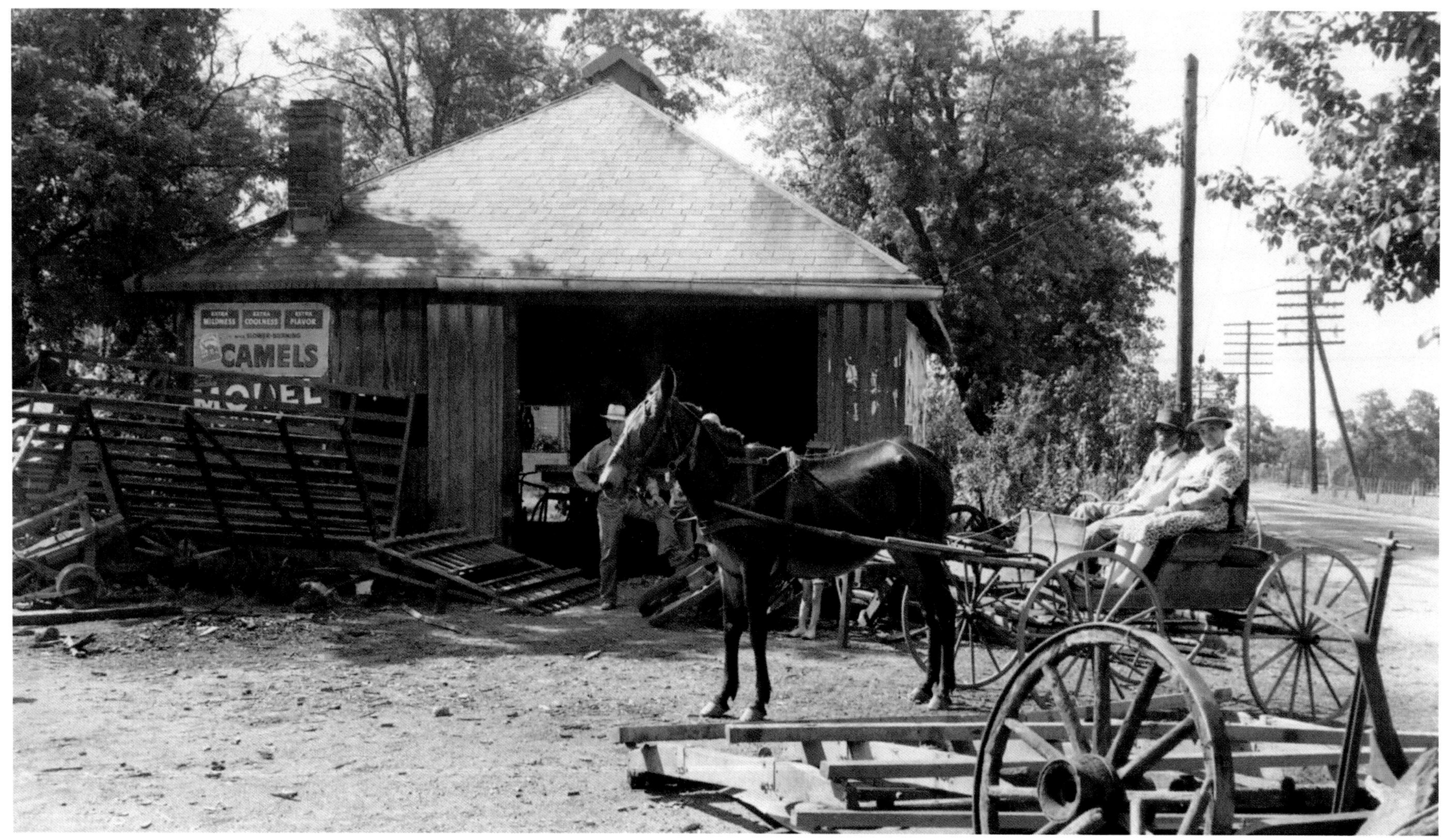

Blacksmith shop of Stanley Bryant at Donerail, north of Lexington, 1942.

Locally sponsored "Stop over Station" for the troops on the Esplanade, 1942.

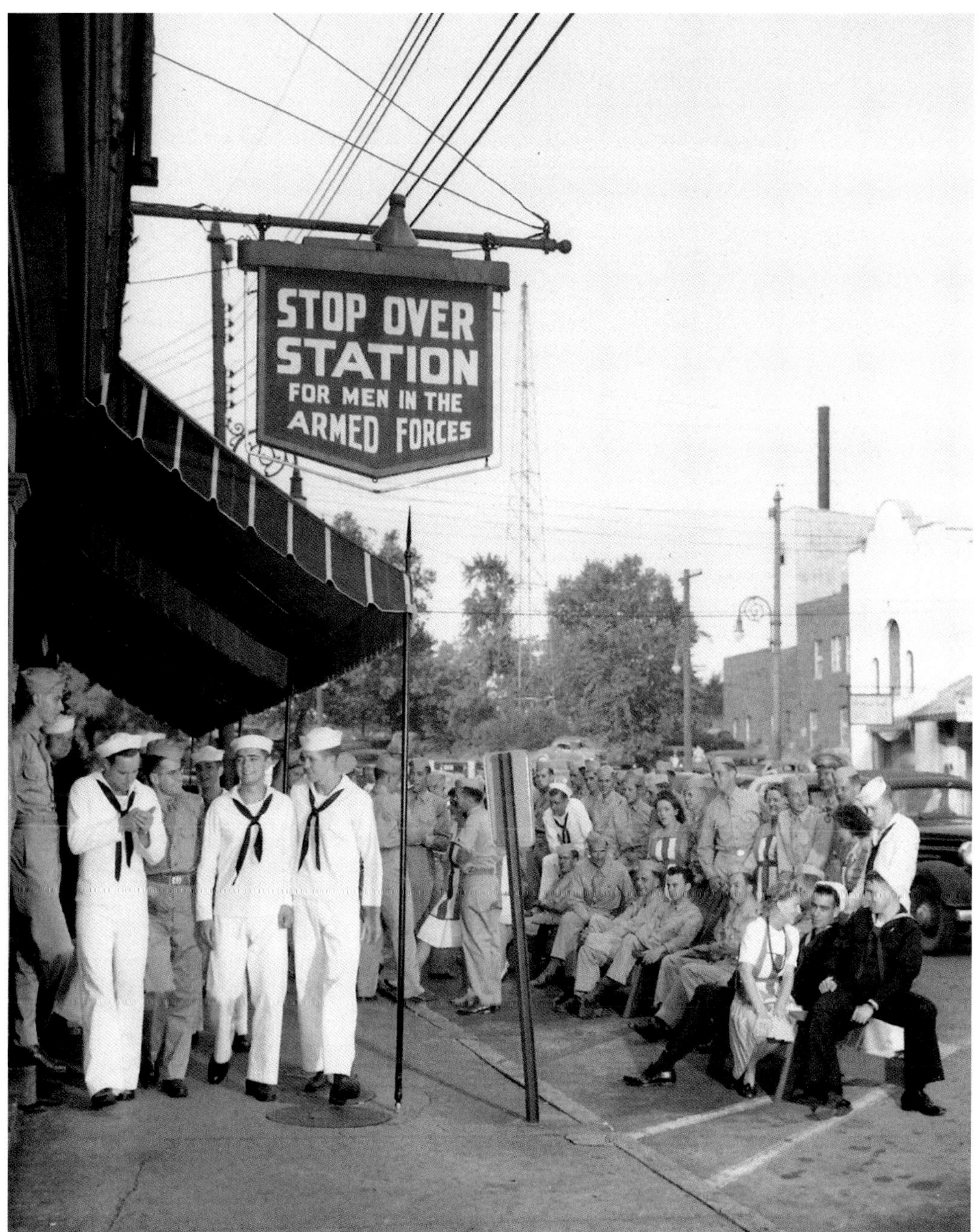

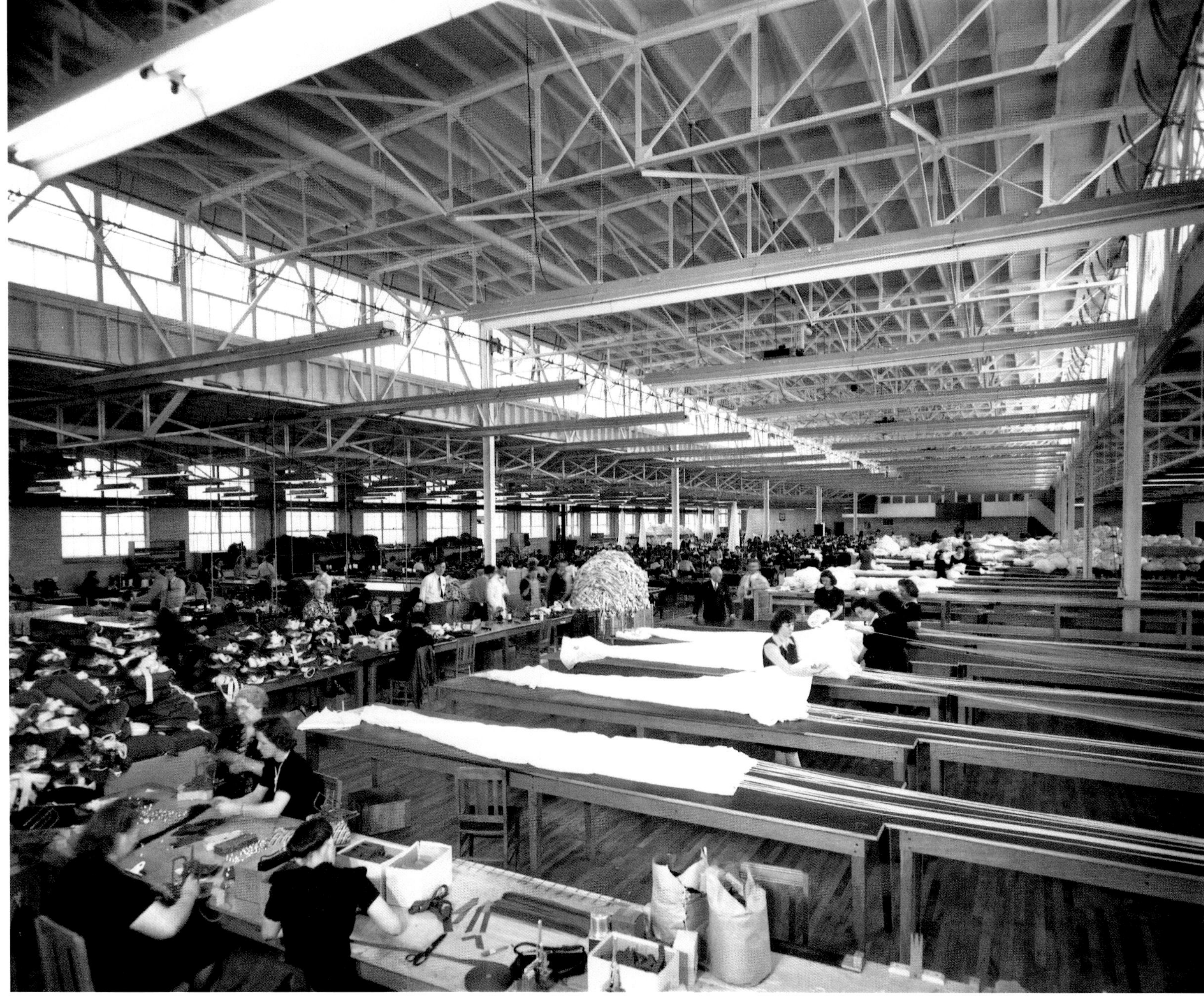

Women working at Irving Air Chute Company on Versailles Road during wartime in 1943. The plant had moved from Main Street and expanded in 1942.

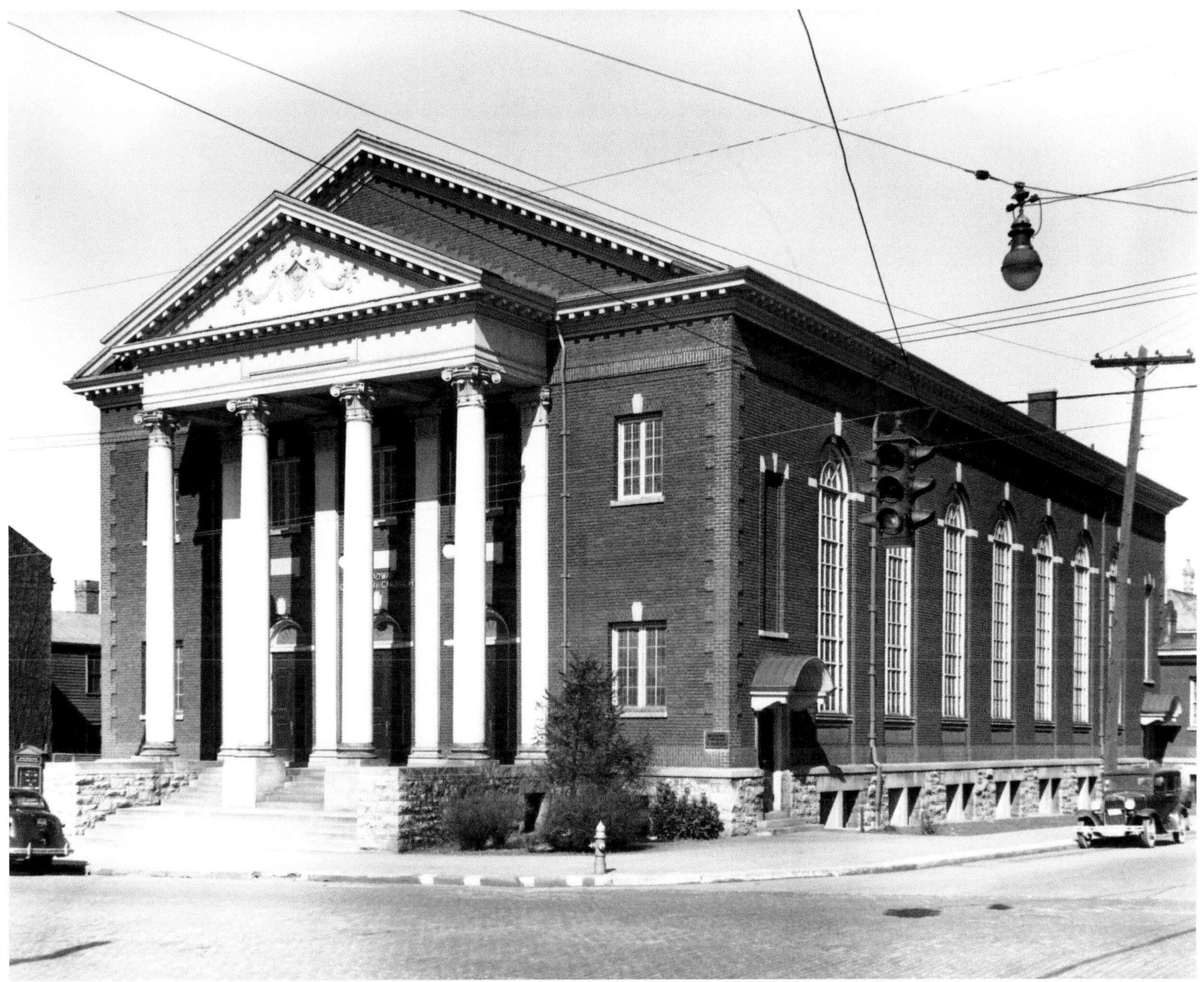

Broadway Christian Church (built 1917), as it appeared in 1943.

Christ Church Episcopal Cathedral on Market Street (built in 1847), as it appeared in 1943.

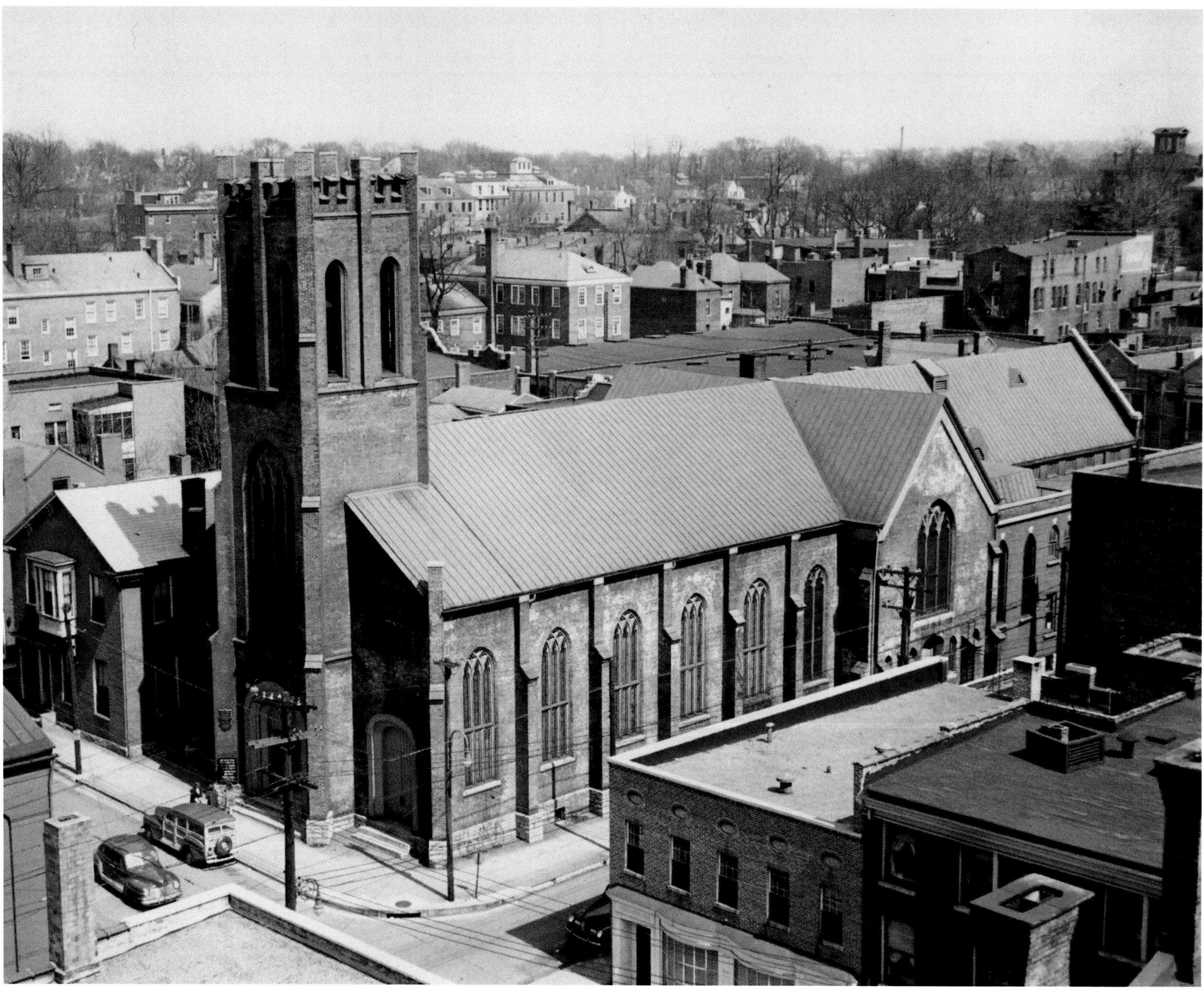

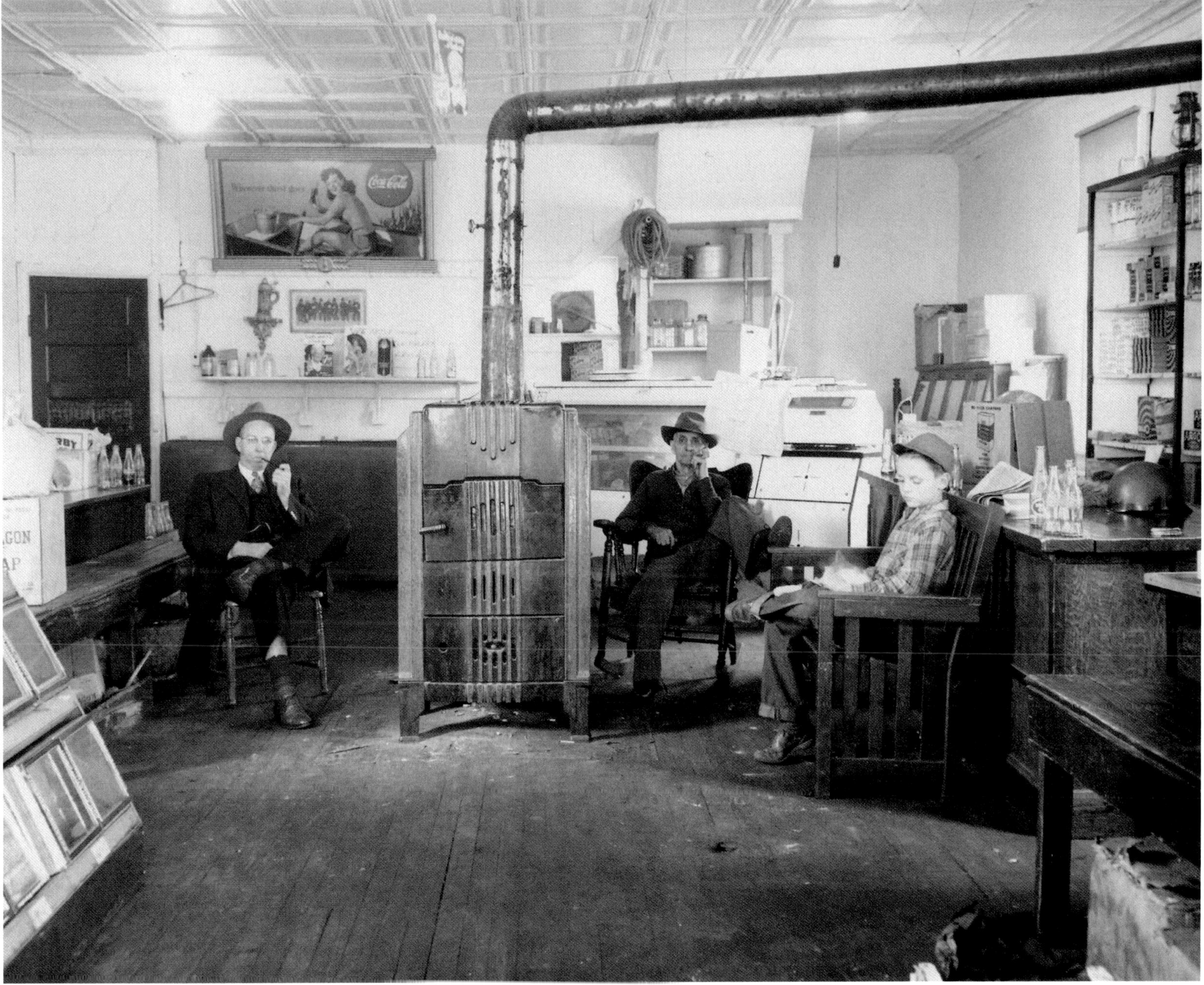

"Jot 'em Down" country store interior at Iron Work Pike and Russell Cave Road, 1944.

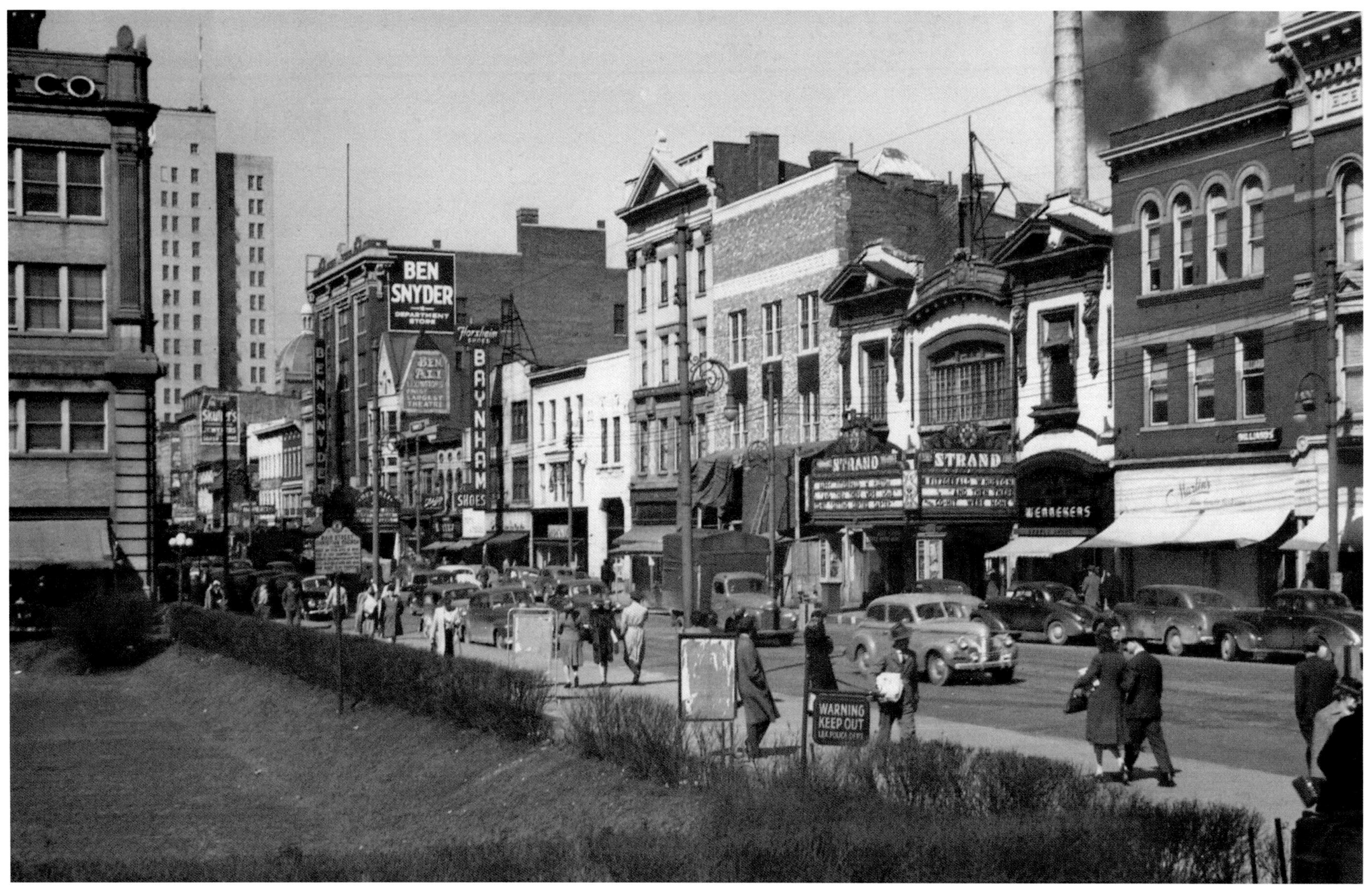

A view across the courthouse lawn toward Main Street, mid-1940s.

Interior of Keith's Restaurant (later the Golden Horseshoe) on Main Street, 1946.

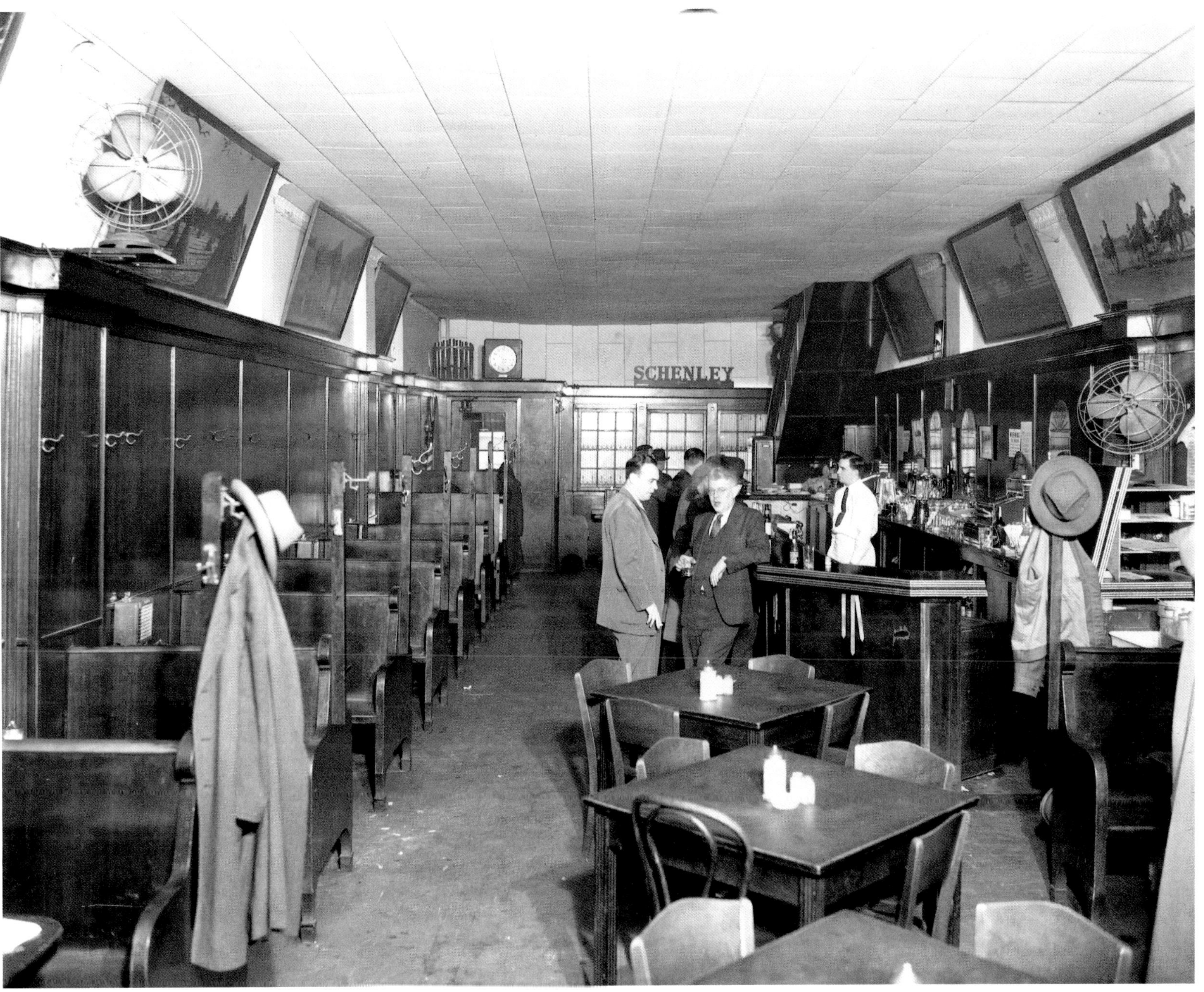

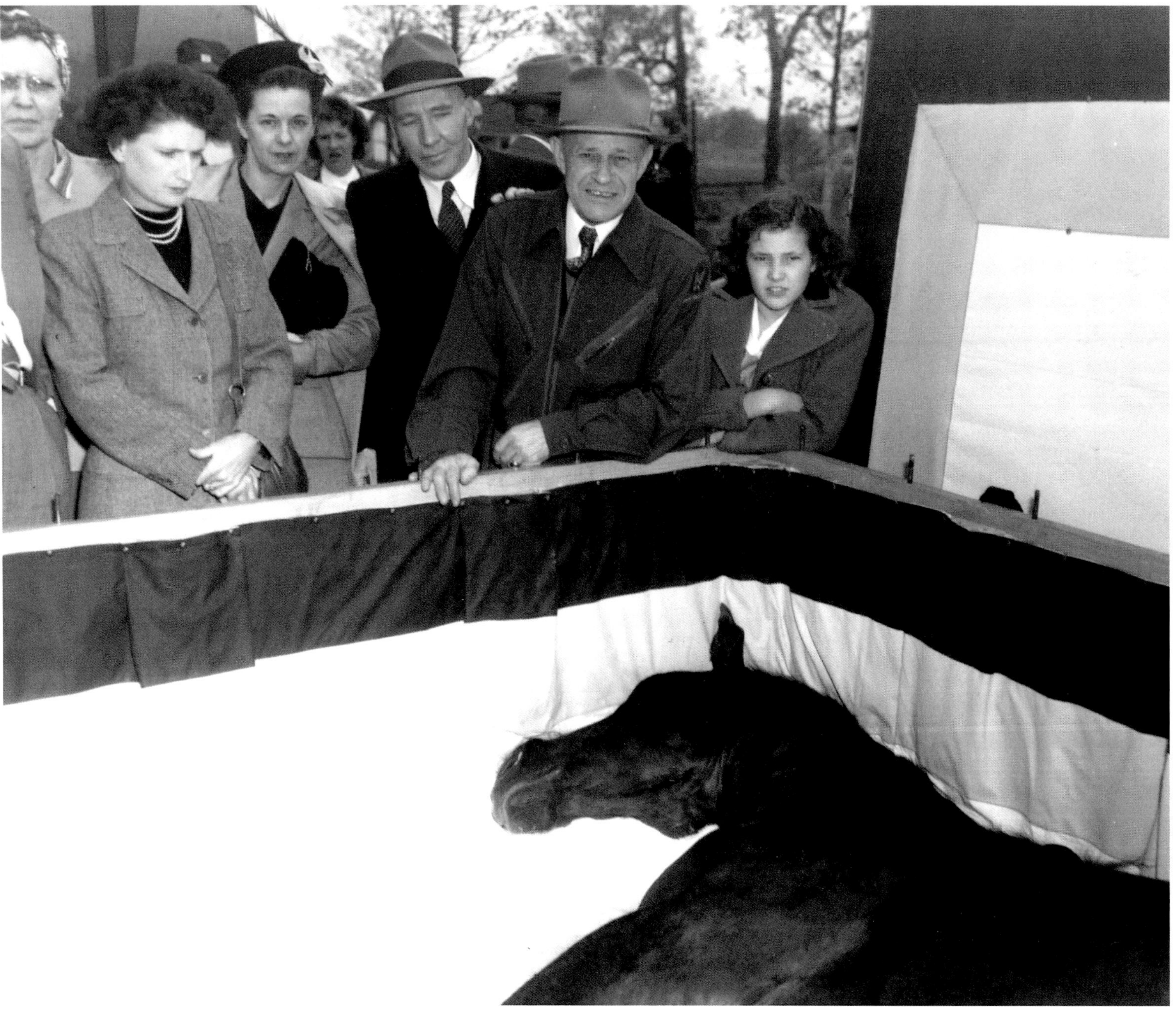

Funeral of Man O'War. November 1947.

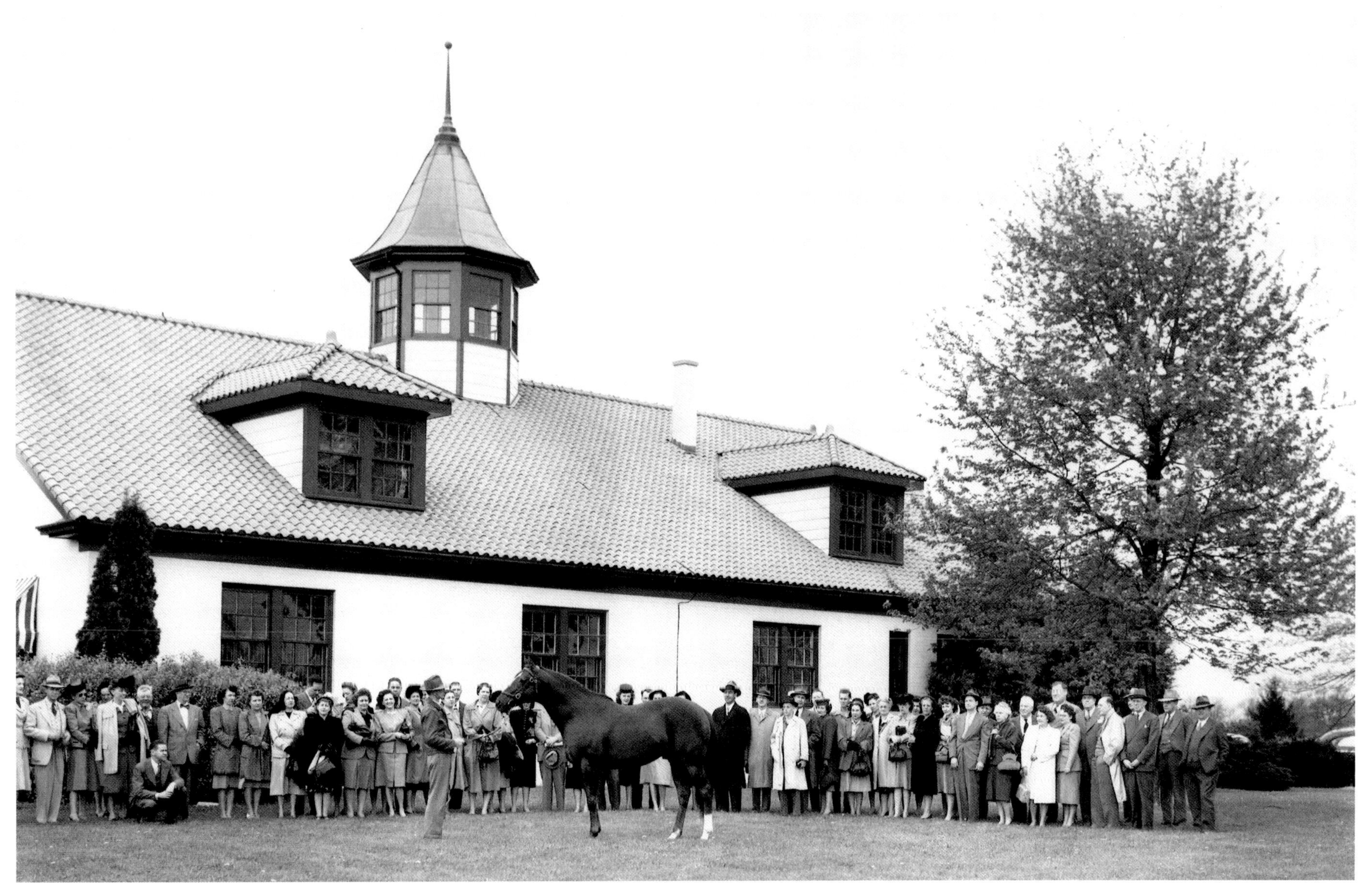

Whirlaway, the 1941 Triple Crown winner, is admired by visitors to Calumet Farm on Versailles Road in 1947.

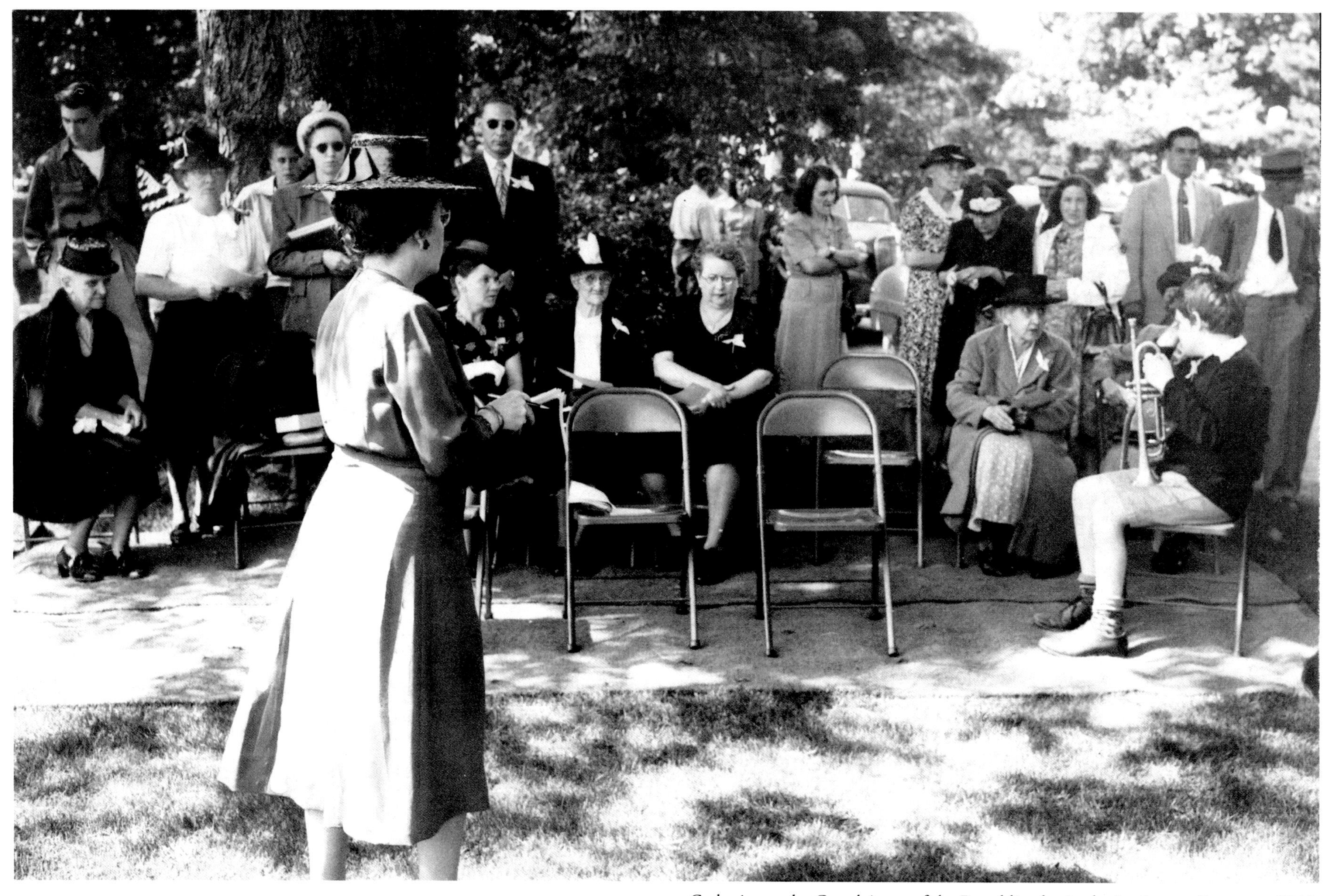

Gathering at the Grand Army of the Republic plot in the Lexington Cemetery, 1948.

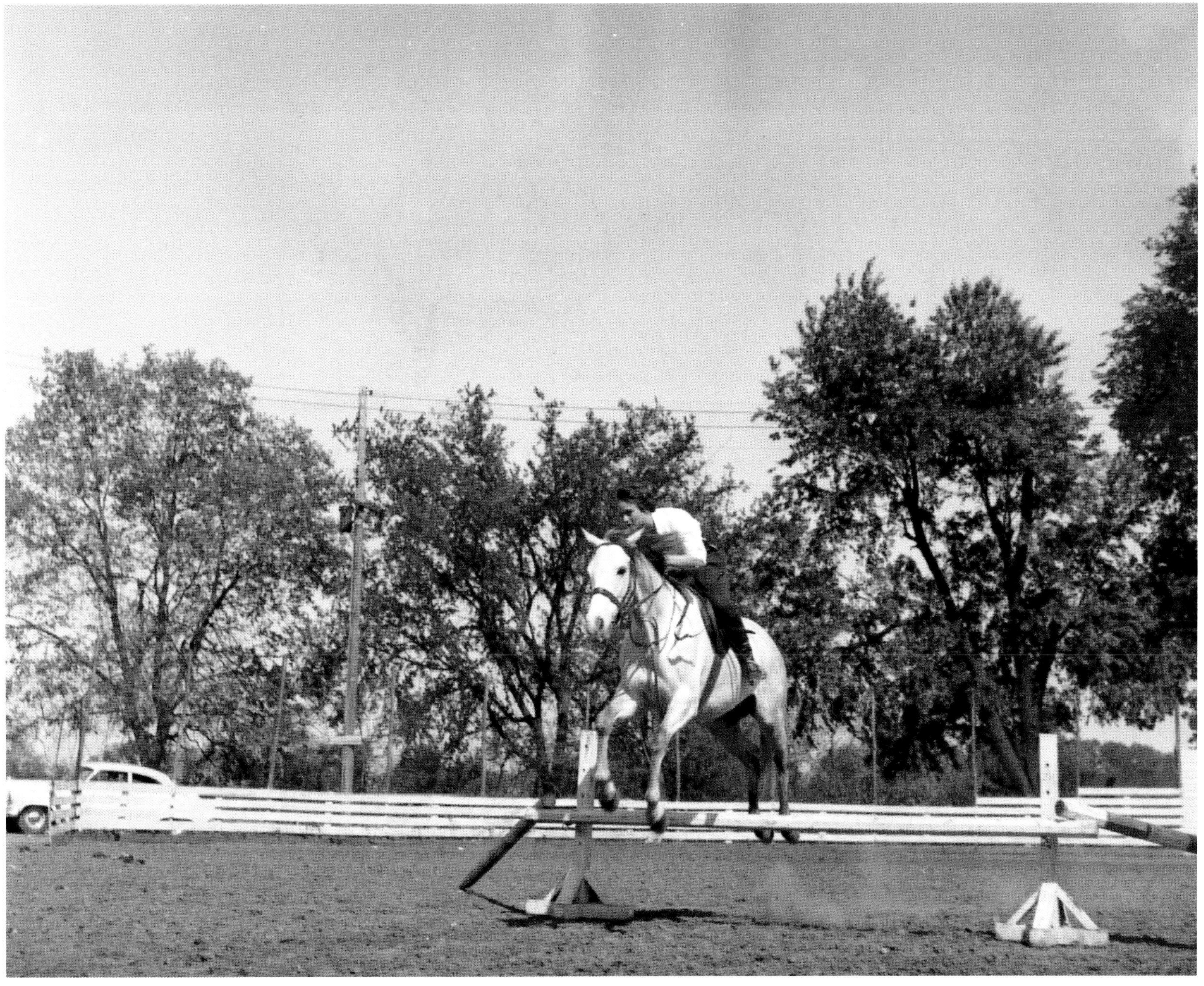

A University of Kentucky equestrienne prepares for the Block and Bridle Horse Show at the trotting track in 1958.

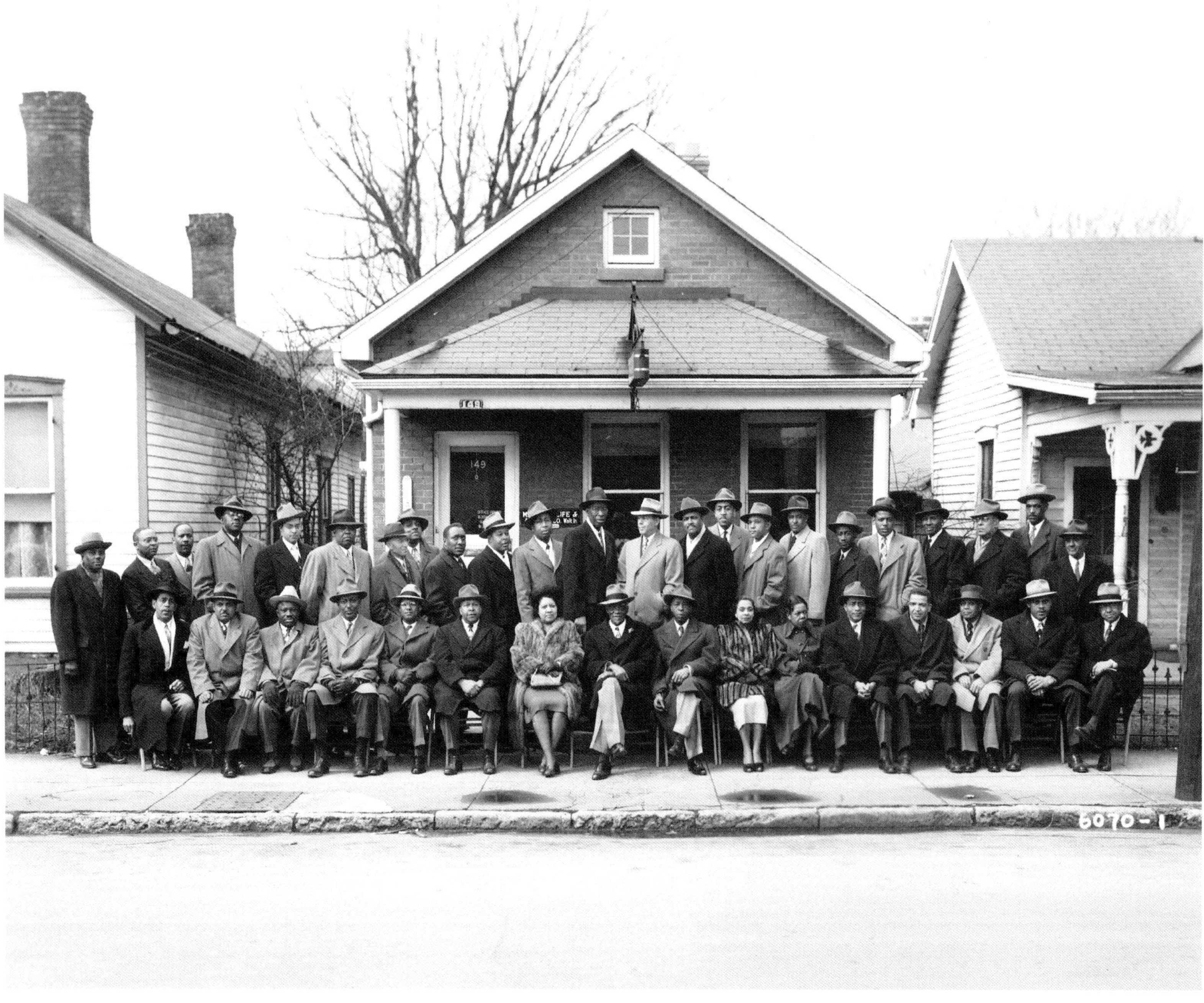

Mammoth Life Insurance Company (Kentucky's largest African-American owned business, founded in 1915) on Deweese Street, 1949.

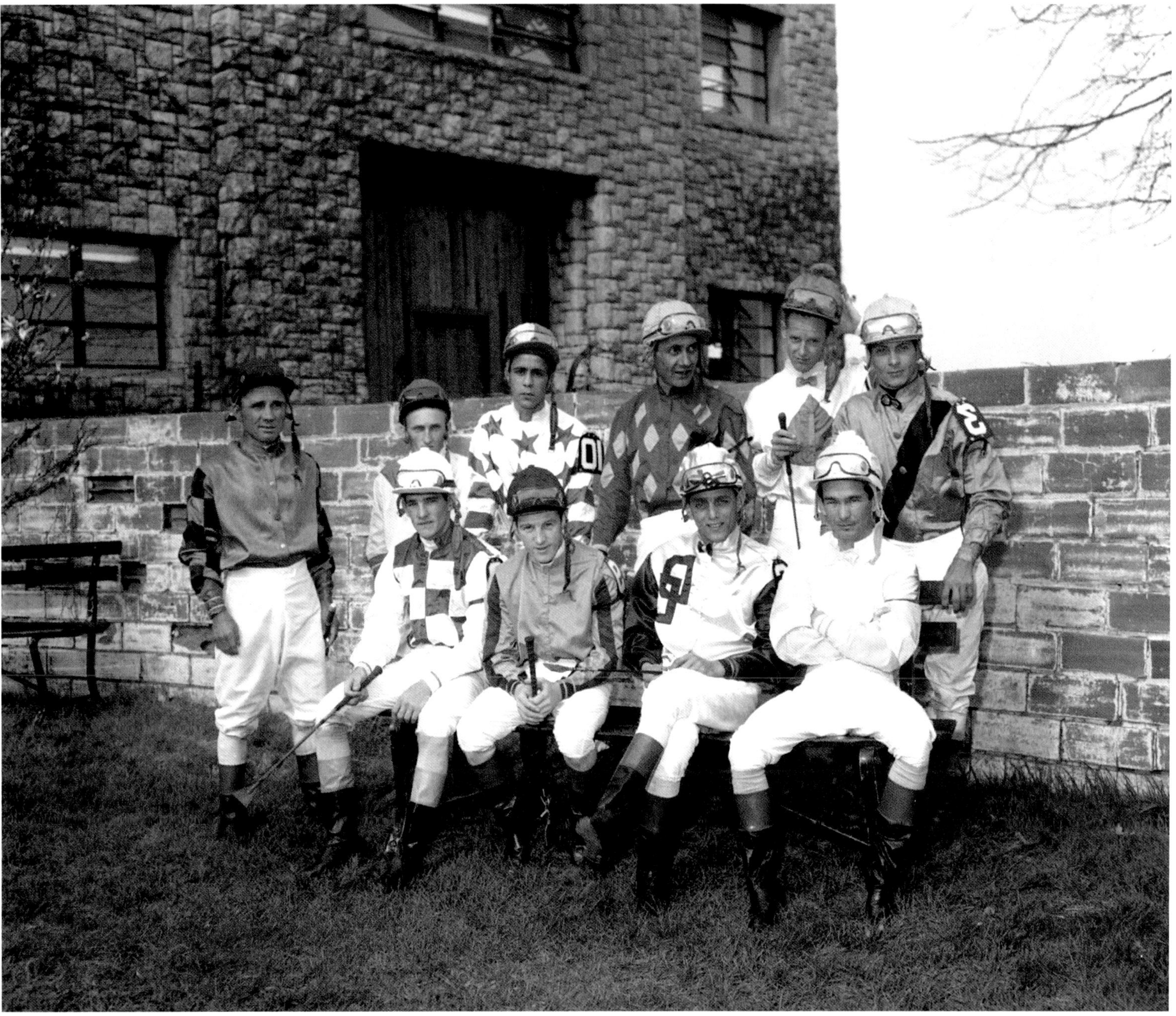

Jockeys at Keeneland, ca. 1950.

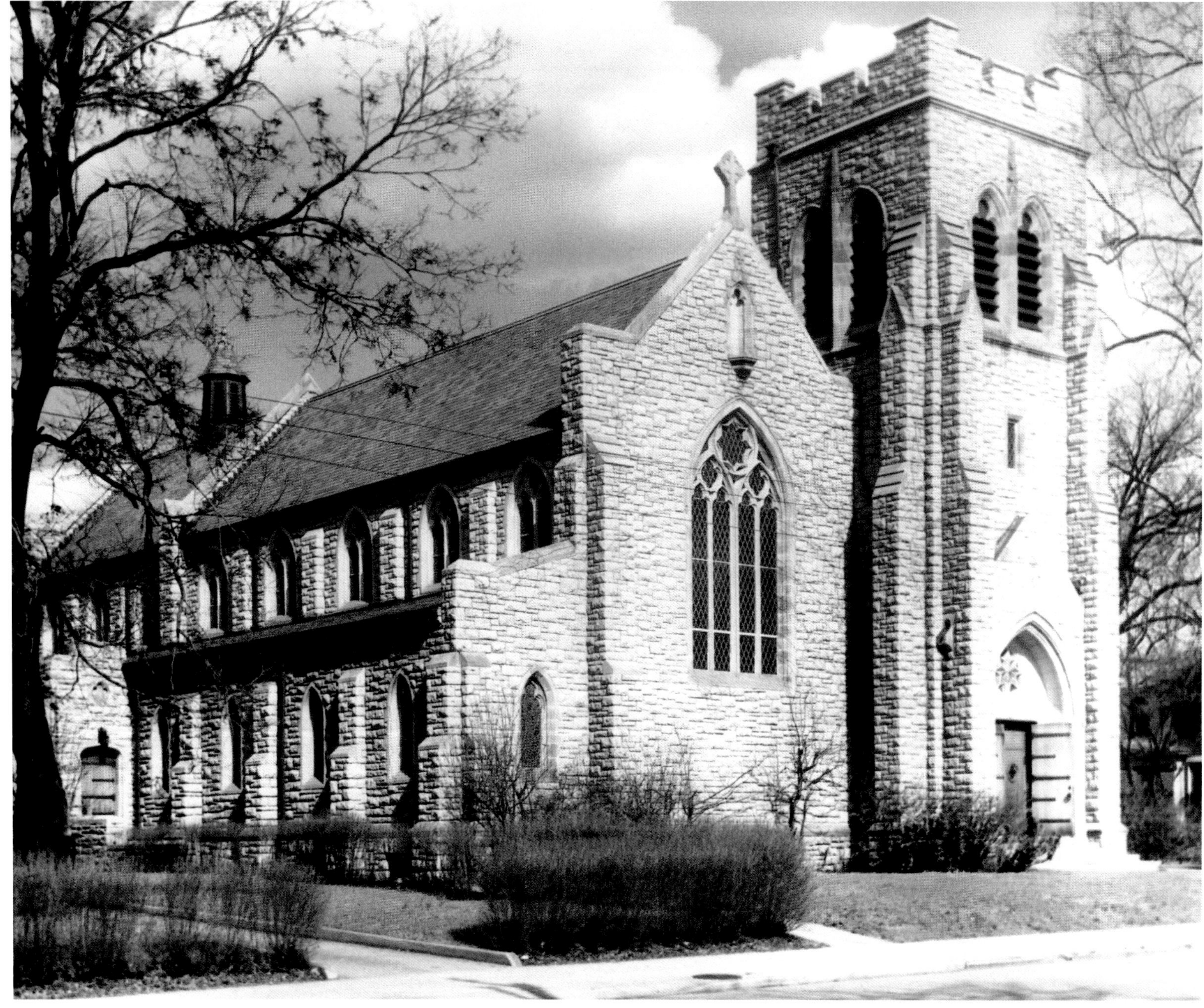

Good Shepherd Episcopal Church on East Main Street (built 1927), 1956.

Cooke Memorial Library, Georgetown University.

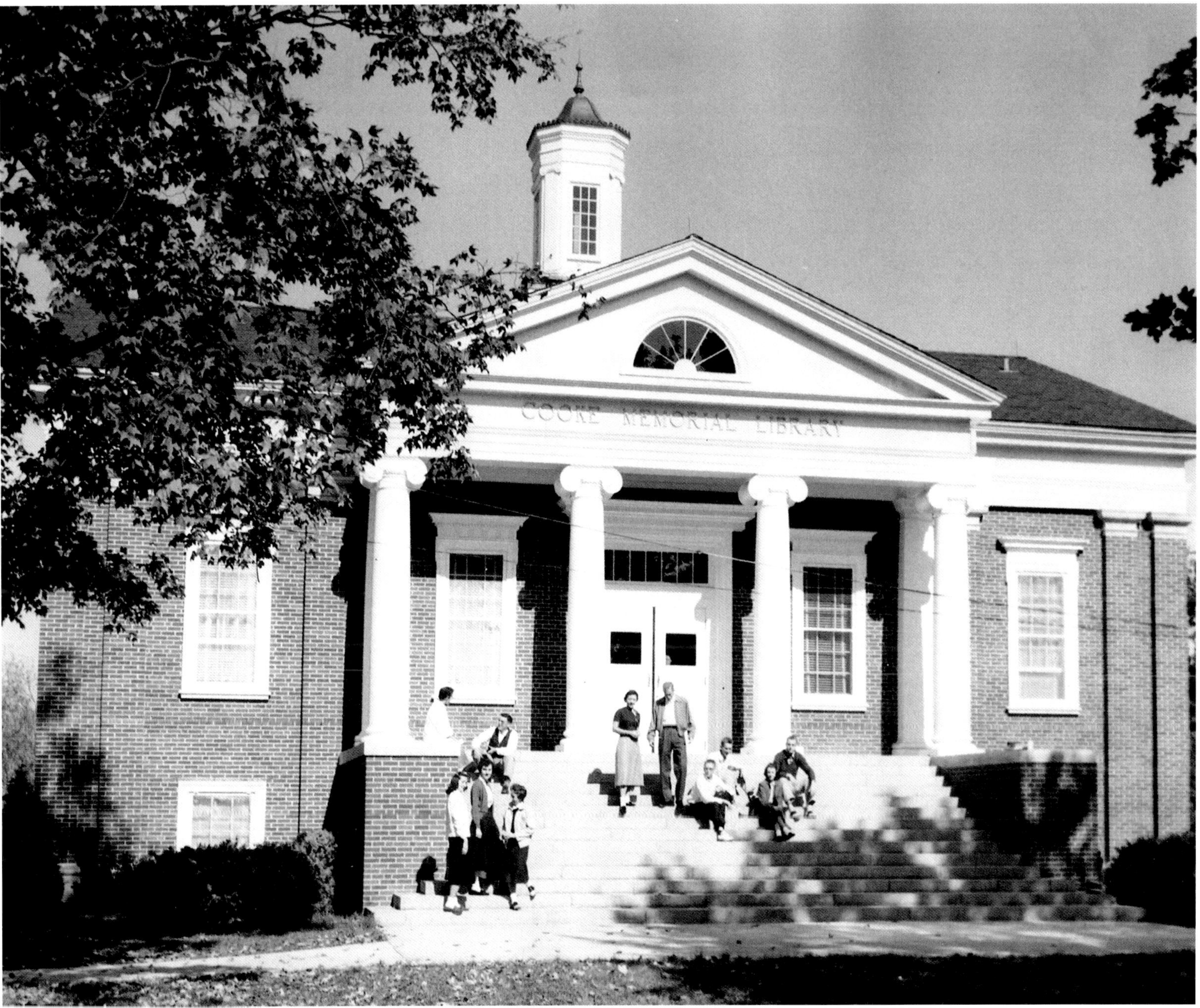

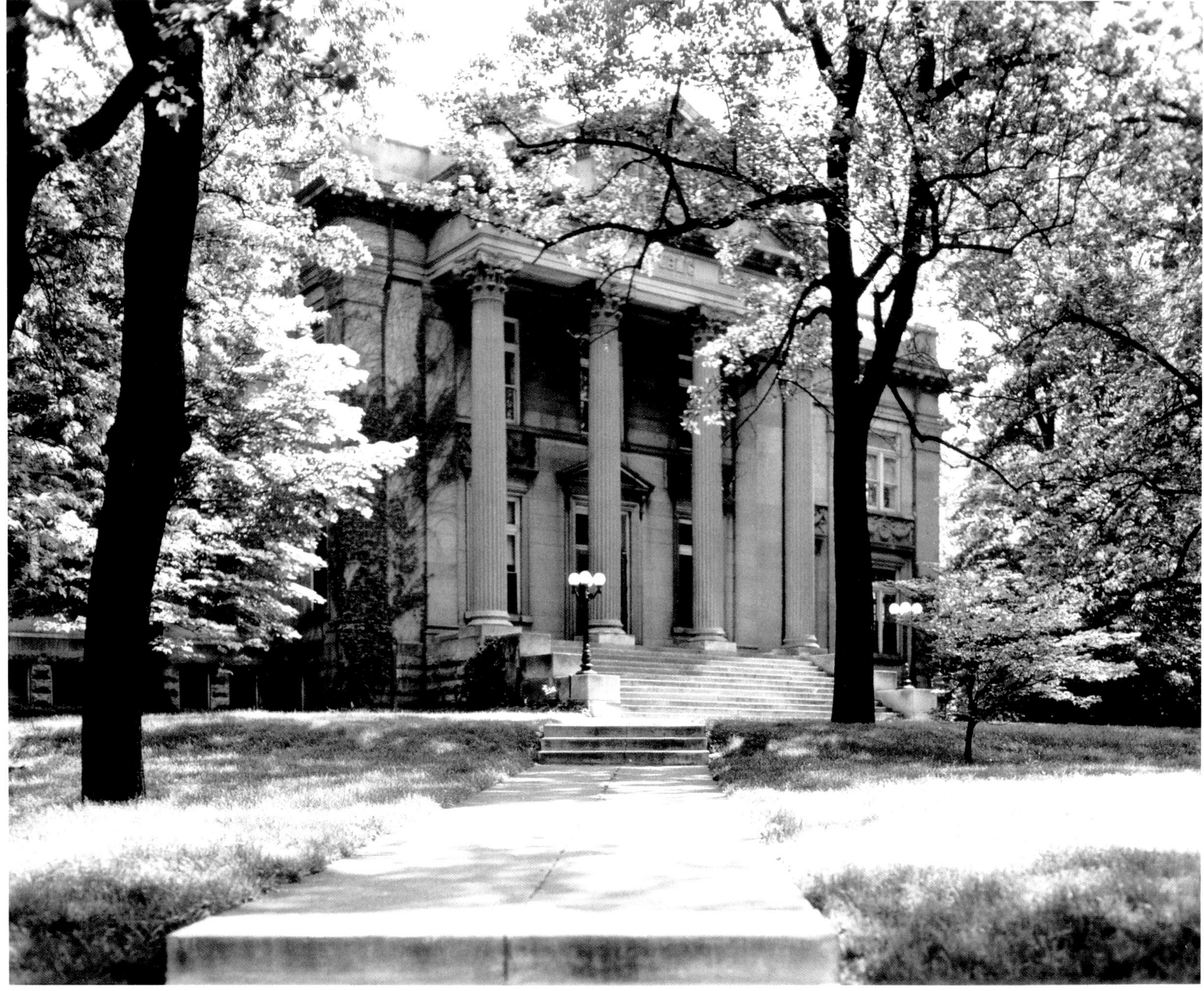

Lexington Public Library (built with a Carnegie grant in 1902) in Gratz Park, mid twentieth century.

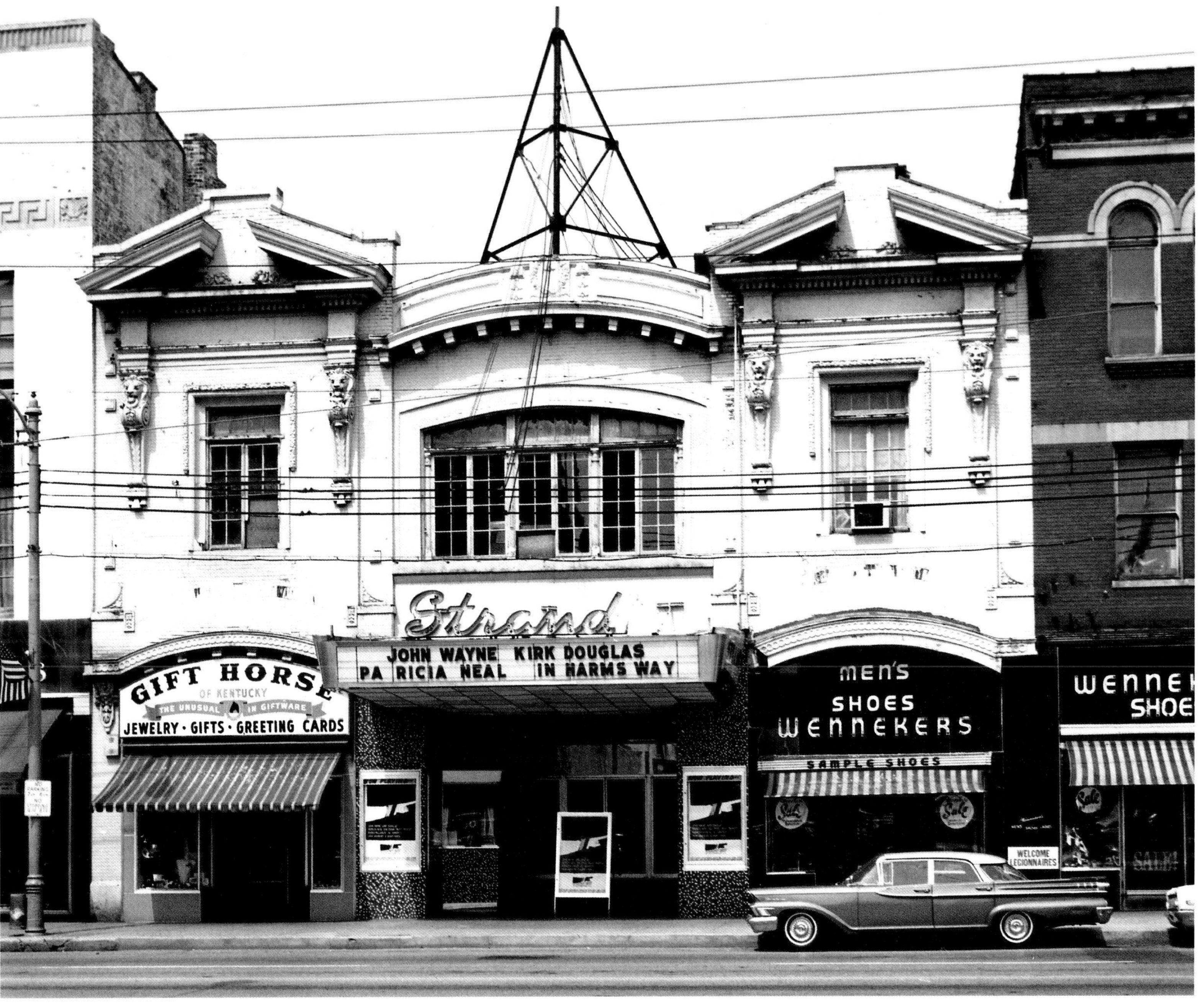

The Strand Theater on Main Street (built as a livery stable about 1907, operated as a theater from 1915 to 1973), mid twentieth century.

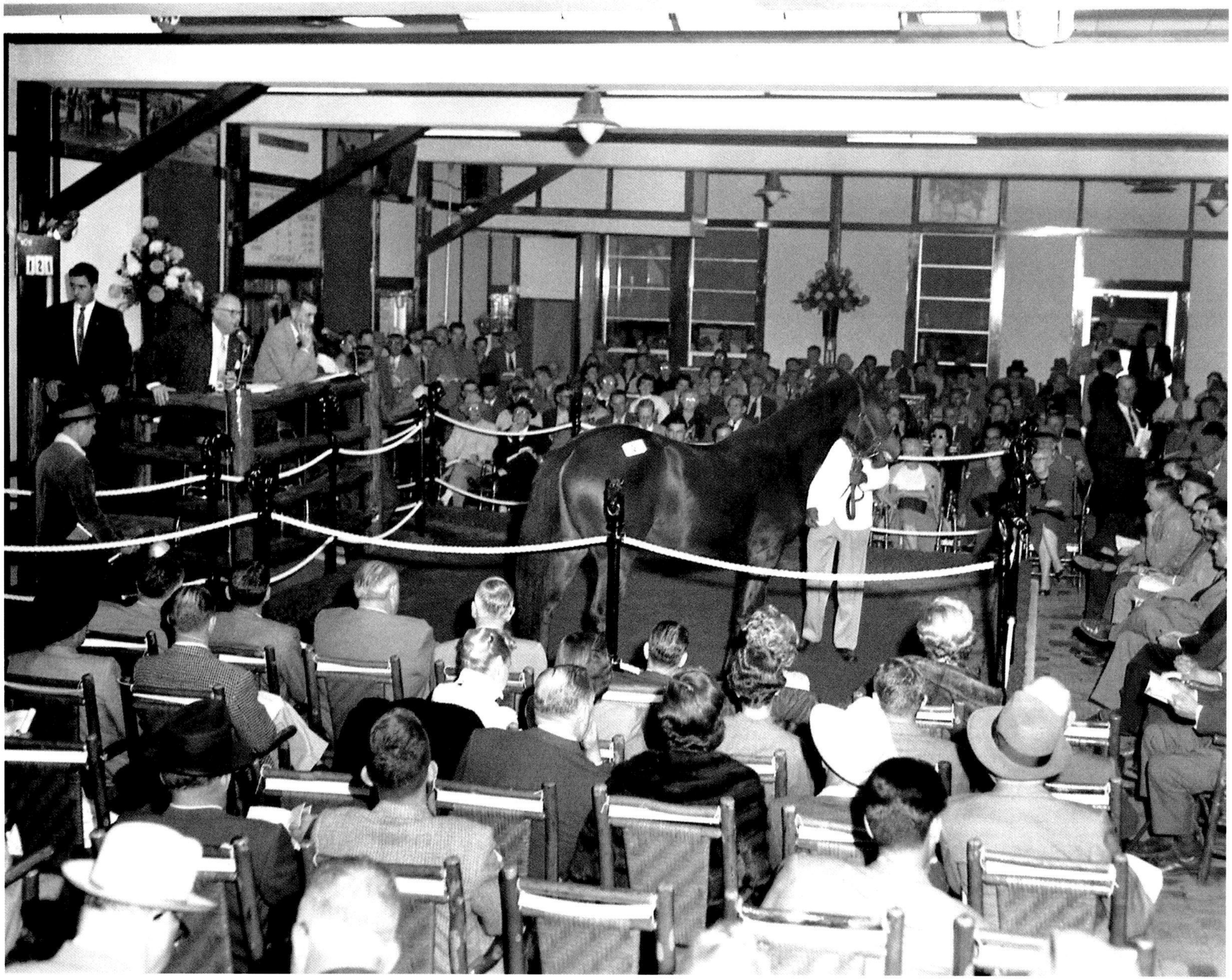

Sale of Tige o' My Heart at Keeneland, 1957.

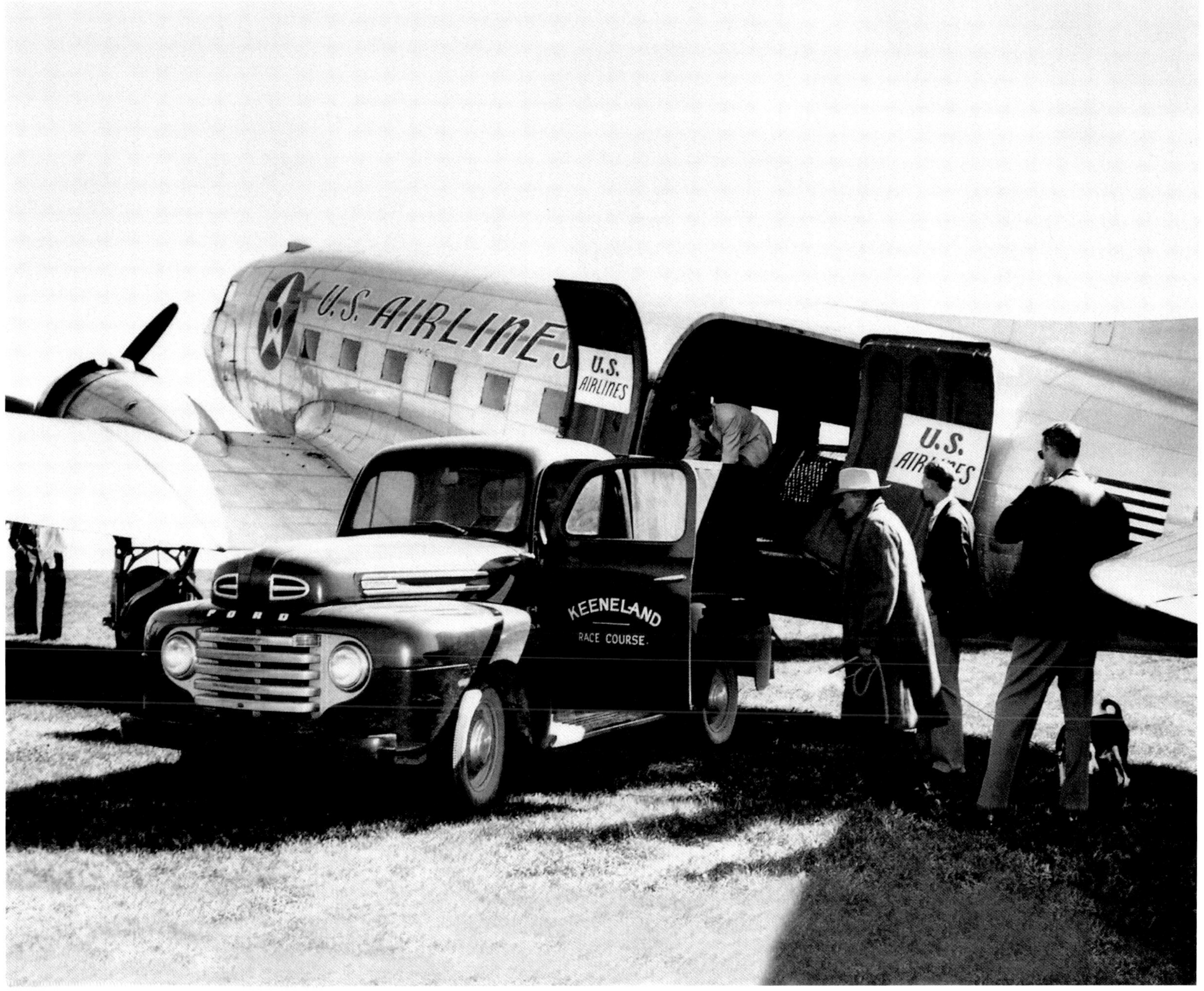

Tige o' My Heart being loaded onto transport plane at Blue Grass Airport, 1957.

Vogt Reel House (a firehouse built in 1904) on Jefferson Street, 1965.

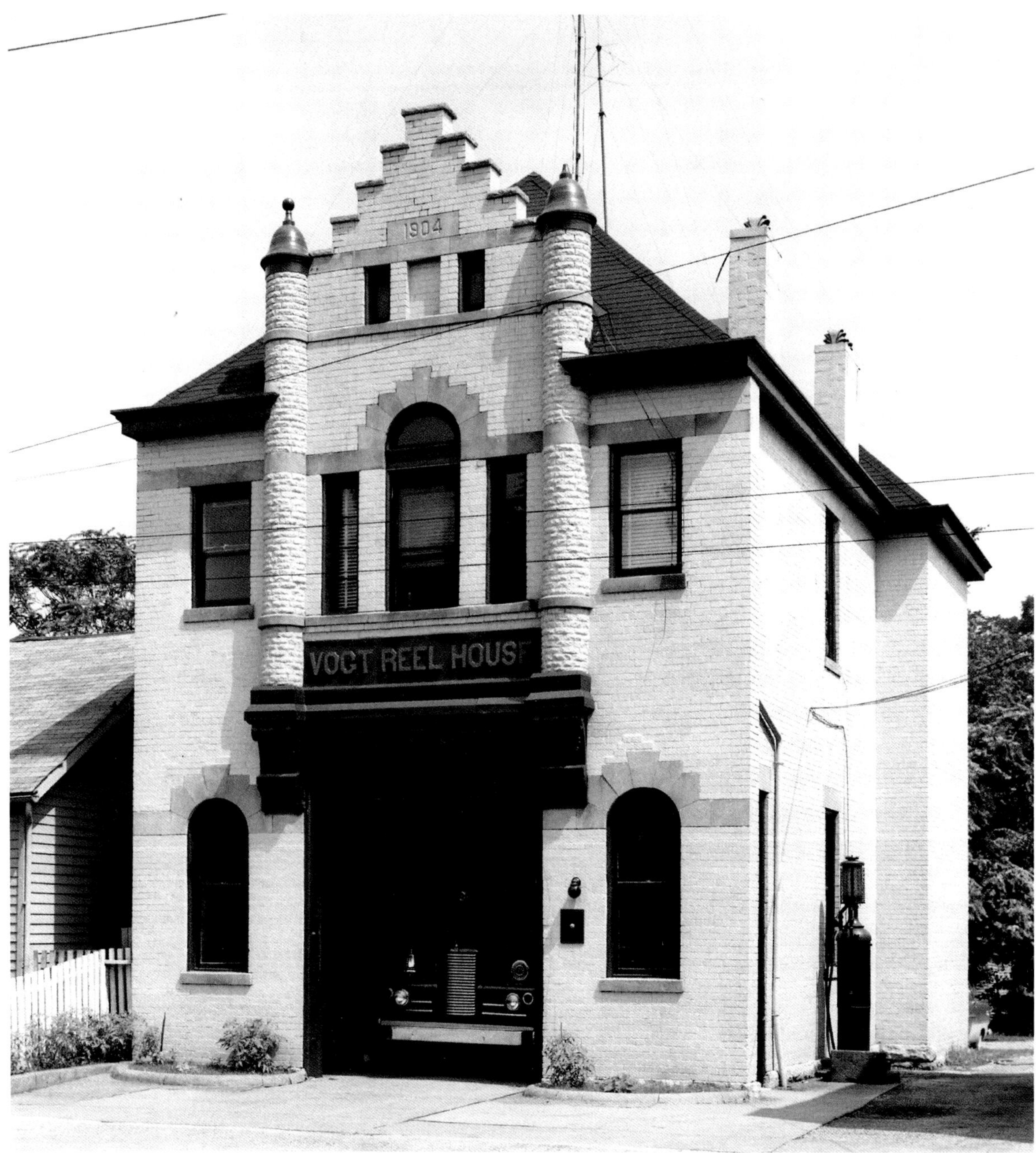

Notes on the Photographs

These notes attempt to include all aspects known of the photographs. Each of the photographs is identified by the page number, photograph's title or description, photographer and collection, archive, and call or box number when applicable. Although every attempt was made to include all data, in some cases complete data may have been unavailable.

ii **College of the Bible**
kukav:2002:017
J. Soule Smith
Art Work of the Blue Grass Region of Kentucky
University of Kentucky Libraries

vi **View of Third Street**
kukav:2002av02:075
J. Soule Smith
Art Work of the Blue Grass Region of Kentucky
University of Kentucky Libraries

x **Streetcar Center at Courthouse**
ktu:pa1:364
Bullock Photograph Collection
Transylvania University Library, Lexington, Ky.

2 **Lexington Fire Department**
J. Winston Coleman, Jr. Photographic
Transylvania University Library, Lexington, Ky.

3 **Stagecoach**
ktu:pa1:52
Bullock Photograph Collection
Transylvania University Library, Lexington, Ky.

4 **Phoenix Hotel**
kukav:2002av02:091
J. Soule Smith
Art Work of the Blue Grass Region of Kentucky
University of Kentucky Libraries

5 **Kentucky Association Racetrack**
ktu:pa1:44b
Bullock Photograph Collection
Transylvania University Library, Lexington, Ky.

6 **Red Mile Grandstand**
J. Winston Coleman, Jr. Photographic
Transylvania University Library, Lexington, Ky.

7 **Graz Kitchen**
Ktu:pa1:211
Bullock Photograph Collection
Transylvania University Library, Lexington, Ky.

8 **Old Soldiers' Reunion**
ktu:pa1:36
Transylvania University Library, Lexington, Ky.
Bullock Photograph Collection

9 **Lexington's Third Courthouse**
kukav:pa62w8:0189
Wilson Family Photographic Collection
University of Kentucky Libraries

10 **Sheriff's Office**
ktu:pa1:31b
Bullock Photograph Collection
Transylvania University Library, Lexington, Ky.

11 **Hemp Field**
kukav:2002av02:042
J. Soule Smith
Art Work of the Blue Grass Region of Kentucky
University of Kentucky Libraries

12 **Aerial View of Short Street**
ktu:pa1:370
Bullock Photograph Collection
Transylvania University Library, Lexington, Ky.

13 **Kentucky State Guard**
ktu:pa1:41
Transylvania University Library, Lexington, Ky.
Bullock Photograph Collection

14 **African-American Baptism**
ktu:pa1:19
Bullock Photograph Collection
Transylvania University Library, Lexington, Ky.

15 **Lexington's Post Office**
kukav:2002av02:002
J. Soule Smith
Art Work of the Blue Grass Region of Kentucky
University of Kentucky Libraries

16 **Courthouse at Main and Cheapside**
kukav:80pa121:0071
Louis Edward Nollau High Bridge Collection
University of Kentucky Libraries

17 **Cheapside**
kukav:pa62w8:0191
Wilson Family Photographic Collection
University of Kentucky Libraries

18 **The Straus Building**
ktu:pa1:25a
Bullock Photograph Collection
Transylvania University Library, Lexington, Ky.

19 **Broadway**
kukav:2002av02:090
J. Soule Smith
Art Work of the Blue Grass Region of Kentucky
University of Kentucky Libraries

20 **Central Christian Church**
kukav:2002av02:027
J. Soule Smith
Art Work of the Blue Grass Region of Kentucky
University of Kentucky Libraries

21 **Lexington Cemetery Entrance**
kukav:2002av02:007
J. Soule Smith
Art Work of the Blue Grass Region of Kentucky
University of Kentucky Libraries

22 **Hanover**
Kukav:2002av02:033
J. Soule Smith
Art Work of the Blue Grass Region of Kentucky
University of Kentucky Libraries

23 **Chenosa Lake**
ktu:pa1:340
Bullock Photograph Collection
Transylvania University Library, Lexington, Ky.

24 **Eastern Kentucky Asylum for the Insane**
kukav:2002av02:030
J. Soule Smith
Art Work of the Blue Grass Region of Kentucky
University of Kentucky Libraries

25 **Mule-drawn Trolleys**
ktu:pa1:46b
Bullock Photograph Collection
Transylvania University Library, Lexington, Ky.

26 **Lexington Opera House**
kukav:2002av02:031
J. Soule Smith
Art Work of the Blue Grass Region of Kentucky
University of Kentucky Libraries

27 **View of Broadway, 1898**
kukav:2002av02:088
J. Soule Smith
Art Work of the Blue Grass Region of Kentucky
University of Kentucky Libraries

28 **Bryan Station Memorial**
Kukav:2002av02:001
J. Soule Smith
Art Work of the Blue Grass Region of Kentucky
University of Kentucky Libraries

29 **Old Morrison**
ktu:pa1:451a
Bullock Photograph Collection
Transylvania University Library, Lexington, Ky.

30 **Monument to John C. Breckinridge**
kukav:2002av02:032
J. Soule Smith
Art Work of the Blue Grass Region of Kentucky
University of Kentucky Libraries

31 **Masterson's Station**
kukav:2002av02:023
J. Soule Smith
Art Work of the Blue Grass Region of Kentucky
University of Kentucky Libraries

32 **Lyon Firehouse**
ktu:pa1:452
Bullock Photograph Collection
Transylvania University Library, Lexington, Ky.

33 **Revival In Woodlawn Park**
ktu:pa1:45b
Bullock Photograph Collection
Transylvania University Library, Lexington, Ky.

34 **Main Street, 1898**
kukav:2002av02:051
J. Soule Smith
Art Work of the Blue Grass Region of Kentucky
University of Kentucky Libraries

35 **Hamilton College**
Kukav:2002av02:038
J. Soule Smith
Art Work of the Blue Grass Region of Kentucky
University of Kentucky Libraries

36 **Short Street**
kukav:2002av02:108
J. Soule Smith
Art Work of the Blue Grass Region of Kentucky
University of Kentucky Libraries

37 **Women and Christian Temperance Union**
kukav:2002av02:060
J. Soule Smith
Art Work of the Blue Grass Region of Kentucky
University of Kentucky Libraries

38 **Agricultural and Mechanical College of Kentucky**
kukav:2002av02:070
J. Soule Smith
Art Work of the Blue Grass Region of Kentucky
University of Kentucky Libraries

39 **Johnson School**
kukav:2002av02:060
J. Soule Smith
Art Work of the Blue Grass Region of Kentucky
University of Kentucky Libraries

40 **Stable on Limestone**
J. Winston Coleman, Jr. Photographic
Transylvania University Library, Lexington, Ky.

41 **Sayre Female Institute**
ktu:pa1:600
Transylvania University Library, Lexington, Ky.
Bullock Photograph Collection

42 **Floral Hall**
J. Winston Coleman, Jr. Photographic
Transylvania University Library, Lexington, Ky.

43 **County Officials on Courthouse Steps**
ktu:pa1:38
Bullock Photograph Collection
Transylvania University Library, Lexington, Ky.

44 **Police Station on Water Street**
ktu:pa1:48b
Bullock Photograph Collection
Transylvania University Library, Lexington, Ky.

46 **Mary Dodd's Class at East Hickman School**
kukav:80pa132:0023
Massillon Alexander Cassidy
Fayette County Schools Photographic Collection
University of Kentucky Libraries

47 **Choir of Second Presbyterian Church**
kukarp:1998ua01:360_0001
Louis Edward Nollau Collection
University of Kentucky Libraries

48 **Fire Companies Race at Trotting Track**
J. Winston Coleman, Jr. Photographic
Transylvania University Library, Lexington, Ky.

49 **Henry Howard Gratz**
ktu:pa1:520
Bullock Photograph Collection
Transylvania University Library, Lexington, Ky.

50 **Giddings Hall at Georgetown College**
Georgetown College Library
Special Collections

51 **Northern Bank Building**
ktu:pa1:278
Bullock Photograph Collection
Transylvania University Library, Lexington, Ky.

52 Davidson School
ktu:pa1:210
Bullock Photograph Collection
Transylvania University Library, Lexington, Ky.

53 Lexington State College Band
kukarp:1998ua001:042_0036
Louis Edward Nollau Collection
University of Kentucky Libraries

54 Police Station
Ktu:pa1:218
Bullock Photograph Collection
Transylvania University Library, Lexington, Ky.

55 Streetcar Accident
Ktu:pa1:366
Bullock Photograph Collection
Transylvania University Library, Lexington, Ky.

56 Electric Streetcar Passing Phoenix Hotel
Ktu:pa1:368
Bullock Photograph Collection
Transylvania University Library, Lexington, Ky.

57 Main and Broadway
ktu:pa1:367
Bullock Photograph Collection
Transylvania University Library, Lexington, Ky.

58 Woodland Park Auditorium
J. Winston Coleman, Jr. Photographic
Transylvania University Library, Lexington, Ky.

59 Short Street During Construction of National Bank
J. Winston Coleman, Jr. Photographic
Transylvania University Library, Lexington, Ky.

60 Coal Company on Broadway
J. Winston Coleman, Jr. Photographic
Transylvania University Library, Lexington, Ky.

61 Mary Todd Lincoln's Girlhood Home
pa62w8:0188
Wilson Family Photographic Collection
University of Kentucky Libraries

62 Jail on Short Street
J. Winston Coleman, Jr. Photographic
Transylvania University Library, Lexington, Ky.

63 Streetcar Strikers
J. Winston Coleman, Jr. Photographic
Transylvania University Library, Lexington, Ky.

64 St. Joseph Hospital
J. Winston Coleman, Jr. Photographic
Transylvania University Library, Lexington, Ky.

65 Carty Building
J. Winston Coleman, Jr. Photographic
Transylvania University Library, Lexington, Ky.

66 Golden Jubilee
kukarp:1998au001:175_0001
Louis Edward Nollau Collection
University of Kentucky Libraries

67 Town Branch
J. Winston Coleman, Jr. Photographic
Transylvania University Library, Lexington, Ky.

68 Soldiers at Union Station
Kukarp:1998au001:53_002
Louis Edward Nollau Collection
University of Kentucky Libraries

69 Training Recruits Arrive
kukarp:1998ua002:53_0003
Louis Edward Nollau Collection
University of Kentucky Libraries

70 Fire department Volunteers
kukarp:1998ua001:392_0003
Louis Edward Nollau Collection
University of Kentucky Libraries

72 Piggly Wiggly
kukav:lstudio:0890202
Lafayette Studio Collection
University of Kentucky Libraries

73 Cannon in front of the Main Building at UK
kukuarp:1998ua001:182_0002
Louis Edward Nollau
University of Kentucky Libraries

74 Professor Granville Terrel
kukarp:2001ua028:4613
Louis Edward Nollau Collection
University of Kentucky Libraries

75 Flooded Alumni Gymnasium
kukarp:1998ua001:186_0005
Louis Edward Nollau Collection
University of Kentucky Libraries

76 Main Street during 1928 Flood
J. Winston Coleman, Jr. Photographic
Transylvania University Library, Lexington, Ky.

77 Main Street in flood
kukav:lstudio:0890122
Lafayette Studio Collection
University of Kentucky Libraries

78 Ice Plant
J. Winston Coleman, Jr. Photographic
Transylvania University Library, Lexington, Ky.

79 Main and Limestone with Crowler Bus
kukuarp:1998ua002:3960
Louis Edward Nollau Collection
University of Kentucky Libraries

80 Dunn's Drug Store on South Limestone Street
Kukav:lstudio:0890101
Lafayette Studio Collection
University of Kentucky Libraries

81 Kentucky Theater
Kukav:lstudio:0890238
Lafayette Studio Collection
University of Kentucky Libraries

82 Spotswood Specialty Company
Kukav:lstudio:0890053
Lafayette Studio Collection
University of Kentucky Libraries

83 American Legion Parade
kukav:lstudio:0890024
Lafayette Studio Collection
University of Kentucky Libraries

84 Hoisting a Signal
kukuarp:1998ua002:4226
Louis Edward Nollau Collection
University of Kentucky Libraries

85 Hamburg Place
Kukav:lstudio:0890081
Lafayette Studio Collection
University of Kentucky Libraries

86 Blessing of the Hounds
J. Winston Coleman, Jr. Photographic
Transylvania University Library, Lexington, Ky.

87 Mayor O'Brien with Nubian Lion Cub
kukav:lstudio:0890241
Lafayette Studio Collection
University of Kentucky Libraries

88 Kelley's Liquor Dispensary
kukav:lstudio:0890206
Lafayette Studio Collection
University of Kentucky Libraries

89 Clark's Hardware
Kukav:lstudio:0890030
Lafayette Studio Collection
University of Kentucky Libraries

90 Christmas Parade on Main Street
kukav:lstudio:0890034
Lafayette Studio Collection
University of Kentucky Libraries

91 Marion Miley
Kukav:lstudio:0890138
Lafayette Studio Collection
University of Kentucky Libraries

92 **Democratic Convention**
Kukav:lstudio:0890128
Lafayette Studio Collection
University of Kentucky Libraries

93 **Banquet at Phoenix Hotel**
J. Winston Coleman, Jr. Photographic
Transylvania University Library,
Lexington, Ky.

94 **Prior to Race at Keeneland**
Keeneland Library

95 **Man O' War with Jeannette McDonald**
kukav:lstudio:0890011
Lafayette Studio Collection
University of Kentucky Libraries

96 **Jockey Weighing In**
Keeneland Library

97 **At the Start of the Race**
Keeneland Library

98 **Hutchinson Drugs on West Main Street**
kukav:lstudio:0890152
Lafayette Studio Collection
University of Kentucky Libraries

100 **Robert J. Long**
kukav:lstudio:0890193
Lafayette Studio Collection
University of Kentucky Libraries

101 **Betty Coed and the Debs**
lstudio:0890156
Lafayette Studio Collection
University of Kentucky Libraries

102 **Roller Coaster at Joyland Park**
lstudio:0890123
Lafayette Studio Collection
University of Kentucky Libraries

103 **Renovated Floral Hall**
J. Winston Coleman, Jr. Photographic
Transylvania University Library,
Lexington, Ky.

104 **Margaret I. King Library**
kukav:lstudio:0890042
Lafayette Studio Collection
University of Kentucky Libraries

105 **Federal Post Office**
J. Winston Coleman, Jr. Photographic
Transylvania University Library,
Lexington, Ky.

106 **Lexington Brewery**
J. Winston Coleman, Jr. Photographic
Transylvania University Library,
Lexington, Ky.

107 **Goodwin Brothers**
lstudio:0890171
Lafayette Studio Collection
University of Kentucky Libraries

108 **Sesquicentennial Monument**
kukav:pa51w13:3
Samuel M. Wilson: Kentucky
Sesquicentennial Collection
University of Kentucky Libraries

109 **Epping Bottling Works**
kukav:lstudio:0890201
Lafayette Studio Collection
University of Kentucky Libraries

110 **Blacksmith shop**
J. Winston Coleman, Jr. Photographic
Transylvania University Library,
Lexington, Ky.

111 **Stop Over Station**
J. Winston Coleman, Jr. Photographic
Transylvania University Library,
Lexington, Ky.

112 **Irving Air Chute Company**
lstudio:0890179
Lafayette Studio Collection
University of Kentucky Libraries

113 **Broadway Christian**
J. Winston Coleman, Jr. Photographic
Transylvania University Library,
Lexington, Ky.

114 **Christ Church Episcopal Cathedral**
J. Winston Coleman, Jr. Photographic
Transylvania University Library,
Lexington, Ky.

115 **Jot 'Em Down**
J. Winston Coleman, Jr. Photographic
Transylvania University Library,
Lexington, Ky.

116 **View Across Courthouse Lawn**
J. Winston Coleman, Jr. Photographic
Transylvania University Library,
Lexington, Ky.

117 **Keith's Restaurant**
Kukav:lstudio:0890187
Lafayette Studio Collection
University of Kentucky Libraries

118 **Funeral for Man O' War**
J. Winston Coleman, Jr. Photographic
Transylvania University Library,
Lexington, Ky.

119 **Whirlaway**
Kukav:lstudio:0890189
Lafayette Studio Collection
University of Kentucky Libraries

120 **GAR at Lexington Cemetery**
kukav:61m158:020
Neville Family Papers
University of Kentucky Libraries

121 **University of Kentucky Equestrienne**
kukarp:2001ua028:1962
Portrait Print Collection
University of Kentucky Libraries

122 **Mammoth Life Insurance**
lstudio:0890195
Lafayette Studio Collection
University of Kentucky Libraries

123 **Jockeys at Keeneland**
Keeneland Library

124 **Good Shepherd**
J. Winston Coleman, Jr. Photographic
Transylvania University Library,
Lexington, Ky.

125 **Cooke Memorial Library**
Georgetown University
Special Collections

126 **Lexington Public Library**
kukav:1997av27:2535
James Edwin Ed Weddle Photographic
Collection
University of Kentucky Libraries

127 **Strand Theater**
J. Winston Coleman, Jr. Photographic
Transylvania University Library,
Lexington, Ky.

128 **Sale of Tige O' My Heart**
Keeneland Library

129 **Tige O' My Heart Loaded onto Airplane**
Keeneland Library

130 **Vogt Reel House**
J. Winston Coleman, Jr. Photographic
Transylvania University Library,
Lexington, Ky.